BIG DATA AND DATA SCIENCE INITIATIVE IN INDIA

A. K. ROY

Dedication:

Dedicated to my granddaughter
'ANGANA'

(Blank even page)

Preface

Prime Minister Narendra Modi has launched an ambitious initiative to digitize India by making Internet access available to over two lakh villages by 2019, promoting e-governance, e-banking, e. education and e-health, and transforming India into a knowledge economy. Covering issues ranging from cyber security and promoting startups to digital highways and "Design in India," Government will invest Rs4.5 lakh crores in the Digital India program which will generate 18 lakh jobs."Reliance Industries (RIL) Chairman Mukesh Ambani said that he will invest Rs2.5 lakh crores which will create employment for over five lakh people. Cyrus Mistry said that Tata Group will hire 60,000 IT professionals, this year. K.M. Birla said that the Aditya Birla Group would invest Rs.44,500 crores in next five years in the infra and digital space. That is why Data Scientists are in high demand. The scarcity of data analytics talent is acute and demand for talent is expected to be on the higher because of the present digital India initiative besides many global organizations are outsourcing their work at India.

According to the Gartner, Big Data is high-volume, high-velocity and high-variety information assets that demand cost effective, innovative forms of information processing for enhanced insight and decision making. Big Data is data whose scale, diversity, and complexity require new architecture, techniques, algorithms, and analytics to manage it and extract value and hidden knowledge from both structured and unstructured data. Such large data is difficult to process using traditional database and software techniques. One of the greatest scientific challenges of the 21st century is to effectively understand and make use of the vast amount of information being produced. Data analytics will be among our most important tools in helping to understand such large-scale information.

Data science sits at the intersection of statistics, business intelligence, sociology, computer science, and communication. Data scientists use their data and analytical ability to find and interpret rich data sources; manage large amounts of data, merge data sources; ensure consistency of datasets; create visualizations to aid in understanding data and build mathematical model. Researchers from India are active, in the fields of astrophysics, materials science, earth and atmospheric observations, energy, computational biology, bioinformatics, cognitive science, statistics etc., which generate a lot of data. To deal with these data it requires the development of advanced algorithms, visualization techniques, data streaming methodologies and analytics. Keeping in mind the momentum that big data analytics is gaining in India, there is a need to build a sustainable eco-system that brings in a strong partnership across the industry players, government, and academia. With this objective, the Indian government has launched a *Big Data Initiative. Digital India is an initiative of Government of India to integrate the government departments and the people of India. It aims at ensuring the government services are made available to citizens electronically by reducing paperwork.* The NIC has created the Open Government Data portal, data.gov.in. Currently 85 government ministries, departments and agencies have contributed more than 12,000 datasets across segments such as population census, water and sanitation, health and family welfare, transportation and agriculture to data.gov.in. Present government's pet project of building *'one hundred smart cities'* which has been allocated Rs 7,060crores is another major project that would rely strongly on technology, calling for a robust cloud computing backend coupled with real-time surveillance and big data analytics technologies. The UID-Aadhaar project will be the largest such citizen database on the planet. NASSCOM 10,000 Startups launched a report on "Institutionalization of Analytics in India: Big Opportunity, Big Outcome.

Keeping in view the giant initiative by Govt. of India the book entitled 'Big Data and Data Science Initiative in India-Upcoming Job Opportunities' is compiled with latest developments in this sector. The recent trend in methods and tools that Data Scientists use and are covered in the following chapters: **Chapter 1:Basics of Big Data and Application; Chapter 2: Fundamentals of Data Science / Data Scientist; Chapter 3: India's Initiative in Data Science and Big Data Application; Chapter 4: Skill Development for Data Science Jobs; Chapter 5: Data Science and Big Data Courses Offered in India; Chapter 6: Best Data Science and Big Data Courses Offered Abroad; Chapter 7: Ways to become Data Scientist by Oneself; Chapter 8: Job Prospect of Data Science.** With respect to Job creation and opportunities of data scientists in India and abroad suggested that the Analytics and Big Data sector has seen a consistent growth in the last five years and is expected to further grow at a CAGR of 33.2% and 26.4% respectively, almost six to eight times that of the overall IT sector. According to NASSCOM, the Indian market is expected to grow to US$ 2.3 billion by the year 2018. Big data analytics accounted for some 29,000 jobs in India in 2014. The book may be helpful for a large pool of English-speaking engineering, mathematics &management graduates to equip themselves with skill to grab forthcoming data science jobs as India is an attractive destination for the off-shoring of big data analytics, which Indian tech entrepreneurs are well placed to exploit as well as major initiatives taken by the present government to uplift the analytics sector that is going to create huge job opportunities in data science and big data analytics.

(Blank even page)

CONTENTS

List of Figures

List of Tables

Chapter 1: Basics of Big Data and Application

1.1 Definitions of Big Data by Thought Leaders

What is Big Data? **"Big data" - It seems like the phrase is everywhere. The term was added to the Oxford English Dictionary in 2013** [1] **and appeared in Merriam-Webster's Collegiate Dictionary in 2014** [2]**. Now, Gartner's just-released 2014 Hype Cycle** [3] **shows "big data" passing the "peak of inflated expectations" and moving on its way down into the "trough of disillusionment." Big data is all the rage. But what does it actually mean?**

Figure 1: Conceptual Sketch of Big data

A commonly repeated definition [4] cites the three Vs: volume, velocity, and variety. But others argue that it's not the size of data [5] that counts, but the tools being used or the insights that can be drawn from a dataset.

Top recurring themes in our thought leaders' definitions (word cloud via Wordle).To settle the question once and for all, we asked more than 40 thought leaders in publishing, fashion, food, automobiles, medicine, marketing, and every industry in between how exactly they would define the phrase "big data." Answers of thought leaders' definitions look below to find out what big data is:

John Akred

Founder and CTO, Silicon Valley Data Science (http://svds.com/)

"Big Data" refers to a combination of an approach to informing decision making with analytical insight derived from data, and a set of enabling technologies that enable that insight to be economically derived from at times very large, diverse sources of data. Advances in sensing technologies, the digitization of commerce and communications, and the advent and growth in social media are a few of the trends which have created the opportunity to use large scale, fine grained data to understand systems, behavior and commerce; while innovation in technology makes it viable economically to use that information to inform decisions and improve outcomes.

Philip Ashlock

Chief   Architect, Data.gov   (http://www.data.gov/) Twitter: @philipashlock (https://twitter.com/philipashlock)

While the use of the term is quite nebulous and is often co-opted for other purposes, I've understood "big data" to be about analysis for data that's really messy or where you don't know the right questions or queries to make — analysis that can help you find patterns, anomalies, or new structures amidst otherwise chaotic or complex data points. Usually this revolves around datasets with a byte size that seems fairly large relative to our frame of reference using files on a desktop PC (e.g., larger than a terabyte) and many of the tools around big data are to help deal with a large volume of data, but to me the most important concepts of big data don't actually have much to do with it being "big" in this sense (especially since that's such a relative term these days). In fact, they can often be applied to smaller datasets as well. Natural language processing and lucene based search engines are good examples of big data techniques and tools that are often used with relatively small amounts of data.

Jon Bruner

Editor-at-Large, O'Reilly Media (http://www.oreilly.com/)
Twitter: @JonBruner (https://twitter.com/JonBruner)

Big Data is the result of collecting information at its most granular level — it's what you get when you instrument a system and keep all of the data that your instrumentation is able to gather.

Reid Bryant

Data Scientist, Brooks Bell (http://www.brooksbell.com/)

As computational efficiency continues to increase, "big data" will be less about the actual size of a particular dataset and more about the specific expertise needed to process it. With that in mind, "big data" will ultimately describe any dataset large enough to necessitate high-level programming skill and statistically defensible methodologies in order to transform the data asset into something of value.

Mike Cavaretta

Data Scientist and Manager, Ford Motor Company (http://www.ford.com/)
Twitter: @mjcavaretta(https://twitter.com/mjcavaretta)

You cannot give me too much data. I see big data as storytelling — whether it is through information graphics or other visual aids that explain it in a way that allows others to understand across sectors. I always push for the full scope of the data over averages and aggregations — and I like to go to the raw data because of the possibilities of things you can do with it.

Drew Conway

Head of Data, Project Florida (http://sum.com/) Twitter: @drewconway (https://twitter.com/drewconway)

Big data, which started as a technological innovation in distributed computing, is now a cultural movement by which we continue to discover how humanity interacts with the world — and each other — at large-scale.

Rohan Deuskar

CEO and Co-Founder, Stylitics (https://www.stylitics.com/) Twitter: @RohanD (https://twitter.com/RohanD)

Big data refers to the approach to data of "collect now, sort out later"…means you capture and store data on a very large volume of actions and transactions of different types, on a continuous basis, in order to make sense of it later. The low cost of storage and better methods of analysis mean that you generally don't need to have a specific purpose for the data in mind before you collect it.

Amy Escobar

Data Scientist, 2U, Inc (http://2u.com/)

Big data is an opportunity to gain a more complex understanding of the relationships between different factors and to uncover previously undetected patterns in data by leveraging advances in the technical aspects of collecting, storing, and retrieving data along with innovative ideas and techniques for manipulating and analyzing data.

Josh Ferguson

Chief Technology Officer, Mode Analytics (https://modeanalytics.com/)

Big data is the broad name given to challenges and opportunities we have as data about every aspect of our lives becomes available. It's not just about data though; it also includes the people, processes, and analysis that turn data into meaning.

John Foreman

Chief Data Scientist, Mail Chimp (http://mailchimp.com/) Twitter: @John4man (https://twitter.com/John4man)

I prefer a flexible but functional definition of big data. Big data is when your business wants to use data to solve a problem, answer a question, produce a product, etc., but the standard, simple methods (maybe it's SQL, maybe it's k-means, maybe it's a single server with a cron job) break down on the size of the data set, causing time, effort, creativity, and money to be spent crafting a solution to the problem that leverages the data without simply sampling or tossing out records.

The main consideration here, then, is to weigh the cost of using "all the data" in this complex (and potentially brittle) solution versus the benefits gained over using a smaller data set in a cheaper, faster, more stable way.

Daniel Gillick

Senior Research Scientist, Google

Historically, most decisions — political, military, business, and personal — have been made by brains [that] have unpredictable logic and operate on subjective experiential evidence. "Big data" represents a cultural shift in which more and more decisions are made by algorithms with transparent logic, operating on documented immutable evidence. I think "big" refers more to the pervasive nature of this change than to any particular amount of data.

Vincent Granville

Co-Founder, Data   Science   Central (http://www.datasciencecentral.com/) Twitter: @AnalyticBridge (https://twitter.com/AnalyticBridge)

Big data is data that even when efficiently compressed still contains 5-10 times more information (measured in entropy or predictive power, per unit of time) than what you are used to right now. It may require a different approach to extract value.

Annette Greiner

Lecturer, UC   Berkeley   School   of   Information (http://www.ischool.berkeley.edu/) Web Application Developer at NERSC, Lawrence   Berkeley   National   Lab Twitter: @annettegreiner (https://twitter.com/annettegreiner)

Big data is data that contains enough observations to demand unusual handling because of its sheer size, though what are unusual changes over time and varies from one discipline to another. Scientific computing is accustomed to pushing the envelope, constantly developing techniques to address relentless growth in dataset size, but many other disciplines are now just discovering the value — and hence the challenges — of working with data at the unwieldy end of the scale.

Seth Grimes

Principal Consultant, Alta Plana Corporation (http://altaplana.com/ sethgrimes.html) Twitter: @SethGrimes (https://twitter.com/SethGrimes)

Big data has taken a beating in recent years, the accusation being that marketers and analysts have stretched and squeezed the term to cover a multitude of disparate problems, technologies, and products. Yet the core of big data remains what it has been for over a decade, framed by Doug Laney's 2001 three Vs, Volume, Velocity, and Variety, and indicating data challenges sufficient to justify non-routine computing resources and processing techniques.

Joel Gurin

Author of *Open Data Now* (http://www.opendatanow.com/) Twitter: @JoelGurin (https://twitter.com/JoelGurin)

Big data describes datasets that are so large, complex, or rapidly changing that they push the very limits of our analytical capability. It's a subjective term: What seems "big" today may seem modest in a few years when our analytic capacity has improved. While big data can be about anything, the most important kinds of big data and perhaps the only ones worth the effort are those that can have a big impact through what they tell us about society, public health, the economy, scientific research, or any number of other large-scale subjects.

Quentin Hardy

Deputy Tech Editor, *The New York Times* Twitter: @qhardy (https://twitter.com/qhardy)

What's "big" in big data isn't necessarily the size of the databases, it's the big number of data sources we have, as digital sensors and behavior trackers migrate across the world. As we triangulate information in more ways, we will discover hitherto unknown patterns in nature and society — and pattern-making is the wellspring of new art, science, and commerce.

Harlan Harris

Director, Data Science at Education Advisory Board (https://www.eab.com/) President and Co-Founder, Data Community DC (https://www.eab.com/) Twitter: @HarlanH (https://twitter.com/HarlanH)

To me, "big data" is the situation where an organization can (arguably) say that they have access to what they need to reconstruct, understand, and model the part of the world that they care about. Using their big data, then, they can (try to) predict future states of the world, optimize their processes, and otherwise be more effective and rational in their activities.

Jessica Kirkpatrick

Director of Data Science, Insta EDU (https://instaedu.com/tutors/) Twitter: @berkeleyjess (https://twitter.com/berkeleyjess)

Big data refers to using complex datasets to drive focus, direction, and decision making within a company or organization. This is done by deriving actionable insights from the analysis of your organization's data.

David Leonhardt

Editor, The Upshot (http://www.nytimes.com/upshot/?_r=2) , *The New York Times* Twitter: @DLeonhardt (https://twitter.com/DLeonhardt)

Big Data is nothing more than a tool for capturing reality — just as newspaper reporting, photography and long-form journalism are. But it's an exciting tool, because it holds the potential of capturing reality in some clearer and more accurate ways than we have been able to do in the past.

Hilary Mason

Founder, Fast Forward Labs (http://www.fastforwardlabs.com/) Twitter: @hmason (https://twitter.com/hmason)

Big data is just the ability to gather information and query it in such a way that we are able to learn things about the world that were previously inaccessible to us.

Deirdre Mulligan

Associate Professor, UC Berkeley School of Information (http://www.ischool.berkeley.edu/)

Big data: Endless possibilities or cradle-to-grave shackles, depending upon the political, ethical, and legal choices we make.

Sharmila Mulligan

CEO and Founder, ClearStory Data (http://www.clearstorydata.com/)
Twitter: @ShahaniMulligan (https://twitter.com/ShahaniMulligan)

[Big data means] harnessing more sources of diverse data where "data variety" and "data velocity" are the key opportunities. (Each source represents "a signal" on what is happening in the business.) The opportunity is to harness data variety [and] automate "harmonization" of data sources to deliver fast-updating insights consumable by the line-of-business users.

Sean Patrick Murphy

Consulting Data Scientist and Co-Founder of a stealth startup
Twitter:@sayhitosean (https://twitter.com/sayhitosean)

While "big data" is often large in size relative to the available tool set, "big" actually refers to being important. Scientists and engineers have long known that data is valuable, but now the rest of the world, including those in control of purse strings, understand the value that can be created from data.

Prakash Nanduri

Co-Founder, CEO and President, Paxata, Inc (http://www.paxata.com/)

Everything we know spits out data today — not just the devices we use for computing. We now get digital exhaust from our garage door openers to our coffee pots, and everything in between. At the same time, we have become a generation of people who demand instantaneous access to information — from what the weather is like in a country thousands of miles away to which store has better deals on toaster ovens. Big data is at the intersection of collecting, organizing, storing, and turning all of that raw data into truly meaningful information.

Chris Neumann

CEO and Co-Founder, Data Hero (https://datahero.com/) Twitter: @ckneumann (https://twitter.com/ckneumann)

At Aster Data, we originally used the term big data in our marketing to refer to analytical MPP databases like ours and to differentiate them from traditional data warehouse software. While both were capable of storing a "big" volume of data (which, in 2008, we defined as 10 TB or greater), "big data" systems were capable of performing complex analytics on top of that data — something that legacy data warehouse software could not do. Thus, our original definition was a system that was capable of storing 10 TB of data or more and was capable of executing advanced workloads, such as behavioral analytics or market basket analysis, on those large volumes of data. As time went on, diversity of data started to become more prevalent in these systems (particularly the need to mix structured and unstructured data), which led to more widespread adoption of the "3 Vs" (volume, velocity, and variety) as a definition for big data, which continues to this day.

Cathy O'Neil

Program Director, the Lede Program (http://www.journalism.columbia. edu/page/1058-the-lede-program-an-introduction-to-data-practices/906) at Columbia University
Twitter: @mathbabedotorg (https://twitter.com/ mathbabedotorg)

"Big data" is more than one thing, but an important aspect is its use as a rhetorical device, something that can be used to deceive or mislead or overhype. It is thus vitally important that people who deploy big data models consider not just technical issues but the ethical issues as well.

Brad Peters

Chief Product Officer, Chairman at Birst (https://www.birst.com/)

In my view, big data is data that requires novel processing techniques to handle. Typically, big data requires massive parallelism in some fashion (storage and/or compute) to deal with volume and processing variety.

Gregory Piatetsky-Shapiro

President and Editor1, KDnuggets.com (http://www.kdnuggets.com/)
Twitter: @kdnuggets (https://twitter.com/kdnuggets)

The best definition I saw is, "Data is big when data size becomes part of the problem." However, this refers to the size only. Now the buzzword "big data" refers to the new data-driven paradigm of business, science and technology, where the huge data size and scope enables better and new services, products, and platforms. # *Big Data also generates a lot of hype and will probably be replaced by a new buzzword, like "Internet of Things," but "big data"-enabled services companies, like Google, Face book, Amazon, location services, personalized/precision medicine, and many more will remain and prosper.*

Jake Porway

Founder   and   Executive   Director, Data   Kind (http://www.datakind.org/)   Twitter: @DataKind (https://twitter.com/DataKind) , @jakeporway (https://twitter.com/jakeporway)

As our lives have moved from the physical to the digital world, our everyday tools like smart phones and ubiquitous Internet create vast amounts of data. **One of the best interpretations of the "big" in "big data" is expansive — whether you are a Fortune 500 company who just released an app that is creating a torrent of user data about every click and every activity of every user or a nonprofit who just launched a cell phone based app to find the closest homeless shelters that are now spewing forth information about every search and every click, we all have data.** *Dealing with this so-called big data requires a massive shift in technologies for storing, processing, and managing data — but also presents tremendous opportunity for the social sector to gather and analyze information faster to address some of our world's most pressing challenges.*

Kyle Rush

Head of Optimization, Optimizely (https://www.optimizely.com/) Twitter: @kylerush (https://twitter.com/kylerush)

There is certainly a colorful variety of definitions for the term big data out there. **To me it means working with data at a large scale and velocity.**

Anna Lee Saxenian

Dean, UC Berkeley School of Information (http://www.ischool.berkeley.edu/)   Twitter: @annosax (https://twitter.com/annosax)

I'm not fond of the phrase "big data" because it focuses on the volume of data, obscuring the far-reaching changes are making data essential to individuals and organizations in today's world. But if I have to define it I'd say that "big data" is data that can't be processed using standard databases because it is too big, too fast-moving, or too complex for traditional data processing tools.

Josh Schwartz

Chief Data Scientist, Chartbeat (https://chartbeat.com/) Twitter: @joshuadschwartz (https://twitter.com/joshuadschwartz)

The rising accessibility of platforms for the storage and analysis of large amounts of data (and the falling price per TB of doing so) has made it possible for a wide variety of organizations to store nearly all data in their purview — every log line, customer interaction, and event — unaggregated and for a significant period of time. The associated ethos of "store everything now and ask questions later" to me more than anything else characterizes how the world of computational systems looks under the lens of modern "big data" systems.

Peter Skomoroch

Entrepreneur, former Principal Data Scientist, LinkedIn (https://www.linkedin.com/nhome/)Twitter: @peteskomoroch (https://twitter.com/peteskomoroch)

Big data originally described the practice in the consumer Internet industry of applying algorithms to increasingly large amounts of disparate data to solve problems that had suboptimal solutions with smaller datasets. Many features and signals can only be observed by collecting massive amounts of data (for example, the relationships across an entire social network), and would not be detected using smaller samples. Processing large datasets in this manner was often difficult, time consuming, and error prone before the advent of technologies like MapReduce and Hadoop, which ushered in a wave of related tools and applications now collectively called big data technologies.

Anna Smith

Analytics Engineer, Rent the Runway (https://www.renttherunway.com/) Twitter: @OMGannaks (https://twitter.com/OMGannaks)

Big data is when data grows to the point that the technology supporting the data has to change. It also encompasses a variety of topics relating to how disparate data can be combined, processed into insights, and/or reworked into smart products.

Ryan Swanstrom

Data Science Blogger, Data Science 101 (http://101.datascience.community/) Twitter: @swgoof (https://twitter.com/swgoof)

Big data used to mean data that a single machine was unable to handle. Now big data has become a buzzword to mean anything related to data analytics or visualization.

Shashi Upadhyay

CEO and Founder, Lattice Engines (http://www.lattice-engines.com/) ;Twitter: @shashiSF (https://twitter.com/shashiSF)

*Big data is an umbrella term that means a lot of different things, but to me, **it means the possibility of doing extraordinary things using modern machine learning techniques on digital data.** Whether it is predicting illness, the weather, the spread of infectious diseases, or what you will buy next, it offers a world of possibilities for improving people's lives.*

Mark van Rijmenam

CEO/Founder, BigData-Startups (http://bigdata-startups.com/) Author of Think Bigger (http://www.amazon.com/gp/product/0814434150) Twitter: @VanRijmenam (https://twitter.com/VanRijmenam)

Big data is not all about volume; it is more about combining different data sets and to analyze it in real-time to get insights for your organization. Therefore, the right definition of big data should in fact be: mixed data.

Hal Varian

Chief Economist, Google Twitter: @halvarian (https://twitter.com/halvarian)

Big data means data that cannot fit easily into a standard relational database.

Timothy Weaver

CIO, Del Monte Foods (http://www.delmonte.com/) Twitter: @DelMonteCIO (https://twitter.com/DelMonteCIO)

I'm happy to repeat the definition I've heard used and think appropriately defines the over [all] subject. I believe its Forrester's definition of Volume, Velocity, Variety, and Variability. A lot of different data is coming fast and in different structures.

Steven Weber

Professor, UC   Berkeley   School   of   Information (http://www.ischool.berkeley.edu/) and Department of Political Science

*For me, the technological definitions (like "too big to fit in an Excel spreadsheet" or "too big to hold in memory") are important, but aren't really the main point. **Big data for me is data at a scale and scope that changes in some fundamental way (not just at margins) the range of solutions that can be considered when people and organizations face a complex problem.** Different solutions, not just 'more, better.'*

John Myles White

Twitter: @johnmyleswhite (https://twitter.com/johnmyleswhite)

***The term big data is really only useful if it describes a quantity of data that's so large that traditional approaches to data analysis are doomed to failure.** That can mean that you're doing complex analytics on data that's too large to fit into memory or it can mean that you're dealing with a data storage system that doesn't offer the full functionality of a standard relational database. What's essential is that your old way of doing things doesn't apply anymore and can't just be scaled out.*

Brian Wilt

Senior   Data   Scientist, Jawbone   (https://jawbone.com/) Twitter: @brianwilt (https://twitter.com/brianwilt)

*The joke is that **big data is data that breaks Excel**, but we try not to be snooty about whether you measure your data in MBs or PBs. Data is more about your team and the results they can get.*

Raymond Yee, Ph.D.

Software   Developer, unglue.it   (https://unglue.it/)
Twitter: @rdhyee (https://twitter.com/rdhyee)

Big data enchants us with the promise of new insights. Let's not forget the knowledge hidden in the small data right before us.

1.2   A Comprehensive List of Big Data Statistics

The team at Wikibon is pretty excited about the future of Big Data. From Big Data info graphics [6] to revenue forecasts [7] and funding reports [8] to our own Big Data Manifesto [9], the market is literally exploding with innovation and development. But the sheer magnitudes of the numbers we're analyzing around Big Data are tremendous in and of themselves.

Here are **over thirty significant Big Data statistics** to consider, broken out by the current environment, the growth of unstructured (user generated) data, the marketplace, and business issues related to Big Data.

Big Data in Today's Business and Technology Environment

- 2.7 Zetabytes of data exist in the digital universe today. (Source: https://www.marketingtechblog.com/ibm-big-data-marketing/)

- 235 Terabytes of data has been collected by the U.S. Library of Congress in April 2011. (Source: https://www.marketingtechblog.com/ibm-big-data-marketing/)

- The Obama administration is investing $200 million in big data research projects. (Source: http://wikibon.org/blog/taming-big-data/)

- IDC Estimates that by 2020, business transactions on the internet- business-to-business and business-to-consumer – will reach 450 billion per day. (Source: http://wikibon.org/blog/ unstructured-data/)

- Face book stores, accesses, and analyzes 30+ Petabytes of user generated data. (Source: http://wikibon.org/blog/taming-big-data/)

- Akamai analyzes 75 million events per day to better target advertisements. (Source: http://wikibon.org/blog/taming-big-data/)

- 94% of Hadoop users perform analytics on large volumes of data not possible before; 88% analyze data in greater detail; while 82% can now retain more of their data. (Source: http://www.sys-con.com/node/1920943)

- Walmart handles more than 1 million customer transactions every hour, which is imported into databases estimated to contain more than 2.5 petabytes of data. (Source)

- More than 5 billion people are calling, texting, tweeting and browsing on mobile phones worldwide. (Source)

- Decoding the human genome originally took 10 years to process; now it can be achieved in one week. (Source: http://www.economist.com/node/15557443)

- In 2008, Google was processing 20,000 terabytes of data (20 petabytes) a day. (Source: http://techcrunch.com/2008/

01/09/google-processing-20000-terabytes-a-day-and-growing/)

- The largest AT&T database boasts titles including the largest volume of data in one unique database (312 terabytes) and the second largest number of rows in a unique database (1.9 trillion), which comprises AT&T's extensive calling records. (Source: http://www.searcheduncovered.com/?dn=searchfusion.com&pid=9POK8YGH5)

The Rapid Growth of Unstructured Data

- YouTube users upload 48 hours of new video every minute of the day. (Source: http://wikibon.org/blog/big-data-infographics/)

- 571 new websites are created every minute of the day. (Source: http://wikibon.org/blog/big-data-infographics/)

- Brands and organizations on Face book receive 34,722 Likes every minute of the day. (Source: http://wikibon.org/blog/big-data-infographics/)

- 100 terabytes of data uploaded daily to Face book. (Source: http://wikibon.org/blog/big-data-infographics/)

- According to Twitter's own research in early 2012, it sees roughly 175 million tweets every day, and has more than 465 million accounts. (Source: http://www.mediapost.com/publications/article/173109/a-conversation-on-the-role-of-big-data-in-marketin.html)

- 30 Billion Pieces of content shared on Face book every month. (Source:

http://www.mckinsey.com/insights/business_
technology/big_data_the_next_frontier_for_innovation)

- Data production will be 44 times greater in 2020 than it was in 2009. (Source: http://wikibon.org/blog/big-data-infographics/)

- In late 2011, IDC Digital Universe published a report indicating that some 1.8 zettabytes of data will be created that year. (Source: https://www.siliconrepublic.com/companies/2003/11/19/security-giants-team-up-to-defeat-virus-threats)

In other words, the amount of data in the world today is equal to:

- Every person in the US tweeting three tweets per minute for 26,976 years.

- Every person in the world having more than 215m high-resolution MRI scans a day.

- More than 200bn HD movies – this would take a person 47m years to watch.

The Market and the Marketers' Challenge with Big Data

- Big data is a top business priority and drives enormous opportunity for business improvement. Wikibon's own study projects that big data will be a $50 billion business by 2017. (Source: http://siliconangle.com/blog/2012/07/13/studies-confirm-big-data-as-key-business-priority-growth-driver/)

- As recently as 2009 there were only a handful of big data projects and total industry revenues were under $100 million. By the end of 2012 more than 90 percent of the Fortune 500 will likely have at least some big data initiatives under way. (Source)

- Market research firm IDC has released a new forecast that shows the big data market is expected to grow from $3.2 billion in 2010 to $16.9 billion in 2015. (Source: http://statspotting.com/big-data-statistics-16-9-billion-market-by-2015/)

- In the developed economies of Europe, government administrators could save more than €100 billion ($149 billion) in operational efficiency improvements alone by using big data, not including using big data to reduce fraud and errors and boost the collection of tax revenues. (Source: http://www.mckinsey.com/insights/business_technology/big_data_the_next_frontier_for_innovation)

- Poor data across businesses and the government costs the U.S. economy $3.1 trillion dollars a year. (Source: http://www-new.insightsquared.com/2012/01/7-facts-about-data-quality-infographic/)

- 140,000 to 190,000. Too few people with deep analytical skills to fill the demand of Big Data jobs in the U.S. by 2018. (Source: http://www.mckinsey.com/insights/business_technology/big_data_the_next_frontier_for_innovation)

- 14.9 percent of marketers polled in Crain's B to B Magazine are still wondering "What is Big Data?" (Source: http://www.mckinsey.com/insights/business_technology/big_data_the_next_frontier_for_innovation)

- 39 percent of marketers say that their data is collected "too infrequently or not real-time enough." (Source: http://www. prnewswire.com/news-releases/study-finds-marketers- struggle-with-the-big-data-and-digital-tools-of-today- 142312475.html)

- 29 percent report that their marketing departments have "too little or no customer/consumer data." When data is collected by marketers, it is often not appropriate to real- time decision making. (Source: http://www.prnewswire. com/news-releases/study-finds-marketers-struggle-with- the-big-data-and-digital-tools-of-today-142312475.html)

Big Data & Real Business Issues

- According to estimates, the volume of business data worldwide, across all companies, doubles every 1.2 years. (Source)

- Poor data can cost businesses 20%–35% of their operating revenue. (Source): http://www.fathomdelivers.com/blog/ analytics-and-big-data/big-data-facts-and-statistics-that- will-shock-you/)

- Bad data or poor data quality costs US businesses $600 billion annually. (Source: http://www.fathomdelivers.com/ blog/analytics-and-big-data/big-data-facts-and-statistics- that-will-shock-you/)

- According to execs, the influx of data is putting a strain on IT infrastructure. 55 percent of respondents reporting a slowdown of IT systems and 47 percent citing data security problems, according to a global survey from Avanade. (Source)

- In that same survey, by a small but noticeable margin, executives at small companies (fewer than 1,000 employees) are nearly 10 percent more likely to view data as a strategic differentiator than their counter parts at large enterprises. (Source)

- Three-quarters of decision-makers (76 per cent) surveyed anticipate significant impacts in the domain of storage systems as a result of the "Big Data" phenomenon. (Source: http://www.btplc.com/news/articles/showarticle.cfm?article id={74889611-be1c-4f91-bbed-ab9e72e25918})

- A quarter of decision-makers surveyed predict that data volumes in their companies will rise by more than 60 per cent by the end of 2014, with the average of all respondents anticipating a growth of no less than 42 per cent. (Source)

- 40% projected growth in global data generated per year vs. 5% growth in global IT spending. (Source)

Wikibon in Analytics: (http://wikibon.org/blog/category/ analytics/) & Big Data (http://wikibon.org/blog/category/big-data/) on August 1, 2012

1.3   20 Shocking Facts and Figures about "Big Data"

Here at eSpatial (https://www.espatial.com/) we are very interested in the subjects surrounding big data, data management and data visualization. After all, our goal is to help businesses and organizations make the most of data of any kind by turning it into engaging and useful visuals. (You can see examples of how we do this here https://www.espatial.com/features/ public-maps).

The volume, velocity and variety of data created in the modern digital world are truly astounding. Here are some facts and figures that come across in the last while that illustrate that point.

1. The volume of data created by U.S. companies alone each year is enough to fill ten thousand Libraries of Congress. (http://www. sapvirtualevents.com/sapphirenow/sessiondetails.aspx?sId=2310)

2. According to McKinsey – a retailer using big data to the full could increase its operating margin. (http://www. mckinsey.com/Insights/MGI/Research/Technology_and_Innovation/Big_data_The_n ext_frontier_for_innovation)

3. Zuckerberg noted that 1 billion pieces of content are shared via Face book's Open Graph daily. (http://thenextweb.com/facebook/2012/07/ 26/facebook-says-that-1-billion-pieces-of-content-is-shared-via-open-graph-daily/)

4. Google's Eric Schmidt claims that every two days now we create as much information as we did from the dawn of civilization up until 2003 (http://techcrunch.com/2010/08/04/schmidt-data/)

5. Bad data or poor data quality costs US businesses $600 billion annually. (http://www.fathomdelivers.com/big-data-facts-and-statistics- that-will-shock-you/)

6. According to Gartner Big data will drive $232 billion in spending through 2016. (http://onvab.com/blog/big-data-facts-statistics-trends/)

7. 48 hours of video are uploaded to YouTube every minute, resulting in nearly 8 years of content every day (Source: http://www.pc- wholesale.com/graphics.html)

8. Data collection volume increased by 400% in 2012, from an average of 10 collection events per page to 50 (http://www.krux.com/ pro/broadcasts/krux_research/CIS2012/)

9. By 2015, 4.4 million IT jobs globally will be created to support big data, generating 1.9 million IT jobs in the United States (http://www.dailyfinance.com/2012/10/22/gartner-says-big-data-creates-big-jobs-44-million-/)

10. 70% of data is created by individuals – but enterprises are responsible for storing and managing 80% of it. (http://www.csc.com/insights/flxwd/78931-big_data_growth_just_beginning_to_explode).

11. By 2020 one third of all data will be stored, or will have passed through the cloud, and we will have created 35 zeta bytes worth of   data (http://www.csc.com/insights/flxwd/78931-big_data_growth_just_beginning_to_explode)

12. 1.5 million more data-savvy managers are needed to take full advantage of big data in the United States (http://www.mckinsey.com/Insights/MGI/Research/Technology_and_Innovation/Big_data_The_next_frontier_for_innovation)

13. There was an estimated 1.8 zettabytes of business data in use in 2011 up by 30 percent from 2010 (http://www.kpmg.com/Global/en/IssuesAndInsights/ArticlesPublications/accelerating-innovation/Documents/ehealth-implementation.pdf)

14. The Obama administration in the US announced $200 million in new R&D investments for "Big Data" initiative in 2012 (http://www.whitehouse.gov/sites/default/files/microsites/ostp/big_data_press_release.pdf)

15. Big Data is set to create 1.9M IT Jobs in U.S. By 2015 (http://www.cio.com/article/719484/Big_Data_to_Create_1.9M_IT_Jobs_in_U.S._By_2015?taxonomyId=3006)

16. Stacking a pile of CD-ROMs on top of one another until you'd reached the current global storage capacity for digital information would stretch 80,000 km beyond the moon

(http://smartdatacollective.com/ yellowfin/35139/digital-data-explosion-highlights-need-new-age-database-and-business-intelligence-te)

17. Up to 80% of the 247 billion email messages sent each day is spam (http://www.kurtosys.com/blog/12-big-facts-about-big-data/)

18. There are nearly as many pieces of digital information as there are stars in the universe (Source: http://realcomm.com/advisory/advisoryPrint.asp?AdvisoryID=544)

19. A survey reported that more than 37.5% of large organizations said that analyzing big data is their biggest challenge. (http://www.informationweek.com/big-data/news/big-data-analytics/240005662/big-data-development-challenges-talent-cost-time)

20. Visualization is in demand because it makes data-analysis easier. An InformationWeek Business survey found 45% of the 414 respondents cited "ease-of-use challenges with complex software/less-technically savvy employees" as the second-biggest barrier to adopting BI/analytics products. (http://www.informationweek.com/big-data/commentary/software/business-intelligence/240004277/how-to-choose-advanced-data-visualization-tools)

1.4   Actual and Potential Uses of Big Data for Development

Supplying new knowledge: The appeal of potentially leaping ahead is also shaped by the 'supply side' of big data. There is early practical evidence and a growing body of work on big data's novel potential to understand and affect human populations and processes. For example, big data has been used to track inflation online, estimate and predict changes in GDP in near real-time, monitor traffic or even a dengue outbreak. Monitoring social media data to analyze people's sentiments is opening new ways to measure welfare, while email and

Twitter data could be used to study internal and international migration. And an especially rich and growing academic literature is using CDRs to study migration patterns, socioeconomic levels and malaria spread, among others.

Guidance for analyzing big data, published by UN Global Pulse, has focused on four fields: *disaster response, public health, poverty and socioeconomic levels, and human mobility and transportation.*

Meanwhile, various other authors have proposed how big data could benefit development. The UN Global Pulse distinguished the 'early warning' uses from 'real-time awareness', or from 'real-time monitoring' of the impact of a policy. Others contrast its descriptive function (such as a real-time map) from predictive and diagnostic functions (Table 1).

Table 1: Actual and potential uses of big data for development

Applications	Explanation	Examples	Comments and Caveats
UN GLOBAL PULSE TAXONOMY			
1. Early warning	Big data can document and convey what is happening	This application is quite similar to the 'real-time awareness' application — although it is less ambitious in its objectives. Any info graphic, including maps, that renders vast amounts of data legible to the reader is an example of a descriptive application	Describing data always implies making choices and assumptions — about what and how data are displayed — that need to be made explicit and understood; it is well known that even bar graphs and maps can be misleading

Applications	Explanation	Examples	Comments and Caveats
2. Real-time awareness	Big data could give a sense of what is likely to happen, regardless of why	One kind of 'prediction' refers to what may happen *next* — the predictive policing mentioned above is one example. Another kind refers to predicting prevailing conditions through big data — as in the cases of socioeconomic levels using CDRs in Latin America and Ivory Coast	Similar comments as those made for the 'early-warning' and 'real-time awareness' applications apply
3.Real-time feedback	Big Data might shed light on why things may happen and what could be done about it	So far there have been next to no clear-cut examples of this application in development contexts. The example of CDR data used to show that bus routes in Abidjan could be 'optimized' falls closest to a case where the analysis identifies causal links and can shape policy	Most comments about 'real-time feedback' application apply. Strictly speaking, an example of the diagnostics application would require being able to assign causality. The prescriptive application works best in theory when supported by feedback systems and loops on the effect of policy actions
ALTERNATIVE TAXONOMY			
1. Descrip-tive	Early detection of anomalies in how populations	Predictive policing based upon the notion that analysis of historical data can reveal certain combinations of factors	This application assumes that certain regularities in human behaviors can be observed and modeled.

Applications	Explanation	Examples	Comments and Caveats
	use digital devices and services can enable faster response in times of crisis	associated with greater likelihood of increased criminality in a given area; it can be used to allocate police resources. Google is another example, where searches for particular terms ("runny nose", "itchy eyes") are analyzed to detect the onset of the flu season — although its accuracy	Key challenges for policy include the tendency of most malfunction-detection systems and forecasting models to over-predict — i.e. to have a higher prevalence of 'false positives'
2. Predictive	Big data can paint a fine-grained and current representation of reality which can inform the design and targeting of programs and policies	Using data released by Orange, researchers found a high degree of association between social networks and language distribution in Ivory Coast — suggesting that such data may provide information about language communities in countries where it is unavailable	The appeal and underlying argument for this application is the notion that big data may be a substitute for bad or scarce data; however models that show high correlations between 'big data-based' and 'traditional' indicators often require the availability of the latter to be trained and built. 'Real-time' here means using high frequency digital data to get a picture of reality at any given time
3. Prescrip-tive or	The ability to monitor a	Private corporations already. For development,	Although appealing, few (if any) actual

Applications	Explanation	Examples	Comments and Caveats
diagnostic	population in real time makes it possible to understand where policies and programs are failing, and make the necessary adjustments	this might include analyzing the impact of a policy action — e.g. the introduction of new traffic regulations — in real-time.	examples of this application exist; a challenge is making sure that any observed change can be attributed to the intervention or 'treatment'. However high-frequency data can also contain 'natural experiments' — such as a sudden drop in online prices of a given good — that can be leveraged to infer causality

*Sources: **Emmanuel Letouzé. Big data for development: opportunities and challenges. (UN Global Pulse, 29 May 2012), Robert Kirkpatrick. Digital smoke signals. (UN Global Pulse, 21 April 2011)***

1.5   Big Data, Big Comprehensive Advantage

The value that big data offers marketing executives, combined with the competition that drives businesses to seek market advantage, means we should expect to see increased investment in digital infrastructures. As discussed, such technology can help retailers optimize and narrow the gap between what their clients want and what they actually receive. Financial services [10], healthcare [11] and many other sectors will seek the opportunities and benefits that big data offers as well.

This overview of big data analytics will help you to understand what big data analytics is, which business value it brings and how organizations across different industries are applying it to address their unique business requirements. You'll also learn how Qubole, a leading self-service <u>big data platform</u> [12] works with leading analytics tools and engines as well as CRM and online marketing solutions to support the broad range of use-case requirements across industries all from one centralized location.

What is big data analytics?

The definition of big data holds the key to understanding big data analytics. According to the Gartner IT Glossary, Big Data is high-volume, high-velocity and high-variety information assets that demand cost effective, innovative forms of information processing for enhanced insight and decision making.

Volume refers to the amount of data. Many factors are contributing to high volume: sensor and machine-generated data, networks, social media, and much more. Enterprises are awash with terabytes and, increasingly, petabytes of big data.

Variety refers to the number of types of data. Big data extends beyond structured data such as numbers, dates and strings to include unstructured data such as text, video, audio, click streams, 3D data and log files.

Velocity refers to the speed of data processing. The pace at which data streams in from sources such as mobile devices, clickstreams, high-frequency stock trading, and machine-to-machine processes is massive and continuously fast moving.

Like conventional analytics and business intelligence solutions, big data mining and analytics helps uncover hidden patterns, unknown correlations, and other useful business information. However, big data tools can analyze high-volume, high-velocity and high-variety information assets far better than conventional tools and relational databases that struggle to capture, manage, and process big data within a tolerable elapsed time and at an acceptable total cost of ownership.

Organizations are using new big data technologies and solutions such as Hadoop, MapReduce, Hadoop Hive, Spark, Presto, Yarn, Pig, NoSQL databases and more to support their big data requirements.

1.6   Three Big Benefits of Big Data Analytics

Google, eBay and LinkedIn were among the first to experiment with big data. They developed proof of concept and small-scale projects to learn if their analytical models could be improved with new data sources. In many cases, the results of these experiments were positive. Today, big data analytics is no longer just an experimental tool. Many companies have begun to achieve real results with the approach, and are expanding their efforts to encompass more data and models.

After interviewing more than 50 companies for a SAS-sponsored project called *"Big Data in Big Companies"*, Tom Davenport (IIA Director of Research and faculty leader) reveals the true value of big data at work. Here's how they're getting value:

1. Cost reduction: Big data technologies like Hadoop and cloud-based analytics can provide substantial cost advantages. While comparisons between big data technology and traditional architectures (data warehouses and marts in particular) are difficult because of differences in functionality, a price comparison alone can suggest order-of-magnitude improvements. Virtually every large company I interviewed, however, is employing big data technologies not to replace existing architectures, but to augment them. Rather than processing and storing vast quantities of new data in a data warehouse, for example, companies are using Hadoop clusters for that purpose, and moving data to enterprise warehouses as needed for production analytical applications. Well-established firms like City, Wells Fargo and USAA all have substantial Hadoop projects underway that exist alongside existing storage and processing capabilities for analytics. While the long-term role of these technologies in enterprise architecture is unclear, it's likely that they will play a permanent and important role in helping companies manage big data.

2. Faster, better decision making: Analytics has always involved attempts to improve decision making, and big data doesn't change that. Large organizations are seeking both faster and better decisions with big data, and they're finding them. Driven by the speed of Hadoop and in-memory analytics, several companies I researched were focused on speeding up existing decisions. For example, Caesars, a leading gaming company that has long embraced analytics, is now embracing big data analytics for faster decisions. The company has data about its customers from its Total Rewards loyalty program, web click streams, and real-time play in slot machines. It has traditionally used all those data sources to understand customers, but it has been difficult to integrate and act on them in real time, while the customer is still playing at a slot machine or in the resort.

Caesars has found that if a new customer to its loyalty program has a run of bad luck at the slots; it's likely that customer will never come back. But if it can present, say, a free meal coupon to that customer while he's still at the slot machine, he is much more likely to return to the casino later. The key, however, is to do the necessary analysis in real time and present the offer before the customer turns away in disgust with his luck and the machines at which he's been playing. In pursuit of this objective, Caesars has acquired Hadoop clusters and commercial analytics software. It has also added some data scientists to its analytics group.

Some firms are more focused on making better decisions analyzing new sources of data. For example, health insurance giant United Healthcare is using "natural language processing" tools from SAS to better understand customer satisfaction and when to intervene to improve it. It starts by converting records of customer voice calls to its call center into text and searching for indications that the customer is dissatisfied. The company has already found that the text analysis improves its predictive capability for customer attrition models.

3. New products and services: Perhaps the most interesting use of big data analytics is to create new products and services for customers. Online companies have done this for a decade or so, but now predominantly offline firms are doing it too. GE, for example, has made a major investment in new service models for its industrial products using big data analytics.

Verizon Wireless is also pursuing new offerings based on its extensive mobile device data. In a business unit called Precision Market Insights, Verizon is selling information about how often mobile phone users are in certain locations, their activities and backgrounds. Customers thus far have included malls, stadium owners and billboard firms. For the Phoenix Suns, an NBA basketball team, Verizon's Precision Market Insights offered information on where people attending the team's games live, what percentage of game attendees are from out of town, and how often game attendees combine a basketball game with a baseball spring training game or a visit to a fast food chain. Such insights are obviously valuable to the Suns in targeting advertising and promotions.

1.7   How Big Data is changing the way we do business

Big Data is increasingly being used by prominent companies to outpace the competition. Be it established companies or startups; they are embracing data-focused strategies to outpace the competition.

In **healthcare**, clinical data can be reviewed treatment decisions based on big data algorithms that work on aggregate individual data sets to detect nuances in subpopulations that are so rare that they are not readily apparent in small samples.

Banking and retail have been early adopters of Big Data-based strategies. Increasingly, other industries are utilizing Big Data like that from sensors embedded in their products to determine how they are actually used in the real world.

Big Data is useful not just for its **scale** but also for its **real-time** and **high-frequency nature** that enables real-time testing of business strategies. While creating new growth opportunities for existing companies, it is also creating entirely new categories of companies that capture and analyze industry data about products and services, buyers and suppliers, consumer preferences and intent.

What can Big Data analytics do for you?

Optimize operations: The advent of advanced analytics, coupled with high-end computing hardware, has made it possible for organizations to analyze data more comprehensively and frequently. Analytics can help organizations answer new questions about business operations and advance decision-making, mitigate risks and uncover insights that may prove to be valuable to the organization. Most organizations are sitting upon heaps of transactional data. Increasingly, they are discovering and developing the capability to collect and utilize this mass of data to conduct controlled experiments to make better management decisions.

React faster: Big Data analytics allows organizations to make and execute better business decisions in very little time. Big Data and analytics tools allow users to work with data without going through complicated technical steps. This kind of abstraction allows data to be mined for specific purposes.

Improve the quality of services: Big Data analytics leads to generation of real business value by combining analysis, data and processing. The ability to include more data, run deeper analysis on it and deliver faster answers has the potential to improve services. It allows ever-narrower segmentation of customers and, therefore, much more precisely tailored products or services.

Big Data analytics helps organizations capitalize on a wider array of new data sources, capture data in flight, analyze all the data instead of sample subsets, apply more sophisticated analytics to it and get answers in minutes that formerly took hours or days.

Deliver relevant, focused customer communications: Mobile technologies tracks can now track where customers are at any point of time, if they're surfing mobile websites and what they're looking at or buying. Marketers can now serve customized messaging to their customers. They can also inform just a sample of people who responded to an ad in the past or run test strategies on a small sample.

Where is the gap? Data is more than merely figures in a database. Data in the form of text, audio and video files can deliver valuable insights when analyzed with the right tools. Much of this happens using natural language processing tools, which are vital to text mining, sentiment analysis, clinical language and name entity recognition efforts. As Big Data analytics tools continue to mature, more and more organizations are realizing the competitive advantage of being a data-driven enterprise.

Social media sites have identified opportunities to generate revenue from the data they collect by selling ads based on an individual user's interests. This lets companies target specific sets of individuals that fit an ideal client or prospect profile. The breakthrough technology of our time is undeniably Big Data and building a data science and analytics capability is imperative for every enterprise.

A successful Big Data initiative, then, can require a significant cultural transformation in an organization. In addition to building the right infrastructure, recruiting the right talent ranks among the most important investments an organization can make in its Big Data initiative. Having the right people in place will ensure that the right questions are asked -- and that the right insights are extracted from the data that's available. Data professionals are in short supply and are being quickly snapped up by top firms- Mahendra Mehta, head of Big Data & analytics programme, SP Jain School of Global Management; and Vibhanshu Bisht, senior consultant with the programme [13].

1.8 Re-imagine your business with Big Data Advanced Analytics

Now is the time to invest in the right technology foundation for your data center—one that will take you from data overload to data insights. Intel is enabling the cost-effective adoption of big-data-and-analytics-driven business models that fuel innovation.

With Intel® architecture-based advanced analytics solutions, you can efficiently and effectively capture process, analyze, and store vast amounts of data of all types. Built in partnership with industry leaders in big data and analytics software, our highly available, performance-optimized, open-standards-based solutions will support your most ambitious analytics-driven initiatives.

1.9 Big Data Challenges and Insights in India

As a stable economy with relatively low inflation, initiatives that leverage data to lower costs or increase productivity are highly prized. Additionally, the country has a low Big Data adoption rate, giving companies with the knowledge and insights a prime opportunity to quickly pull ahead of their competitors. Time is ripe to learn how to maximize innovation using Big Data.

1.10 Winning with Big Data: Maximizing Opportunities for Successful Business Outcomes

Hear from IDC's Chwee Kan Chua, the Associate Vice President for Big Data and Analytics and Cognitive Computing in Asia Pacific, on how Big Data is changing the way companies work. From covering the basics to providing case studies, Chwee Kan provides insights into initiating and developing your Big Data projects.

1.11 Collaborative Analytics for Personalized Cancer Care

Figure 2: Personalized Cancer Care

Intel and the Oregon Health & Science University (OHSU) Knight Cancer Institute (KCI) are using collaborative analytics to advance cancer care via genomics analysis and targeted treatment plans. Get inspired by this video of what happens when IT and the business—in this case, clinician researchers at KCI—collaborate to solve a major problem in medicine: identifying the best cancer care for a specific individual and then creating an effective treatment plan quickly. This is a big data analytics story brought to life through a collaborative cloud that ties together top cancer institutions across the world to share data and advance scientific discovery. The cloud provides access to technology and services (analytics platforms and tools) that dramatically increase the speed, precision, and cost-effectiveness of analyzing a patient's individual genetic profile. New big data technologies across a number of Intel's ecosystem partners are making this vision a reality in a way that can become main stream across large numbers of hospitals and research institutions.

1.12 Medicine with Advanced Analytics

Figure 3: Medicine with Advanced Analytics

Oregon Health & Science University (OHSU) and Intel aim to speed up whole genome analytics for cancer patients to a single day by 2020.

1.13 Combining Wearable Medical Devices and Big Data

Intel and the Michael J. Fox Foundation make a revolutionary step forward in Parkinson's research and a glimpse of future possibilities.

Figure 4: Wearable Medical Devices

1.14 Improving Heart Healthcare with Analytics

The Trusted Analytics Platform and the Internet of Things help the doctors at Penn Medicine's Heart Failure and Transplant Program.

Figure 5: Improving Heart Health Care with Analytics

1.15 Big Data Applications to Healthcare and Social Problems

Many countries are applying big data analytics to solve problems in healthcare and social services. In the United States, the

Pillbox project results in an annual $500 million reduction in healthcare costs through the application of big data analytics. The San Francisco Police Department has developed a big data system designed for crime prevention.

The UK is utilizing big data through establishment and management of the Foresight Horizon Scanning Centre, which serves as a countermeasure to various health and social problems such as obesity, potential risk management (coastal erosion, climate change), and epidemics. The EU is dealing with uncertainty through the iKnow (Interconnect Knowledge) project, which provides opportunities for research on earthquakes, tsunamis, terrorism, networking, and global crisis. The OECD adopted 'evaluating economic benefits of big data' as an agenda for the 15th Working Party on Indicators for the Information Society (WPIIS) by considering big data for business efficiency. Moreover, the Australian Government Information Management Office has saved time and resources by developing an automated tool that can analyze, search, and reuse massive information through government 2.0 (http://www.ncbi.nlm.nih.gov./pmc//article). In 2004, Singapore established the Risk Assessment and Horizon Scanning (RAHS) to prepare for future uncertainty regarding terrorism and epidemics.

In Korea, the National Information Society Agency (NIA) demonstrated the potential for suicide prevention through analysis of online buzzwords. Following this, a 2012 study revealed a relationship between quantity of searching 'suicide' and suicide rate by analyzing Google search trends.

1.16 How can Big Data help your business deal with disruptive competition?

Experts from IDC, Intel, Cloudera, SAS and SAP gathered at an executive roundtable discussion to highlight how big data and analytics allow enterprise companies manage disruption.

Big Data Case Studies: *Discover how these companies are maximizing the potential of big data analytics to capture new opportunities.*

Figure 6: Big data in Oil and Gas Exploration

Taking Oil and Gas Exploration to the Next Level: Down Under Geo Solutions harnesses the power of high-performance computing using a platform based on Intel® Xeon® processor E5-2600 v2 product family and Intel® Xeon Phi™ coprocessors to fast track their clients' exploration.

Big Data Analytics for New Sales Opportunities: Find out how United Daily News Group pushed recommendations to their website visitors and convert existing customer behavior to sales opportunities with fast and stable big data analytics, increasing revenue by almost 50%.

Industry Partnerships Accelerate Big Data: Intel and our network of partners are working together to spread analytics adoption, helping organizations use the data center to generate innovation and discovery. Intel and SAS work closely together to optimize feature-rich SAS analytics software for powerful Intel® architecture generate greater value from data.

Intel: Change the game to real-time business with Intel and SAP. Deploy Intel® Xeon® processors to optimize the power of SAP HANA* software for a blazing-fast, in-memory database solution for your transactional and analytical applications.

Cloudera and Intel: Cloudera and Intel are bringing data management and analytics innovations to the enterprise for the power, speed, and security to accelerate business insights. See which enterprises are benefiting [14].

1.17   Six real-world examples of how Healthcare can use Big Data Analytics

1. Ditch the Cookbook, Move to Evidence-Based Medicine

Cookbook medicine refers to the practice of applying the same battery of tests to all patients who come into the emergency department with similar symptoms. This is efficient, but it's rarely effective. As Dr. Leana Wan, an ED physician and co-author of When Doctors Don't Listen, puts it, "Having our patient is 'ruled out' for a heart attack while he has gallstone pain doesn't help anyone."

Dr. John Halamka, CIO at Boston's Beth Israel Deaconess Medical Center, says access to patient data—even from competing institutions—helps caregivers take an evidence-based approach to medicine. To that end, Beth Israel is rolling out a smart phone app that uses a Web-based- drag-and-drop UI to give caregivers self-service access to 200 million data points about 2 million patients. Admittedly, the health information exchange process necessary for getting that patient data isn't easy, Halamka says. Even when data's in hand, analytics can be complicated; what one electronic health record (EHR) system calls "high blood pressure" a second may call "elevated blood pressure" and a third "hypertension." To combat this, Beth Israel is encoding physician notes using the SNOMED CT standard. In addition to the benefit of standardization, using SNOMED CT makes data more searchable, which aids the research query process.

2. Give Everyone a Chance to Participate

The practice of medicine cannot succeed without research, but the research process itself is flawed, says Leonard D'Avolio, associate center director of biomedical informatics for MAVERIC within the U.S. Department of Veterans Affairs. Randomized controlled trials can last many years and cost millions of dollars, he says, while observational studies can suffer from inherent bias.

The VA's remedy has been the Million Veteran Program, a voluntary research program that's using blood samples and other health information from U.S. military veterans to study how genes affect one's health. So far, more than 150,000 veterans have enrolled, D'Avolio says.

All data is available to the VA's 3,300 researchers and its hospital academic affiliates. The idea, he says, is to embed the clinical trial within VistA, the VA EHR system, with the data then used to augment clinical decision support.

3. Build Apps That Make EHR 'Smart'

A data warehouse is great, says John D'Amore, founder of clinical analytics software vendor Clinfometrics, but it's the healthcare equivalent of a battleship that's big and powerful but comes with a hefty price tag and isn't suitable for many types of battles. It's better to use lightweight drones—in this case, applications—which are easy to build in order to accomplish a specific task.

To accomplish this, you'll need records that adhere to the Continuity of Care Document (CCD) standard. A certified EHR must be able to generate a CCD file, and this is often done in the form of a patient care summary. In addition, D'Amore says, you'll need to use SNOMED CT as well as LOINC to standardize your terminology. Echoing Halamka, co-presenter Dean Sittig, professor in the School of Biomedical Informatics at the University of Texas Health Science Center at Houston, acknowledges that this isn't easy. Stage 1 of meaningful use, the government incentive program that encourages EHR use, only makes the testing of care summary exchange optional, and at the moment fewer than 25 percent of hospitals are doing so.The inability or EHR, health and wellness apps to communicate among themselves is a "significant limitation," Sittig says. This is something providers will learn the hard way when stage 2 of meaningful use begins in 2014, D'Amore adds.

That said, the data that's available in CCD files can be put to use in several ways, D'Amore says, ranging from predictive analytics that can reduce hospital readmissions to data mining rules that look at patient charts from previous visits to fill gaps in current charts. The latter scenario has been proven to nearly double the number of problems that get documented in the patient record, he adds.

4. 'Domesticate' Data for Better Public Health Reporting, Research

Stage 2 of meaningful use requires organizations to submit syndrome surveillance data, immunization registries and other information to public health agencies. This says Brian Dixon, assistant professor of health informatics at Indiana University and research scientist with the Regenstrief Institute, offers a great opportunity to "normalize" raw patient data by mapping it to LOINC and SNOMED CT, as well as by performing real-time natural and using tools such as the Notifiable Condition Detector to determine which conditions are worth reporting.

Dixon compares this process to the Neolithic Revolution that refers to the shift from hunter-gatherer to agrarian society about 12,000 years ago. Healthcare organizations no longer need to hunt for and gather data; now, he says, the challenge is to domesticate and tame the data for an informaticist's provision and control.

The benefits of this process—in addition to meeting regulatory requirements—include research that takes into account demographic information as well as corollary tests related to specific treatments. This eliminates gaps in records that public health agencies often must fill with phone calls to already burdened healthcare organizations, Dixon notes. In return, the community data that physicians receive from public health agencies will be robust enough to offer what Dixon dubs "population health decision support."

5. Make Healthcare IT Vendors Articulate SOA Strategy

Dr. Mark Dente, managing director and chief medical officer for MBS Services, recommends that healthcare organizations "aggregate clinical data at whatever level you can afford to do it," then normalize data (as others explain above). This capability to normalize data sets in part explains the growth and success of providers such as Kaiser Permanente and Intermountain Healthcare, he says.

To do this, you need to create modules and apps such as the ones D'Amore describes. This often requires linking contemporary data sets to legacy IT architecture. The MUMPS programming language, originally designed in 1966, has served healthcare's data processing needs well, but data extraction is difficult, Dente says.

Service oriented architecture is the answer, Dente says, because it can be built to host today's data sets as well as tomorrow's, from sources that organizations don't even know they need yet. (This could range from personal medical devices to a patient's grocery store rewards card.) Challenge vendors on their SOA strategy, Dente says, and be wary of those who don't have one.

6. Use Free Public Health Data for Informed Strategic Planning

Strategic plans for healthcare organizations often resort to reactive responses to the competitive market and a "built it and they will come" mentality, says Les Jebson, director of the Diabetes Center of Excellence within the University of Florida Academic Health System. Taking a more proactive approach requires little more than a some programming know-how.

Using Google Maps and free public health data, the University of Florida created heat maps for municipalities based on numerous factors, from population growth to chronic disease rates, and compared those factors to the availability of medical services in those areas. When merged with internal data, strategic planning becomes both visually compelling (critical for C-level executives) and objective (critical for population health management), Jebson says. With this mapping, for example, the university found three Florida countries that were underserved for breast cancer screening and thus redirected its mobile care units accordingly.

1.18   Extracting the Value from Big Data

By definition, *big data* exceeds the processing capacity of conventional relational database management systems. The amount of information stored worldwide topped 2.8 zettabytes of data in 2012; by 2020, this is expected to be 50 times larger than it is today. Dealing with that onslaught requires high-performance analytics, also known as *big data analytics.* By some estimates, only 0.5 percent of available data are analyzed. What benefits are global communities missing because those insights remain untapped and trapped in the relational database systems of the past? The emerging technology of big data analytics brings us to a tipping point. The power to analyze huge amounts of data gives us an unprecedented ability to make better, more insightful decisions in each of the areas needed for inclusive growth. With big data analytics, we are shifting from a world in which we *think* we know how to elevate the human condition into a world in which we *know* how to do this and we can *prove* it.

The needs are certainly considerable for the following social issues:

- ✓ Unemployment is a global problem. Could we proactively address it by identifying patterns and countering them at their source, using methods such as "predict to prevent" and "predict to prepare"?
- ✓ The food and water supply is not secure in many areas of the world. By expanding on emerging approaches to data for development (D4Development) to include D4Water, D4Food, D4Energy, and so on, can big data analytics identify the areas of greatest need and optimize the flow of resources to the right places?

✓ Developing nations do not yet have access to first-rate education. Can our digital resources change that through virtual self-learning platforms combined with common certification standards?

✓ Disease and natural disasters provide further setbacks to already-challenged nations. Can analytics level the playing field and bring stricken economies to competitive strength faster?

✓ Huge sums of money that could be spent on bettering the world are currently lost through waste, leakage, and fraud. Can big data analytics stop the drain and divert the money back where it belongs?

The answer to all of those questions is now "yes," thanks to the modern ability to tap into vast data sources and use complex models. We can now find solutions to extremely complex problems when it matters the most and uncover new ways to address global issues and foster inclusive growth. Big data analytics breaks free of conventional limitations, helps us influence the impact of actions in advance, and makes it possible to do things never before conceived.

The sense of urgency is strong—all of the data that exist today will represent just 10 percent of the total in three years. That is a truly transformative force that can be addressed only by analyzing the meaning of all those data, and it is also the reason that big data analytics is the path forward to inclusive growth. Returning to driving inclusive growth, we note that education spurs job creation, and education together with jobs lead to societal well-being. In today's digital age, it is data that will drive all three forward to the desired outcome of inclusive growth. This chapter examines each of these components in turn.

1.19 Top Ten free, easy-to-use, and powerful Data Analysis Tools for Business

Ten free, easy-to-use, and powerful tools to help you analyze and visualize data, analyze social networks, do optimization, search more efficiently, and solve your data analysis problems. Although the challenge of collecting and analyzing "*Big Data*" requires some complex and technical solutions, the fact is that most businesses do not realize what they are currently capable of. There are a number of exceptionally powerful analytical tools that are free and open source that you can leverage today to *enhance your business and develop skills that can genuinely propel your career*.

Rather than just leave you to navigate the frightening and giant world of IT tools and software, I have put together a list of what I see as the *Top 10 Data analysis tools for Business*. I picked these because of their **free availability** for personal use, **ease of use** (no coding and intuitively designed), **powerful capabilities** (beyond basic excel), and **well-documented resources** (if you get stuck, you can Google your way through).

1. Tableau Public (https://public.tableau.com/s/): Tableau democratizes visualization in an elegantly simple and intuitive tool. It is exceptionally powerful in business because it communicates insights through data visualization. Although great alternatives exist, Tableau Public's million row limit provides a great playground for personal use and the free trial is more than long enough to get you hooked. In the analytics process, Tableau's visuals allow you to quickly investigate a hypothesis, sanity check your gut, and just go explore the data before embarking on a treacherous statistical journey.

2. OpenRefine (http://openrefine.org/): Formerly GoogleRefine, OpenRefine is a data cleaning software that allows you to get everything ready for analysis. What do I mean by that? Well, let's look at an example. Recently, I was cleaning up a database that included chemical names and noticed that rows had different spellings, capitalization, spaces, etc that made it very difficult for a computer to process. Fortunately, OpenRefine contains a number of clustering algorithms (groups together similar entries) and makes quick work of an otherwise messy problem. Increase Java Heap Space (http://www.wikihow.com/Increase-Java-Memory-in-Windows-7) to run large files (Google the tip for exact instructions!)

3. KNIME (http://www.knime.org/): KNIME allows you to manipulate, analyze, and modeling data in an incredibly intuitive way through visual programming. Essentially, rather than writing blocks of code, you drop nodes onto a canvas and drag connection points between activities. More importantly, KNIME can be extended to run R, python, text mining, chemistry data, etc, which gives you the option to dabble in the more advanced code driven analysis. **TIP- Use "File Reader" instead of CSV reader for CSV files. Strange quirk of the software.

4. RapidMiner (http://sourceforge.net/projects/rapidminer/): Much like KNIME, RapidMiner operates through visual programming and is capable of manipulating, analyzing and modeling data. Most recently, RapidMiner won KDnuggets software poll (http://www.kdnuggets.com/ 2014/06/kdnuggets-annual-software-poll-rapidminer-continues-lead.html); demonstrating that data science does not need to be a counter-intuitive coding endeavor.

5. Google Fusion Tables (https://support.google.com/fusiontables/answer/2571232): Meet Google Spreadsheets cooler, larger, and much needier cousin. Google Fusion tables are an incredible tool for data analysis, large data-set visualization, and mapping. Not surprisingly, Google's incredible mapping software plays a big role in pushing this tool onto the list. Take for instance this map, which I made to look at oil production platforms in the Gulf of Mexico. With just a quick upload, Google Fusion tables recognized the latitude and longitude data and got to work.

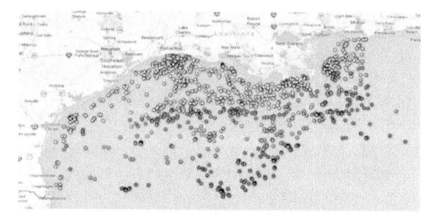

Figure 7: Google Fusion Tables

6.   **NodeXL** (http://nodexl.codeplex.com/): NodeXL is visualization and analysis software of networks and relationships. Think of the giant friendship maps you see that represent LinkedIn or Face book connections. NodeXL takes that a step further by providing exact calculations. If you're looking for something a little less advanced, check out the node graph on Google Fusion Tables, or for a little more visualization try out Gephi (https://gephi.github.io/).

7. **Import.io** (https://import.io/): Web scraping and pulling information off of websites used to be something reserved for the nerds. Now with Import.io, everyone can harvest data from websites and forums. Simply highlight what you want and in a matter of minutes Import.io walks you through and "learns" what you are looking for. From there, Import.io will dig, scrape, and pull data for you to analyze or export.

8. Google Search Operators (http://www.sourcinghacks. com/google-search-operators-and-more/): Google is an undeniably powerful resource and search operators just take it a step up. Operators essentially allow you to quickly filter Google results to get to the most useful and relevant information. For instance, say you're looking for a Data science report published this year from ABC Consulting. If we presume that the report will be in PDF we can search *"Date Science Report" site: ABCConsulting.com File type: PDF* then underneath the search bar, use the "Search Tools" to limit the results to the past year. The operators can be even more useful for discovering new information or market research.

9. Solver: Solver is an optimization and linear programming tool in excel that allows you to set constraints (Don't spend more than this many dollars, be completed in that many days, etc). Although advanced optimization may be better suited for another program (such as R's optim package - http://stat.ethz.ch/R-manual/R-devel/library/ stats/html/optim.html), Solver will make quick work of a wide range of problems.

10. WolframAlpha (http://www.wolframalpha.com/): Wolfram Alpha's search engine is one of the web's hidden gems and helps to power Apple's Siri. Beyond snarky remarks, Wolfram Alpha is the nerdy Google, provides detailed responses to technical searches and makes quick work of calculus homework. For business users, it presents information charts and graphs, and is excellent for high level pricing history, commodity information, and topic overviews. Although these tools make analysis easier, they're only as valuable as the information put in and analysis that you conduct. So take a moment to learn a few new tricks, challenge yourself, and let these tools enhance and complement the logic and reasoning skills that you already have [15, 16].

1.20   Big Data Trends 2016

As we are coming towards the end of 2015 we have seen a considerable amount of change in big data and its perception. We believe that 2016 is going to throw even more up for the industry, so we are taking a look at what we think are going to be the top trends in the next 12 months.

Quantum Computing To Grow

The concept of quantum computing has been around for a long time, but has always been seen as something that we are going to see become a real possibility in some undefined future. However, 2016 may be when its use becomes more commonplace.

After recent work by Australian researchers at the University of NSW it has become possible to code the machines in a more cohesive and understandable way. They have managed to entangle a pair of quits for the first time, allowing for more complex coding to be created and therefore the use of quantum computers to potentially become more widespread.

2016 will not see the use of quantum computing becoming common, but its presence within data will become far more pronounced and some of the more experimental and forward thinking tech giants may begin to use it more frequently.

AI & Machine Learning

As the IOT moves steadily along the Gartner Hype Cycle, one of its most powerful foundations is going to become increasingly important and companies are likely to adopt machine learning and AI within their own systems.

It will allow devices to automatically collect, store and analyze data, of which there will again be a huge increase in the next 12 months. Through the use of both AI and Machine learning, it becomes possible for these huge amounts of information to be processed, stored and mined without needing human interactions to do so. It creates the ultimate tool for modern data driven organizations and 2016 will see even more businesses realize this.

Improved Security Scrutiny

Data in 2015 has been in the media spotlight, but not for the ways that many would want. Unfortunately, the data hacks have become more common than many would have predicted, from the Ashley Madison hack to the Talk hack, it has shown up that companies could do more to protect their data.

2016 will therefore see an increased scrutiny on how data is dealt with and protected. This will also come at a time when many countries around at the world are looking at implementing new data protection and data access laws, meaning that the waters are going to become increasingly muddied.

Within this, companies will need to increase their security spending, improve database safety and prepare for seismic changes in the way that hackers work. It is going to be a difficult year for data security, but it will build the foundation on which future stable and robust data security is created.

Big Data to Become Small

This is a twofold prediction. Firstly the use of masses of data as an indicator of success will turn to the quality of the data being collected. This will mean that the variety for each company is likely to decrease, but the specific data that will be collected will become far more efficient, useful and plentiful. As companies realize that most of what they collect isn't being used and just taking up storage space, this will become more apparent and the use of this data will come under increased scrutiny. Secondly, the term big data is likely to become used more infrequently as a business function; instead this is likely to be broken down into the sum of its parts. Database management and data science technically fall under the same category at the moment, when the reality is that they are different. Companies are likely to realize this and use the term as a catch all rather than a function in itself.

Analytics to Be Simplified & Outsourced

We have seen the use of new data visualization and automation software breaking down the barriers between the data initiated and uninitiated. Through a continuation of this trend, we are going to see that conducting analysis on datasets become considerably simpler; we have already seen software that has a drag and drop analysis option available on tablets which is useable by almost anybody. This comes not only from the needs of the untrained, but because we are still in the midst of a skills gap in the data scientist market, meaning that companies need to look at how they can leverage their data without necessarily having the skills in house to do so. Therefore we have these pieces of software that can do relatively simple analysis for companies, but for the more complex analysis needed we are likely to see this being outsourced to companies who have the expertise. This is likely to be a growth area in 2016 and we already have a number of companies leading the way in this regard.

Data in the Hands of the Masses

Data is no longer just something being discussed in boardrooms and laboratories at the highest levels. Every day people get out of bed and look at the data collected on their sleep patterns, investigate what they are spending money on through apps or even just looking at the possession and running stats from their favourite sports teams. Data is now everywhere in our society, which means that the general population is becoming increasingly clued up on using it. It is not to say that the general population are going to suddenly become data scientists, but it means that the kind of data shared can become more complex as the understanding of it across a population increases. When discussing important matters, informed discussions can be had with data rather than conjecture. There will still be many who throw themselves at things with blind faith and gut instinct, but 2016 will see a growing segment of the population who can engage with matters through data in a way that they never could before, both through increased access and understanding of it.

1.21   The Future of Big Data

Experts predict big possibilities for 'Big Data' and some problems, too. While many see promise in the future of data analysis, some fear that work with gigantic stores of information could lead to privacy abuses and mistaken forecasts. The growing technological ability to collect and analyze massive sets of information, known as Big Data, could lead to revolutionary changes in business, political and social enterprises, according to a new survey of internet experts and stakeholders. But while leading technologists and researchers around the world look forward to the positive impact of Big Data, many also worry about potential drawbacks.

A new Pew Internet / Elon University survey of 1,021 Internet experts, observers and stakeholders measured current opinions about the potential impact of human and machine analysis of newly emerging large data sets in the years ahead. The survey is an opt-in, online canvassing. Some 53% of those surveyed predicted that the rise of Big Data is likely be "a huge positive for society in nearly all respects" by the year 2020. Some 39% of survey participants said it is likely to be "a big negative."

"The analysts who expect we will see a mostly positive future say collection and analysis of Big Data will improve our understanding of ourselves and the world," said researcher Lee Rainie, director of the Pew Research Center's Internet & American Life Project. "They predict that the continuing development of real-time data analysis and enhanced pattern recognition could bring revolutionary change to personal life, to the business world and to government."

Survey respondent Hal Varian, chief economist at Google, said, "This is likely to lead to a better informed, more pro-active fiscal and monetary policy." Bryan Trogdan, a consultant and entrepreneur, said, "Big Data is the new oil." And David Weinberger of Harvard University's Berkman Center observed, "We are just beginning to understand the range of problems Big Data can solve, even though it means acknowledging that we're less unpredictable, free, madcap creatures than we'd like to think. It also raises the prospect of some of our most important knowledge will consist of truths we can't understand because our pathetic human brains are just too small."

As with all technological evolution, the experts also anticipate some negative outcomes. "The experts responding to this survey noted that the people controlling the resources to collect, manage and sort large data sets are generally governments or corporations with their own agendas to meet," said Janna Anderson, director of Elon's Imagining the Internet Center and a co-author of the study. "They also say there's a glut of data and a shortage of human curators with the tools to sort it well, there are too many variables to be considered, the data can be manipulated or misread, and much of it is proprietary and unlikely to be shared."

Survey participant John Pike, director of GlobalSecurity.org, said, "The world is too complicated to be usefully encompassed in such an undifferentiated Big Idea. Who's 'Big Data' are we talking about? Wall Street, Google, the NSA? I'm small, so I do not like Big."

Survey respondent Danah Boyd, a Microsoft research scientist and expert on the societal impacts of the Internet, observed, "The Internet magnifies the good, bad and ugly of everyday life. Of course these things will be used for good. And of course they'll be used for bad and ugly. Science fiction gives us plenty of templates for imagining where that will go. What will be interesting is how social dynamics, economic exchange and information access are inflected in new ways that open up possibilities that we cannot yet imagine. This will mean a loss of some aspects of society that we appreciate but also usher in new possibilities."

This is the seventh report generated out of an analysis of the results of a Web-based survey fielded in fall 2011 to gather opinions on eight Internet issues from a select group of experts and the highly engaged Internet public. *Details can be found here* [17].

Following is a wide-ranging selection of respondents' remarks

I am a big believer in now casting. Nearly every large company has a real-time data warehouse and has more timely data on the economy than our government agencies. In the next decade we will see a public/private partnership that allows the government to take advantage of some of these private sector data stores. This is likely to lead to a better informed, more pro-active fiscal and monetary policy" —**Hal Varian**, chief economist at Google.

"Big Data allows us to see patterns we have never seen before. This will clearly show us interdependence and connections that will lead to a new way of looking at everything. It will let us see the 'real-time' cause and effect of our actions. What we buy, eat, donate, and throw away will be visual in a real-time map to see the ripple effect of our actions. That could only lead to mores-conscious behavior" — **Tiffany Shlain**, director and producer of the film 'Connected' and founder of The Webby Awards.

"Global climate change will make it imperative that we proceed in this direction of now casting to make our societies more nimble and adaptive to both human-caused environmental events and extreme weather events or decadal scale changes. Coupled with the data, though, we must have a much better understanding of decision making, which means extending knowledge about cognitive biases, about boundary work (scientists, citizens, and policymakers working together to weigh options on the basis not only of empirical evidence but also of values)" —**Gina Maranto**, co-director for ecosystem science and coordinator, graduate program in environmental science at the University of Miami.

"Media and regulators are demonizing Big Data and its supposed threat to privacy. Such moral panics have occurred often thanks to changes in technology…But the moral of the story remains: there is value to be found in this data; value in our new found publishes. Google's founders have urged government regulators not to require them to quickly delete searches because, in their patterns and anomalies, they have found the ability to track the outbreak of the flu before health officials could and they believe that by similarly tracking a pandemic, millions of lives could be saved. Demonizing data, big or small, is demonizing knowledge, and that is never wise" —**Jeff Jarvis**, professor, pundit and blogger.

"Large, publicly available data sets, easier tools, wider distribution of analytics skills, and early stage artificial intelligence software will lead to a burst of economic activity and increased productivity comparable to that of the Internet and PC revolutions of the mid to late 1990s. Social movements will arise to free up access to large data repositories, to restrict the development and use of AIs, and to 'liberate' AIs" —**Sean Mead**, director of analytics at Mead, Mead & Clark, Inter brand.

"The world is too complicated to be usefully encompassed in such an undifferentiated Big Idea. Who's 'Big Data' are we talking about? Wall Street, Google, the NSA? I am small, so generally I do not like Big" —**John Pike**, director of GlobalSecurity.org

"We can now make catastrophic miscalculations in nanoseconds and broadcast them universally. We have lost the balance inherent in 'lag time" —**Marcia Richards Suelzer**, senior analyst at Wolters Kluwer.

"Better information is seldom the solution to any real-world social problems. It may be the solution to lots of business problems, but it's unlikely that the benefits will accrue to the public. We're more likely to lose privacy and freedom from the rise of Big Data" —**Barry Parr**, owner and analyst for Media Savvy.

"Big Data will not be so big. Most data will remain proprietary, or reside in incompatible formats and inaccessible databases where it cannot be used in 'real time.' The gap between what is theoretically possible and what is done (in terms of using real-time data to understand and forecast cultural, economic and social phenomena) will continue to grow" —**Jeff Eisenach**, managing director, Navigant Economics LLC, a consulting business; formerly a senior policy expert with the US Federal Trade Commission.

"Never underestimate the stupidity and basic sinfulness of humanity" —**Tom Rule**, educator, technology consultant, and musician based in Macon, Georgia.

"More information will be beneficial in all sorts of ways we can't even fathom right now. Namely because we don't have the data" —**John Capone**, freelance writer and journalist; former editor of Media Post Communications publications.

"The huge prospects for the 'Internet of Things' tip me to checking the first choice. I tend to think of the Internet of Things as multiplying points of interactivity—sensors and/or actuators— throughout the social landscape. As the cost of connectivity goes down the number of these points will go up, diffusing intelligence everywhere" —**Fred Hapgood**, technology author and consultant; moderator of the Nano systems Interest Group at MIT in the 1990s.

"Data that is much more available in quantity, cost, and quality will be a marked feature of the coming decade, but much of that will be 'Little Data,' which is useful mostly or entirely only locally (for practical or privacy concerns). I will want data possibly related to my health kept as private as possible. My house should enable control for light, heat, sound, image, etc. that enhances my experiences and convenience, and saves resources. For example, lighting will increasingly respond to occupancy or 'presence' (not just that someone is present, but who they are, how many they are, and what activity engaged in), and so provide better lighting services, automatically, and at less net energy than before. However, who outside the building should care about the details? No one - Big Data will be a net plus, but a sizeable amount of problems will be created by it as well, particularly around security and privacy" —**Bruce Nordman**, research scientist at Lawrence Berkeley National Laboratory.

"Big Data should be developed within a context of openness and improved understandings of dynamic, complex whole ecosystems. There are difficult matters that must be addressed, which will take time and support, including: public and private sector entities agreeing to share data; providing frequently updated meta-data; openness and transparency; cost recovery; and technical standards" —**Richard Lowenberg**, director, broadband planner 1st-Mile Institute; network activist since early 1970s.

"The real power of 'Big Data' will come depending largely on the degree to which it is held in private hands or openly available. Openly available data, and widespread tools for manipulating it, will create new ways of understanding and governing ourselves as individuals and as societies" —**Alex Halavais**, associate professor at Quinnipiac University; vice president of the Association of Internet Researchers; author of *Search Engine Society.*

"In order for Big Data to have a positive impact on society overall, it has to be transparent. Ordinary citizens would have to be able to query the data set and discover real answers, regardless of the light that shows on individuals or corporations or governments. There is too much at stake for these parties to allow open, transparent access to this data. As long as some data sets or parts of data sets are hidden, there is room for misuse and manipulation. I think this manipulation is sure to take place. Unless Big Data is democratized on a massive scale, it will overall have a negative impact on society. Right now, I don't see much hope for such democratization" —**Nathan Swartzendruber**, technology education at SWON Libraries Consortium.

Respondents were allowed to keep their remarks anonymous if they chose to do so. Following are predictive statements selected from the hundreds of anonymous comments from survey participants:

I.   "If Big Data is not also Wide Data (that is, dispersed among as many players and citizens as possible) then it will be a negative overall".

II.   "The few people who will understand the dangers of 'Big Data' will have high cognitive abilities and training. The general population will continue to rely on crappy results because they know no better".

III. "Collection is likely to be imperceptible to most, unless law and regulation make it overt and provide the individual choice. Analysis likely will suffer from a divorce in knowledge and context between the orderers and the providers of the analysis. No example currently is better than that between the avaricious ignorance of bank executives and the technologists' naiveté about the realities of collateralized debt obligations. Reliance will lead to increasingly unstable processes where only those able to use Big Data will be able to protect themselves, with the individual increasingly at risk. Rapid program stock trading is a current, pernicious example".

IV.   "We will become more addicted to what the databases tell us. It might impair risk-taking for the good. We'll depend more on models than instincts".

V.   "Big Data is not well matched to tiny minds. The data sets now exceed the capabilities of most businesspeople to know what to do with, about, and for the data. This will lead to huge abuse and misapplication".

VI.   "We still haven't figured out the implications of chaos theory, and if 'Big Data' and future casting aren't perfect examples of chaos-based information, then I don't know what is. Generically, we're not prepared for this great a lack of privacy; we're even less prepared for data of this magnitude available only to the powerful, rich, or connected".

VII. "Legal protections for the citizenry (in those jurisdictions which are not decidedly autocratic) are lacking, and will be essential to prevent corporate or governmental abuse of the insights available about people through widely aggregated data, as well as through new surveillance techniques".

VIII. "The old lesson that correlation is not causation seems never to be learned. The control over data means that inaccurate data is hard to identify and correct. I see that the problems will only increase with the size of the datasets. Most emphasis seems to be given to doing clever things with data rather than ensuring its validity or giving the right people control over it".

IX. "The fact that most data is unstructured is a huge issue, and I doubt that we will solve the problems associated with getting meaning from that morass." Another anonymous survey participant wrote, "Certainly in 2020 Big Data will be more risky than trustworthy. We just won't have enough experience—the equivalent of the 100-year flood in forecasting terms—and so our systems will 'look good' on some basic problems but prove to make whoppers of mistakes".

X. The findings reflect the reactions in an online, opt-in survey of a diverse set of 1,021 technology stakeholders and critics who were asked to choose one of two provided scenarios and explain their choice. While 53 percent selected the statement that that Big Data "will cause more problems than it solves," a significant number of the survey participants who selected that scenario said the true outcome will be a little bit of both scenarios, and many said while they chose the first scenario as a "vote" for what they hope will happen they actually expect the outcome will be closer to the second scenario.

53% agreed with the statement: Thanks to many changes, including the building of "the Internet of Things," human and machine analysis of large data sets will improve social, political, and economic intelligence by 2020. The rise of what is known as "Big Data" will facilitate things like "now casting" (real-time "forecasting" of events); the development of "inferential software" that assesses data patterns to project outcomes; and the creation of algorithms for advanced correlations that enable new understanding of the world. Overall, the rise of Big Data is a huge positive for society in nearly all respects.

39% agreed with the alternate statement, which posited: Thanks to many changes, including the building of "the Internet of Things," human and machine analysis of Big Data will cause more problems than it solves by 2020. The existence of huge data sets for analysis will engender false confidence in our predictive powers and will lead many to make significant and hurtful mistakes. Moreover, analysis of Big Data will be misused by powerful people and institutions with selfish agendas who manipulate findings to make the case for what they want. And the advent of Big Data has a harmful impact because it serves the majority (at times inaccurately) while diminishing the minority and ignoring important outliers. Overall, the rise of Big Data is a big negative for society in nearly all respects.

A total of 8% did not respond. The survey results are based on a non-random online sample of 1,021 Internet experts and other Internet users, recruited via email invitation, conference invitation, or link shared on Twitter, Google Plus or Face book. Since the data are based on a non-random sample, a margin of error cannot be computed, and the results are not projectable to any population other than the people participating in this sample. The "predictive" scenarios used in this tension pair were created to elicit thoughtful responses to commonly found speculative futures thinking on this topic in 2011; this is not a formal forecast. Many respondents remarked that both scenarios will happen to a certain degree.

1.22 Risks and Challenges and Paradox

Risks and challenges: Of course, big data's promise has been met with warnings about its perils. The risks, challenges and more generally the hard questions were articulated as 'early' as 2011.

Perhaps the most severe risks and most urgent avenues for research and debate are to individual rights, privacy, identity, and security [18]. In addition to the obvious intrusion of surveillance activities and issues around their legality and legitimacy, there are important questions about 'data anonymization': what it means and its limits. A study of movie rentals showed that even 'anonymized' data could be 'de-anonymized' linked to a known individual by correlating rental dates of as few as three movies with the dates of posts on an online movie platform. Other research has found that CDRs that record location and time, even when free of any individual identifier could be re-individualized. In that case, four data points were theoretically sufficient to uniquely single out individuals out of the whole dataset with 95 per cent accuracy.

Critics also point to the risks associated with basing decisions on biased data or dubious analyses (sometimes called threats to both external and internal validity). If policymakers come to believe that 'the data don't lie', such risks could be especially worrisome. A key challenge in big data is that the people generating it have selected themselves as data generators through their activity. In technical terms this is a 'selection bias' and it means that analysis of big data is likely to yield a different result from a traditional survey (or poll), which would seek out a representative cross section of the population. For example, trying to answer the question "do people in country A prefer rice or chips?" by mining data on Twitter would be biased in favour of young people's preferences as they make up more of Twitter's users. So analyses based on big data may lack 'external validity', although it is possible that individuals that differ in almost all respects may have similar preferences and display identical behaviors (young people may have the same preferences as older people). Another risk comes from analyses that are flawed because they lack 'internal validity'. For instance, a sharp drop in the volume of CDRs from an area might be interpreted, based on past events, as heralding a looming conflict. But it could actually be caused by something different, such as a mobile phone tower having gone down in the area.

Another risk is that analyses based on big data will focus too much on correlation and prediction — at the expense of cause, diagnostics or inference, without which policy is essentially blind. A good example is 'predictive policing'. Since about 2010, police and law enforcement forces in some US and UK cities have crunched data to assess the likelihood of increased crime in certain areas, predicting rises based on historical patterns. Forces dispatch their resources accordingly, and this has reduced crime in most cases. However, unless there is knowledge of why crime is rising it's not possible to put in place preventive policy that tackles the root causes or contributing factors.

Yet another big risk that has not received the attention it merits is big data's potential to create a 'new digital divide' that may widen rather than close existing gaps in income and power worldwide. One of the 'three paradoxes' of big data is that because it requires analytical capacities and access to data that only a fraction of institutions, corporations and individuals have, the data revolution may disempowered the very communities and countries it promises to serve. People with the most data and capacities would be in the best position to exploit big data for economic advantage, even as they claim to use them to benefit others.

Big data divides opinion. Lou Del Bello talks to Sandy Pent land, director of the MIT human dynamics laboratory, about the potential benefits of conducting research using the world's digital "breadcrumbs". But Patrick Ball, executive director of the Human Rights Data Analysis Group, is skeptical about the accuracy of analyses using big data and emphasizes their potential to misrepresent reality.

A related and basic challenge is that of putting the data to use. All discussions about the 'data revolution' assume that 'data matter'; that poor data are partly to blame for poor policies. But history has shown that lack of data or information has historically played only a marginal role in the decisions leading to bad policies and poor outcomes. And a blind 'algorithmic' future may undercut the very processes that are meant to ensure that the way data are turned into decisions is subject to democratic oversight.

Big Future: But since the growth in data production is highly unlikely to abate, the 'big data bubble' is similarly unlikely to burst in the near future. The world can expect more papers and controversies about big data's potential and perils for development. The future of big data will likely be shaped by three main strands: of academic research, legal and technical frameworks for ethical use of data, and larger societal demands for greater accountability.

Research will continue to examine whether and how methodological and scientific frontiers can be pushed, especially in two areas: drawing stronger inferences, and measuring and correcting sample biases. Policy debate will develop frameworks and standards normative, legal and technical for collecting, storing and sharing big data. These developments fall under the umbrella term 'ethics of big data'. Technical advances will help, for example by injecting 'noise' in datasets to make re-identification of the individuals represented in them more difficult. But a comprehensive approach to the ethics of big data would ideally encompass other humanistic considerations such as privacy and equality, and champion data literacy.

A third influence on the future of big data will be how it engages and evolves alongside the 'open' data movement and its underlying social drivers where 'open data' refers to data that is easily accessible, machine-readable, accessible for free or at negligible cost, and with minimal limitations on its use, transformation, and distribution.

For example, big data has been used to track inflation online, estimate and predict changes in GDP in near real-time, monitor traffic or even a dengue outbreak. Monitoring social media data to analyze people's sentiments is opening new ways to measure welfare, while email and Twitter data could be used to study internal and international migration. And an especially rich and growing academic literature is using CDRs to study migration patterns, socioeconomic levels and malaria spread, among others.

Guidance for analyzing big data, published by UN Global Pulse, has focused on four fields: *disaster response, public health, poverty and socioeconomic levels, and human mobility and transportation.*

Mobile phone data analysis examples, based on UN Global Pulse's primer and the 2013 World Disaster Report:

Data on mobile money transfers in the aftermath of the 2008 earthquake in Rwanda was used to analyze the timing, magnitude, and motivation of donations to affected communities — revealing notably that transfers were more likely to benefit wealthier individuals.

CDR analysis has been used to study infectious disease spread and control in an urban slum in Kibera, Kenya. An especially promising avenue is using CDRs to predict socio-economic levels. This is done by overlaying and matching CDR-based indicators (such as average call volumes in an area) with known socioeconomic variables (such as income levels) to build statistical models able to 'predict' patterns and trends.

Big data is all the rage. Its proponents tout the use of sophisticated analytics to mine large data sets for insight as the solution to many of our society's problems. These big data evangelists insist that data-driven decision making can now give us better predictions in areas ranging from college admissions to dating to hiring [19]. And it might one day help us better conserve precious resources, track and cure lethal diseases, and make our lives vastly safer and more efficient. Big data is not just for corporations. Smart phones and wearable sensors enable believers in the "Quantified Self" to measure their lives in order to improve sleep, lose weight, and get fitter [20]. And recent revelations about the National Security Agency's efforts to collect a database of all caller records suggest that big data may hold the answer to keeping us safe from terrorism as well.

Consider *The Human Face of Big Data*, a glossy coffee table book that appeared last holiday season, which is also available as an iPad app. Such products are thinly disguised advertisements for big data's potential to revolutionize society. The book argues that "Big Data is an extraordinary knowledge revolution that's sweeping, almost invisibly, through business, academia, government, healthcare, and everyday life" [21]. The app opens with a statement that frames both the promise and the peril of big data: "Every animate and inanimate object on earth will soon be generating data, including our homes, our cars, and yes, even our bodies." Yet the app and the book, like so many proponents of big data, provide no meaningful analysis of its potential perils, only the promise.

We don't deny that big data holds substantial potential for the future, and that large dataset analysis has important uses today. But we would like to sound a cautionary note and pause to consider big data's potential more critically.

In particular, we want to highlight three paradoxes in the current rhetoric about big data to help move us toward a more complete understanding of the big data picture.

First, while big data pervasively collects all manner of private information, the operations of big data itself are almost entirely shrouded in legal and commercial secrecy. We call this the *Transparency Paradox*.

Second, though big data evangelists talk in terms of miraculous outcomes, this rhetoric ignores the fact that big data seeks to identify at the expense of individual and collective identity. We call this the *Identity Paradox*.

And *third*, the rhetoric of big data is characterized by its power to transform society, but big data has power effects of its own, which privilege large government and corporate entities at the expense of ordinary individuals. We call this the *Power Paradox*. Recognizing the paradoxes of big data, which show its perils alongside its potential, will help us to better understand this revolution. It may also allow us to craft solutions to produce a revolution that will be as good as its evangelists predict.

The Transparency Paradox

Big data analytics depend on small data inputs, including information about people, places, and things collected by sensors, cell phones, click patterns, and the like. These small data inputs are aggregated to produce large datasets which analytic techniques mine for insight. This data collection happens invisibly and it is only accelerating. Moving past the Internet of Things to the "Internet of Everything," Cisco projects that thirty-seven billion intelligent devices will connect to the Internet by 2020 [22]. These devices and sensors drive exponentially growing mobile data traffic, which in 2012 was almost twelve times larger than all global Internet traffic was in 2000 [23]. Highly secure data centers house these datasets on high-performance, low-cost infrastructure to enable real-time or near real-time big data analytics.

This is the Transparency Paradox. Big data promises to use this data to make the world more transparent, but its collection is invisible, and its tools and techniques are opaque, shrouded by layers of physical, legal, and technical privacy by design. If big data spells the end of privacy, then why is the big data revolution occurring mostly in secret?

Of course, there are legitimate arguments for some level of big data secrecy (just as there remain legitimate arguments for personal privacy in the big data era). To make them work fully, commercial and government big data systems which are constantly pulling private information from the growing Internet of Everything are also often connected to highly sensitive intellectual property and national security assets. Big data profitability can depend on trade secrets and the existence of sensitive personal data in big databases also counsels for meaningful privacy and security. But when big data analytics are increasingly being used to make decisions about individual people, those people have a right to know on what basis those decisions are made. Danielle Citron's call for "Technological Due Process" is particularly important in the big data context, and it should apply to both government and corporate decisions.

We are not proposing that these systems be stored insecurely or opened to the public *en masse*. But we must acknowledge the Transparency Paradox and bring legal, technical, business, government, and political leaders together to develop the right technical, commercial, ethical, and legal safeguards for big data and for individuals [24]. We cannot have a system, or even the appearance of a system, where surveillance is secret [25], or where decisions are made about individuals by a Kafkaesque system of opaque and unreviewable decision makers [26].

The Identity Paradox

Big data seeks to *identify*, but it also threatens *identity*. This is the Identity Paradox. We instinctively desire sovereignty over our personal identity. Whereas the important right to privacy harkens from the right to be left alone [27], the right to identity originates from the right to free choice about who we are. This is the right to define who "I am." I am me; I am anonymous. I am here; I am there. I am watching; I am buying. I am a supporter; I am a critic. I am voting; I am abstaining. I am for; I am against. I like; I do not like. I am a permanent resident alien; I am an American citizen.

How will our right to identity, our right to say "I am," fare in the big data era? With even the most basic access to a combination of big data pools like phone records, surfing history, buying history, social networking posts, and others, "I am" and "I like" risk becoming "you are" and "you will like." Every Google user is already influenced by big-data-fed feedback loops from Google's tailored search results, which risk producing individual and collective echo chambers of thought. In his article, *How Netflix Is Turning Viewers into Puppets*, Andrew Leonard explains how:

The companies that figure out how to generate intelligence from that data will know more about us than we know ourselves, and will be able to craft techniques that push us toward where they want us to go, rather than where we would go by ourselves if left to our own devices [28].

Taking it further, by applying advances in personal genomics to academic and career screening, the dystopian future portrayed in the movie *Gattaca* [29] might not be that outlandish. In *Gattaca*, an aspiring starship pilot is forced to assume the identity of another because a test determines him to be genetically inferior. Without developing big data identity protections now, "you are" and "you will like" risk becoming "you cannot" and "you will not". The power of Big Data is thus the power to use information to nudge, to persuade, to influence, and even to restrict our identities [30].

Such influence over our individual and collective identities risks eroding the vigor and quality of our democracy. If we lack the power to individually say who "I am," if filters and nudges and personalized recommendations undermine our intellectual choices, we will have become identified but lose our identities as we have defined and cherished them in the past.

The Power Paradox

The power to shape our identities for us suggests a third paradox of big data. Big data is touted as a powerful tool that enables its users to view a sharper and clearer picture of the world [31]. For example, many Arab Spring protesters and commentators credited social media for helping protesters to organize. But big data sensors and big data pools are predominantly in the hands of powerful intermediary institutions, not ordinary people. Seeming to learn from Arab Spring organizers, the Syrian regime feigned the removal of restrictions on its citizens' Face book, Twitter, and YouTube usage only to secretly profile, track, and round up dissidents [32].

This is the Power Paradox. Big data will create winners and losers, and it is likely to benefit the institutions who wield its tools over the individuals being mined, analyzed, and sorted. Not knowing the appropriate legal or technical boundaries, each side is left guessing. Individuals succumb to denial while governments and corporations get away with what they can by default, until they are left reeling from scandal aftershock of disclosure. The result is an uneasy, uncertain state of affairs that is not healthy for anyone and leaves individual rights eroded and our democracy diminished.

If we do not build privacy, transparency, autonomy, and identity protections into big data from the outset, the Power Paradox will diminish big data's lofty ambitions. We need a healthier balance of power between those who generate the data and those who make inferences and decisions based on it, so that one doesn't come to unduly revolt or control the other.

Almost two decades ago, Internet evangelist John Perry Barlow penned *A Declaration of the Independence of Cyberspace*, declaring the Internet to be a "new home of [the] Mind" in which governments would have no jurisdiction[33, 34]. Barlow was one of many cyber-exceptionalists who argued that the Internet would change everything. He was mostly right—the Internet did change pretty much everything and it did create a new home for the mind. But the rhetoric of cyber-exceptionalism was too optimistic, too dismissive of the human realities of cyberspace, the problems it would cause, and the inevitability (and potential utility) of government regulation.

We think something similar is happening in the rhetoric of big data, in which utopian claims are being made that overstate its potential and understate the values on the other side of the equation, particularly individual privacy, identity, and checks on power. Our purpose in this Essay is thus twofold.

First, we want to suggest that the utopian rhetoric of big data is frequently overblown, and that a less wild-eyed and more pragmatic discussion of big data would be more helpful. It isn't too much to ask sometimes for data-based decisions about data-based decision making.

Second, we must recognize not just big data's potential, but also some of the dangers that powerful big data analytics will unleash upon society. The utopian ideal of cyberspace needed to yield to human reality, especially when it revealed problems like identity theft, spam, and cyber-bullying. Regulation of the Internet's excesses was (and is) necessary in order to gain the benefits of its substantial breakthroughs. Something similar must happen with big data, so that we can take advantage of the good things it can do, while avoiding as much of the bad as possible. The solution to this problem is beyond the scope of this short symposium essay, but we think the answer must lie in the development of a concept of "Big Data Ethics"—a social understanding of the times and contexts when big data analytics are appropriate, and of the times and contexts when they are not.

Big data will be revolutionary, but we should ensure that it is a revolution that we want, and one that is consistent with values we have long cherished like privacy, identity, and individual power. Only if we do that will big data's potential start to approach the story we are hearing from its evangelists.

How should privacy risks be weighed against big data rewards? The recent controversy over leaked documents revealing the massive scope of data collection, analysis, and use by the NSA and possibly other national security organizations has hurled to the forefront of public attention the delicate balance between privacy risks and big data opportunities. The NSA revelations crystallized privacy advocates' concerns of "sleepwalking into a surveillance society" even as decision makers remain loath to curb government powers for fear of terrorist or cyber security attacks.

Classification is the foundation of targeting and tailoring information and experiences to individuals. Big data promises—or threatens—to bring classification to an increasing range of human activity. While many companies and government agencies foster an illusion that classification is (or should be) an area of absolute algorithmic rule—that decisions are neutral, organic, and even automatically rendered without human intervention—reality is a far messier mix of technical and human curating. Both the datasets and the algorithms reflect choices, among others, about data, connections, inferences, interpretation, and thresholds for inclusion that advance a specific purpose. Like maps that represent the physical environment in varied ways to serve different needs—mountaineering, sightseeing, or shopping—classification systems are neither neutral nor objective, but are biased toward their purposes. They reflect the explicit and implicit values of their designers. Few designers "see them as artifacts embodying moral and aesthetic choices" or recognize the powerful role they play in crafting "people's identities, aspirations, and dignity." But increasingly, the subjects of classification, as well as regulators, do [35].

Big data is transforming individual privacy—and not in equal ways for all. We are increasingly dependent upon technologies, which in turn need our personal information in order to function. This reciprocal relationship has made it incredibly difficult for individuals to make informed decisions about what to keep private. Perhaps more important, the privacy considerations at stake will not be the same for everyone: they will vary depending upon one's socioeconomic status. It is essential for society and particularly policymakers to recognize the different burdens placed on individuals to protect their data [36].

Legal debates over the "big data" revolution currently focus on the risks of inclusion: the privacy and civil liberties consequences of being swept up in big data's net. This Essay takes a different approach, focusing on the risks of exclusion: the threats big data poses to those whom it overlooks. Billions of people worldwide remain on big data's periphery. Their information is not regularly collected or analyzed, because they do not routinely engage in activities that big data is designed to capture. Consequently, their preferences and needs risk being routinely ignored when governments and private industry use big data and advanced analytics to shape public policy and the marketplace. Because big data poses a unique threat to equality, not just privacy, this Essay argues that a new "data anti-subordination" doctrine may be needed [37].

Big data's big utopia was personified towards the end of 2012. Our concern is about big data's power to enable a dangerous new philosophy of preemption. In this Essay, we focus on the social impact of what we call "preemptive predictions." Our concern is that big data's promise of increased efficiency, reliability, utility, profit, and pleasure might be seen as the justification for a fundamental jurisprudential shift from our current ex post facto system of penalties and punishments to ex ante preventative measures that are increasingly being adopted across various sectors of society. It is our contention that big data's predictive benefits belie an important insight historically represented in the presumption of innocence and associated privacy and due process values—namely, that there is wisdom in setting boundaries around the kinds of assumptions that can and cannot be made about people [38].

"Big Data" has attracted considerable public attention of late, garnering press coverage both optimistic and dystopian in tone. Some of the stories we tell about big data treat it as a computational panacea—a key to unlock the mysteries of the human genome, to crunch away the problems of urban living, or to elucidate hidden patterns underlying our friendships and cultural preferences. Others describe big data as an invasive apparatus through which governments keep close tabs on citizens, while corporations compile detailed dossiers about what we purchase and consume. Like so many technological advances before it, our stories about big data generate it as a two-headed creature, the source of both tremendous promise and disquieting surveillance. In reality, like any complicated social phenomenon, big data is both of these, a set of heterogeneous resources and practices deployed in multiple ways toward diverse ends [39].

"Big data" can be defined as a problem-solving philosophy that leverages massive datasets and algorithmic analysis to extract "hidden information and surprising correlations." Not only does big data pose a threat to traditional notions of privacy, but it also compromises socially shared information. This point remains underappreciated because our so-called public disclosures are not nearly as public as courts and policymakers have argued—at least, not yet. That is subject to change once big data becomes user friendly [40].

Debates over information privacy are often framed as an inescapable conflict between competing interests: a lucrative or beneficial technology, as against privacy risks to consumers. Policy remedies traditionally take the rigid form of a complete ban, no regulation, or an intermediate zone of modest notice and choice mechanisms. We believe these approaches are unnecessarily constrained. There is often a spectrum of technology alternatives that trade off functionality and profit for consumer privacy. We term these alternatives "privacy substitutes," and in this Essay we argue that public policy on information privacy issues can and should be a careful exercise in both selecting among, and providing incentives for, privacy substitutes [41].

There are only a handful of reasons to study someone very closely. If you spot a tennis rival filming your practice, you can be reasonably sure that she is studying up on your style of play. Miss too many backhands and guess what you will encounter come match time. But not all careful scrutiny is about taking advantage. Doctors study patients to treat them. Good teachers follow students to see if they are learning. Social scientists study behavior in order to understand and improve the quality of human life.

De-identification is a process used to prevent a person's identity from being connected with information. Organizations de-identify data for a range of reasons. Companies may have promised "anonymity" to individuals before collecting their personal information, data protection laws may restrict the sharing of personal data, and, perhaps most importantly, companies de-identify data to mitigate privacy threats from improper internal access or from an external data breach. This Essay attempts to frame the conversation around de-identification [42].

References:

[1] (http://mashable.com/2013/06/13/dictionary-new-words-2013/)

[2] (http://www.computerworld.com/article/2489571/it-management/selfie--big-data-and---make-the-2014-dictionary.html)

[3] (http://siliconangle.com/blog/2014/08/19/gartners-hype-cycle-big-datas-on-the-slippery-slope/)

[4] (http://www.gartner.com/it-glossary/big-data/)

[5] (http://datascience.berkeley.edu/ big-data-infographic/)

[6] (http://wikibon.org/blog/category/big-data/)

[7] (http://wikibon.org/wiki/v/Big_Data_Market_Size_and_Vendor_Revenues

[8] (http://wikibon.org/wiki/v/Big_Data_Start-up_Funding_by_Vendor)

[9]   (http://wikibon.org/wiki/v/Big_Data:_Hadoop,_Business_An alytics_and_Beyond)

[10] (http://www.cio.com/article/_2368129/data-management/10-trends-driving-big-data-in-financial-services.html

[11] (http://www.cio.com/article/2395713/business-intelligence/coding-contest-shows-how-big-data-can-improve-health-care.html

[12] (http://www.qubole.com/features/)

[13] http://timesofindia.indiatimes.com/tech/it-services/How-Big-Data-is-changing-the-way-we-do-business/articleshow/50417589.cms

[14] https://www-ssl.intel.com/content/www/in/en/big-data/big-data-analytics-turning-big-data-into-intelligence.html

[15] Alex Jones (https://www.linkedin.com/start/join?trk=login_reg_redirect&session_redirect=https%3A%2F%2Fwww.linkedin.com%2Fprofile%2Fview%3Fid%3D111366377)

[16] http://www.kdnuggets.com/2014/06/top-10-data-analysis-tools-business.html

[17] (http://www.elon.edu/e-web/predictions/expertsurveys/).

[18] (http://www.scidev.net/global/data/opinion/big-data-boost-analytical-capacities.html)

[19] Adam Bryant, *In Head-Hunting, Big Data May Not Be Such a Big Deal*, N.Y. Times (June 19, 2013), http://www.nytimes.com/_2013/06/20/business/in-head-hunting-big-data-may-not-be-such-a-big-deal.html?pagewanted=all&_r=0.

[20] Emily Singer, *Is "Self-tracking" the Secret to Living Better,* MIT TECH. REV. (June 9, 2011), http://www.technologyreview. com/view/424252/is-self-tracking-the-secret-to-living-better.

[21] RICK SMOLAN & JENNIFER ERWITT, THE HUMAN FACE OF BIG DATA 3 (2012)

[22] Dave Evans, *How the Internet of Everything Will Change the World for the Better #IoE [Info graphic],* CISCO BLOGS (Nov. 7, 2012, 9:58 AM PST), http://blogs.cisco.com/news/how-the-internet-of-everything-will-change-the-worldfor-the-better-infographic.

[23] CISCO VISUAL NETWORKING INDEX: GLOBAL MOBILE DATA TRAFFIC FORECAST UPDATE, 2012-2017, at 1 (2013), available at http://www.cisco.com/en/US/solutions/collateral/ns341/ns52 5/ns537/ns705/ns827/white_paper_c11-520862.pdf.

[24] Omer Tene & Jules Polonetsky, Big Data for All: Privacy and User Control in the Age of Analytics, 11 NW J. TECH. & INTELL. PROP. 239, 270-72 (2013)

[25] Neil M. Richards, 'The Dangers of Surveillance', 126 HARV. L. REV. 1934, 1959-61 (2013).

[26] Cf. DANIEL J. SOLOVE, THE DIGITAL PERSON (2005).

[27] Julie E. Cohen, What Privacy Is For, 126 HARV. L. REV. 1904, 1906 (2013).

[28] Andrew Leonard, How Netflix Is Turning Viewers into Puppets, SALON (Feb. 1, 2013, 7:45 AM EST), http://www.salon.com/ 2013/02/01/how_netflix_is_turning_viewers_into_puppets.

[29] GATTACA (Columbia Pictures 1997).

[30] RICHARD H. THALER & CASS R. SUNSTEIN, NUDGE: IMPROVING DECISIONS ABOUT HEALTH, WEALTH, AND HAPPINESS (2009); Richards, supra note 8, at 1955-56.

[31] VIKTOR MAYER-SCHÖNBERGER & KENNETH CUKIER, BIG DATA: A REVOLUTION THAT WILL TRANSFORM HOW WE LIVE, WORK, AND THINK 11 (2013).

[32] Stephan Faris, The Hackers of Damascus, BLOOMBERG BUSINESS WEEK (Nov. 15, 2012), http://www.businessweek.com/ articles/2012-11-15/the-hackers-of-Damascus

[33] John Perry Barlow, A Declaration of the Independence of Cyberspace, ELEC. FRONTIER FOUND. (Feb. 8, 1996), https://projects.eff. org/~barlow/Declaration-Final.html

[34] Privacy and Big Data (http://www.stanfordlawreview.org/ online/privacy-and-big-data/privacy-and-big-data) by Jules Polonetsky & Omer Tene.

[35] It's Not Privacy, and It's Not Fair (http://www. stanfordlawreview.org/online/privacy-and-big-data/its-not-privacy-and-its-not-fair) by Cynthia Dwork & Deirdre K. Mulligan.

[36] Buying and Selling Privacy (http://www.stanfordlawreview. org/online/privacy-and-big-data/buying-and-selling-privacy) by Joseph W. Jerome.

[37] Big Data and Its Exclusions (http://www.stanfordlawreview.org/online/privacy-and-big-data/big-data-and-its-exclusions) by Jonas Lerman.

[38] Prediction,   Preemption,   Presumption (http://www.
stanfordlawreview.org/online/privacy-and-big-
data/prediction-preemption-presumption)   by Ian   Kerr   &
Jessica Earle.

[39] Relational   Big
Data (http://www.stanfordlawreview.org/online/ privacy-and-
big-data/relational-big-data) by Karen E.C. Levy.

[40] Big Data in Small Hands (http://www.stanfordlawreview.org/
online/privacy-and-big-data/big-data-small-hands)
by Woodrow Hartzog & Evan Selinger.

[41] Privacy   Substitutes (http://www.stanfordlawreview.org/
online/ privacy-and-big-data/privacy-substitutes) by Jonathan
Mayer & Arvind Narayanan

[42] (http://www.stanfordlawreview.org/online/privacy-and-big-
data/three-paradoxes-big-data).

Chapter 2: Fundamentals of Data Science / Data Scientist

2.1 What is Data?

The word 'Data' comes from the Latin datum – meaning what is given, what is known or assumed and upon which conclusions can be drawn. Factual information in a form that can be input to, created by, processed by, stored in and output by a computer. Data can take the form of characters such as letters, numbers, punctuation marks, mathematical operators, and control characters. Data also can take the form of photographic display elements, such as pixels.

Data is the plural form of the Latin datum, although data is used conversationally to represent both singular and plural.

(1) Technically, raw facts and figures, such as orders and payments, which are processed into information, such as balance due and quantity on hand. However, in common usage, the terms "data" and "information" are used synonymously. In addition, the term data is really the plural of "datum," which is one item of data. But datum is rarely used, and data is used as both singular and plural in practice. The amount of data versus information kept in the computer is a trade off. Data can be processed into different forms of information, but it takes time to sort and sum transactions. Up-to-date information can provide instant answers. A common misconception is that software is also data. Software is executed, or run, by the computer. Data are "processed." Thus, software causes the computer to process data.

(2) Any form of information whether on paper or in electronic form. Data may refer to any electronic file no matter what the format: database data, text, images, audio and video. Everything read and written by the computer can be considered data except for instructions in a program that are executed (software).

(3) May refer only to data stored in a database in contrast with text in a word processing document.

"I think data-scientist is a sexed up term for a statistician.... Statistics is a branch of science. Data scientist is slightly redundant in some way and people shouldn't berate the term statistician." -- Nate Silver (applied statistician)

2.2   What is Data Science?

Data Science is an interdisciplinary field about processes and systems to extract knowledge or insights from data in various forms, either structured or unstructured, which is a continuation of some of the data analysis fields such as statistics, data mining, and predictive analytics, similar to Knowledge Discovery.

Data Science is an interdisciplinary field about processes and systems to extract knowledge or insights from data in various forms, either structured or unstructured, which is a continuation of some of the data analysis fields such as statistics, data mining, and predictive analytics, similar to Knowledge Discovery in Databases (KDD).

Data science employs techniques and theories drawn from many fields within the broad areas of mathematics, statistics, chemo metrics, information science, and computer science, including signal processing, probability   models, machine   learning,   statistical learning, data mining, database, data engineering, pattern recognition and   learning,   visualization, predictive   analytics,   uncertainty modeling, data warehousing, data compression, computer programming, artificial intelligence, and high performance computing. Methods that scale to Big Data are of particular interest in data science, although the discipline is not generally considered to be restricted to such big data, and big data solutions are often focused on organizing and preprocessing the data instead of analysis. The development of machine learning has enhanced the growth and importance of data science.

Data science utilizes data preparation, statistics, predictive modeling and machine learning to investigate problems in various domains; such as agriculture, marketing optimization, fraud detection, risk management, marketing analytics, public policy, etc. It emphasizes the use of general methods such as machine learning that apply without changes to multiple domains. This approach differs from traditional statistics with its emphasis on domain-specific knowledge and solutions (The rationale is that developing tailored solutions does not scale).

Data scientists use their data and analytical ability to find and interpret rich data sources; manage large amounts of data despite hardware, software, and bandwidth constraints; merge data sources; ensure consistency of datasets; create visualizations to aid in understanding data; build mathematical models using the data; and present and communicate the data insights/findings. They are often expected to produce answers in days rather than months, work by exploratory analysis and rapid iteration, and to get/present results with dashboards (displays of current values) rather than papers/reports, as statisticians normally do [1]

Data science affects academic and applied research in many domains, including machine translation, speech recognition, robotics, search engines, digital economy, but also the biological sciences, medical informatics, health care, social sciences and the humanities. It heavily influences economics, business and finance. From the business perspective, data science is an integral part of competitive intelligence, a newly emerging field that encompasses a number of activities, such as data mining and data analysis.

The term "data science" (originally used interchangeably with "datalogy") has existed for over thirty years and was used initially as a substitute for computer science by Peter Naur in 1960. In 1974, Naur published *Concise Survey of Computer Methods*, which freely used the term data science in its survey of the contemporary data processing methods that are used in a wide range of applications. In 1996, members of the International Federation of Classification Societies (IFCS) met in Kobe for their biennial conference. Here, for the first time, the term data science is included in the title of the conference ("Data Science, classification, and related methods").

In November 1997, C.F. Jeff Wu gave the inaugural lecture entitled "Statistics = Data Science?"[2]. For his appointment to the H. C. Carver Professorship at the University of Michigan [3]. In this lecture, he characterized statistical work as a trilogy of data collection, data modeling and analysis, and decision making. In his conclusion, he initiated the modern, non-computer science, usage of the term "data science" and advocated that statistics be renamed data science and statisticians data scientists. Later, he presented his lecture entitled "Statistics = Data Science?" as the first of his 1998 P.C. Mahalanobis Memorial Lectures [4]. These lectures honour Prasanta Chandra Mahalanobis, an Indian scientist and statistician and founder of the Indian Statistical Institute.

In 2001, William S. Cleveland introduced data science as an independent discipline, extending the field of statistics to incorporate "advances in computing with data" in his article "Data Science: An Action Plan for Expanding the Technical Areas of the Field of Statistics," which was published in Volume 69, No. 1, of the April

2001 edition of the International Statistical Review / Revue Internationale de Statistique [5]. In his report, Cleveland establishes six technical areas which he believed to encompass the field of data science: multidisciplinary investigations, models and methods for data, computing with data, pedagogy, tool evaluation, and theory.

In April 2002, the International Council for Science: Committee on Data for Science and Technology (CODATA) started the *Data Science Journal*, a publication focused on issues such as the description of data systems, their publication on the internet, applications and legal issues [6]. Shortly thereafter, in January 2003, Columbia University began publishing *The Journal of Data Science* [7], which provided a platform for all data workers to present their views and exchange ideas. The journal was largely devoted to the application of statistical methods and quantitative research. In 2005, The National Science Board published "Long-lived Digital Data Collections: Enabling Research and Education in the 21st Century" defining data scientists as "the information and computer scientists, database and software and programmers, disciplinary experts, curators and expert annotators, librarians, archivists, and others, who are crucial to the successful management of a digital data collection" whose primary activity is to "conduct creative inquiry and analysis."

In 2008, DJ Patil and Jeff Hammerbacher used the term "data scientist" to define their jobs at LinkedIn and Face book, respectively. Although use of the term "data science" has exploded in business environments, many academics and journalists see no distinction between data science and statistics. Writing in Forbes, Gil Press argues that data science is a buzzword without a clear definition and has simply replaced "business analytics" in contexts such as graduate degree programs [8]. In the question-and-answer section of his keynote address at the Joint Statistical Meetings of American Statistical Association, noted applied statistician Silver said, "I think data-scientist is a sexed up term for a statistician....Statistics is a branch of science. Data scientist is slightly redundant in some way and people shouldn't berate the term statistician" [9].

What is Data Science, Anyway?

Touted as "the sexiest job of the 21st century" the definition of data science has been the subject of many articles. At Parrot Analytics, we prefer to define what data scientists do.

Generally, data scientists are responsible for extracting knowledge from data, which for us and many others usually means Big Data. To succeed, data scientists possess three general skills, famously defined by Drew Conway.

Having these skills is necessary but not sufficient to doing data science. These skills must be utilized in a certain way; to see how, we consider the second and most important word in the phrase: *science*.

Science is, above all else, a *process* by which we learn more about the world around us. A physicist may use data about atoms and quarks while a sociologist may look at data on certain groups of people, but both seek to understand more about their respective areas of research through what is commonly called the scientific method. Similarly, data scientists use whatever data is relevant to their field or company to gain new and valuable information about their area. This area can be an established research field, like medicine or politics, or it can be a new, industry-specific domain, like Parrot Analytics' work in the realm of television. Regardless of the field for a data scientist, the scientific method generally looks like this:

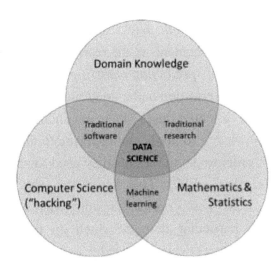

Figure 8: Venn diagram of Big Data

1. *Define the question:* As Drew Conway states in his original diagram: "Questions first, then data." To be valuable, this research question must be driven by the data scientist's specific domain rather than by the tools, data or algorithms available.

2. *Define, and then acquire data set:* Even if all the data is already available, it focuses and streamlines the analysis if the data scientist identifies exactly what is needed and extracts only that. Getting the data often requires computer science knowledge around APIs, big databases, etc.

3. *Process the data:* Up to 80% of a data scientist's time [10] can be spend wrangling the data into a specific form in order for it to be useful in the analysis. "Hacking" skills (knowing enough computer science or programming to get the job done) can help at this stage.

4. *Exploratory data analysis:* After the data is in the proper format, it is important for the data scientist to spend some time understanding what the data contains: variables,

patterns, outliers, basic statistics, etc. This step can also lead to refinements in the research question.

5. *Statistical predicting/modeling:* Armed with a specific research question and a good understanding of the data, the data scientist uses their mathematical and statistical knowledge to apply the appropriate algorithms to the data in order to get the results they need to answer the question.

6. *Interpret results:* This step is the crux of the data science process: based on these results, what can be learned about this particular domain? Such an analysis is impossible without a deep knowledge of the data acquired, the mathematics used, *and* the field the data scientist works in.

7. *Challenge results:* Reviewing one's work is important in any creative process, and data science is no exception. What other conclusions could be drawn from this statistical test? Do these results and their interpretation make sense in a wider context?

8. *Communicate results:* Booz Allen Hamilton defines data science as "the art of turning data into actions" [11]. In order to turn the results of the scientific process to business actions, data scientists must effectively communicate these results to many other people, both technical and non-technical, in the company.

This scientific process is what data scientists do; who they are is harder to quantify. At Parrot Analytics, we find that data scientists are curious, creative and tenacious people. They are the type who will not only find an innovative solution to the problem, but will fight to make sure it has a meaningful impact on their organization and its domain area, in our case measuring global demand for TV content. In our opinion, these qualities and skills make data science the sexiest job around – *Kayla Hegedus, Data Scientist* [12].

Data Science in Simple Terms

Can the author of this chart come back let us know he/she is the author? The article was accidentally deleted when approving it, and I apologize. The chart was interesting and worth discussing, so I decided to include it here. Hopefully, we'll know soon who the author is. I'm curious to know what the colours represent [13].

Data Science: Definitions One Need to Know

Our 7th Annual Media Technology Summit is just a few weeks away, and the subject of data science is going to be front and centre. Each and every one of us creates a wealth of data every day, but... information is not knowledge. The data must be wrangled and put in context to make it actionable. There are many different techniques one can apply to data to accomplish this goal, but an important part of the process falls in to the multi-disciplinary field of data science. Which is what exactly?

- **Data Science** - The analysis of data using the scientific method. (It may be the most overused term of the year, but you're unlikely to have a meeting where the topic does not come up.)
- **Data Scientists** - There are many who say that data scientists (people who practice data science) are not really scientists. That seems unfair. While there are a bunch of charlatans (people and organizations) passing themselves off as data scientists, I would argue that if the scientific method is applied (which if you remember from middle school science class is generally a statistically controlled six-step process: question, research, hypothesize, experiment, analyze and conclude), the professionals doing the work qualify as scientists. Let's not get caught up on whether or not data science is real science. There are

people who use analytical tools to find patterns in data; let's call them data scientists.

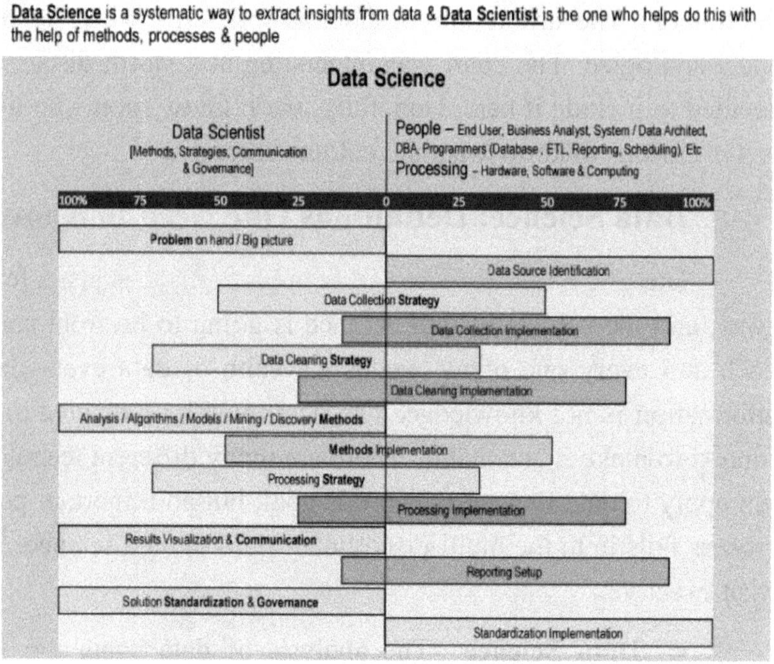

<u>Data Science</u> is a systematic way to extract insights from data & <u>Data Scientist</u> is the one who helps do this with the help of methods, processes & people

Figure 9: Distinction between Data Science& Data Scientist

- **<u>Data Wrangling or Data Munging</u>** - A laborious process of manually extracting, mapping, converting or generally cleaning up data in raw form. Data wranglers use algorithms (a process or set of rules to be followed in calculations or other problem-solving operations, especially by a computer) to parse disparate types of data and fit it into defined structures. The ultimate goal is to prep the data for storage and future use.

- **<u>Big Data</u>** - This can mean anything that anyone wants it to mean. It is on my <u>list of banned words</u> and really is more of a concept than an agreed upon thing. However, it is usually defined as sets of data that are too large and complex to manipulate or interrogate with standard methods or tools - in other words... big. If you collect big amounts of data, go ahead and call it big data. A good example of a big data set is all the digital health records in the United States or all of the viewer data from all of Comcast's set-top boxes.

- **Hadoop** - Apache Hadoop is an open-source software framework for storage and large-scale processing of data-sets on clusters of commodity hardware. It is commonly used in "Hadoop clusters," which are purpose-designed computational clusters.

- **Multivariate statistical analysis** - This is based on the statistical principle of multivariate statistics, which involves observation and analysis of more than one statistical outcome variable at a time. There are several uses for multivariate analysis, such as: capability-based design, inverse design (where variables can be treated independently), AoA (Analysis of Alternatives) and correlations across hierarchical levels.

- **Time-series analysis** - Use of a model to predict future values based on previously observed values. It differs from **regression analysis** (which is often used to test theories that the current values of one or more independent time-series affect the current value of another time-series) in that time-series analysis focuses on comparing values of a single time-series or multiple dependent time-series at different points in time.

- **Multidimensional array** - A data structure that has the semantics of an array of arrays, all of which may be indexed with values of any data type, usually with a supporting syntax built-into a programming language.

These are just a few of the terms that you should know if you're going to discuss data science with your HR department or anyone else for that matter. There is a great deal of myth and mystery around this subject, such as:

- Are data scientists just statisticians with fancy titles?
- Don't we need super-expensive data appliances to support a data science department?
- Aren't all these people just academics who don't know anything about business?

Of course, everyone really wants to know: Where can I find one? These are all great questions. For great answers, come join us at the 7th Annual Media Technology Summit on October 23 at the Sheraton Times Square. BTW, if you've read this far, email me for a discount code -- you deserve it! [14].

2.3   Data Scientist's Qualifications

What Kind of Degree is needed? Broadly speaking, you have 3 education options if you're considering a career as a data scientist:

Degrees and graduate certificates provide structure, internships, networking and recognized academic qualifications for your résumé. They will also cost you significant time and money.

MOOCs and self-guided learning courses are free/cheap, short and targeted. They allow you to complete projects on your own time – but they require you to structure your own academic path.

Boot camps are intense and faster to complete than traditional degrees. They may be taught by practicing data scientists, but they won't give you degree initials after your name.

Academic qualifications may be more important than you imagine. As Burtch Works notes, "it's incredibly rare for someone without an advanced quantitative degree to have the technical skills necessary to be a data scientist."

In its data science salary report, Burtch Works determined that 88% of data scientists have a master's degree and 46% have a PhD. The majority of these degrees are in rigorous quantitative, technical or scientific subjects, including math and statistics (32%), computer science (19%) and engineering (16%).

With that being said, companies are desperate for candidates with real-world skills. Your technical know-how may trump preferred degree requirements.

Cloudera Certified Professional: Data Scientist (CCP: DS)

Targeted towards the elite level, the CCP: DS is aimed at data scientists who can demonstrate advanced skills in working with big data. Candidates are drilled in 3 exams – *Descriptive and Inferential Statistics, Unsupervised Machine Learning and Supervised Machine Learning – and must prove their chops by designing and developing a production-ready data science solution under real-world conditions.*

The EMCDSA certification tests your ability to apply common techniques and tools required for big data analytics. Candidates are judged on their technical expertise (e.g. employing open source tools such as "R", Hadoop, and Postgres, etc.) and their business acumen (e.g. telling a compelling story with the data to drive business action).

Once you've passed the EMCDSA, you can consider the Advanced Analytics Specialty. This works on developing new skills in areas such as Hadoop (and Pig, Hive, HBase), Social Network Analysis, Natural Language Processing, data visualization methods and more.

SAS Certified Predictive Modeler using SAS Enterprise Miner 7

This certification is designed for SAS Enterprise Miner users who perform predictive analytics. Candidates must have a deep, practical understanding of the functionalities for predictive modeling available in SAS Enterprise Miner 7 before they can take the performance-based exam. This exam includes topics such as data preparation, predictive models, model assessment and scoring and implementation.

2.4   Data Scientist's Responsibilities

"A data scientist is someone who is better at statistics than any software engineer and better at software engineering than any statistician."

On any given day, a data scientist may be required to:

- Conduct undirected research and frame open-ended industry questions
- Extract huge volumes of data from multiple internal and external sources
- Employ sophisticated analytics programs, machine learning and statistical methods to prepare data for use in predictive and prescriptive modeling
- Thoroughly clean and prune data to discard irrelevant information
- Explore and examine data from a variety of angles to determine hidden weaknesses, trends and/or opportunities
- Devise data-driven solutions to the most pressing challenges

- Invent new algorithms to solve problems and build new tools to automate work
- Communicate predictions and findings to management and IT departments through effective data visualizations and reports
- Recommend cost-effective changes to existing procedures and strategies

Every company will have a different take on job tasks. Some treat their data scientists as glorified data analysts or combine their duties with data engineers; others need top-level analytics experts skilled in intense machine learning and data visualizations.

As data scientists achieve new levels of experience or change jobs, their responsibilities invariably change. For example, a person working alone in a mid-size company may spend a good portion of the day in data cleaning and munging. A high-level employee in a business that offers data-based services may be asked to structure big data projects or create new products.

An Interview with a Real Data Scientist

We caught up with Lisa Qian, Data Scientist at Airbnb, to find out what it's like to work as a data scientist. Read on to learn about the impact data science has on Airbnb's success, the programming languages they use on the job, and what students need to know in order to succeed.

Q: What are the top PROS & CONS of your job?

A: Things happen very quickly and data scientists have a big impact (see answer to next question). At Airbnb, there are so many interesting problems to work on and so much interesting data to play with. The culture of the company also encourages us to work on lots of different things. I have been at Airbnb for less than two years and I have already worked on three completely different product teams. There's really never a dull moment. This can also be a "con" of the job. Because there are so many interesting things to work on, I often wish that I had more time to go more in depth on a project. I'm often juggling multiple projects at once, and when I'm 90% done with one of them, I'll just move on to something else. Coming from academia where one spends years and years on one project without leaving a single rock unturned (I did a PhD in physics), this has been a delightful, but sometimes frustrating, cultural transition.

Q: How much of an impact do Data Scientists have on Airbnb's overall success?

A: A ton! As a data scientist, I'm involved in every step of a product's life cycle. For example, right now I am part of the Search team. I am heavily involved in research and strategizing where I use data to identify areas that we should invest in and come up with concrete product ideas to solve these problems. From there, if the solution is to come up with a data product, I might work with engineers to develop the product. I then design experiments to quantify the effect and impact of the product, and then run and analyze the experiment. Finally, I will take what I learned and provide insights and suggestions for the next product iteration. Every product team at Airbnb has engineers, designers, product managers, and data scientists. You can imagine the impact data scientists have on the company!

Q: Which Skills or Programming Languages do you most frequently use in your work, and why?

A: At Airbnb, we all use Hive (which is similar to SQL) to query data and build derived tables. I use R to do analysis and build models. I use Hive and R every day of the job. A lot of data scientists use Python instead of R – it's just a matter of what we were familiar with when we came in. There have also been recent efforts to use

Spark to build large-scale machine learning models. I haven't gotten a chance to try it out yet, but plan on doing so in the near future. It seems very powerful.

Q: What kind of person makes the best Data Scientist?

A: Successful data scientists have a strong technical background, but the best data scientists also have great intuition about data. Rather than throwing every feature possible into a black box machine learning model and seeing what comes out, one should first think about if the data makes sense. Are the features meaningful, and do they reflect what you think they should mean? Given the way your data is distributed, which model should you be using? What does it mean if a value is missing, and what should you do with it? The answers to these questions differ depending on the problem you are solving, the way the data was logged, etc., and the best data scientists look for and adapt to these different scenarios.

The best data scientists are also great at communicating, both to other data scientists and non-technical people. In order to be effective at Airbnb, our analyses have to be both technically rigorous and presented in a clear and actionable way to other members of the company.

Q: What advice would you offer students preparing for a position as a Data Scientist?

A: Beyond taking programming and statistics courses, I would recommend doing everything possible to get your hands dirty and work with real data. If you don't have the time to do an internship, sign up to participate in hackathons or offer to help out a local start up by tackling a data problem they have. Courses and books are great for developing fundamental technical skills, but many data science skills can't be properly developed in a classroom where data sets are well groomed.

The Life of a Data Scientist

Data scientists are big data wranglers. They take an enormous mass of messy data points (unstructured and structured) and use their formidable skills in math, statistics and programming to clean, massage and organize them. Then they apply all their analytic powers – industry knowledge, contextual understanding and skepticism of existing assumptions – to uncover hidden solutions to business challenges. Data science was developed to handle the flood of big data engulfing the world. A blend of statisticians, computer scientists and creative thinkers, data scientists have the:

- Skills to collect, process and extract value from giant and diverse data sets
- Imagination to understand, visualize and communicate their findings to non-data scientists
- Ability to create data-driven solutions that boost profits, reduce costs and even help save the world

Data scientists work in every industry – from the Defense Department to Internet start-ups to financial institutions – and tackle big data projects on every level.

Categories of Data Scientists

We are now at 9 categories after a few updates. Just like there are a few categories of statisticians (biostatisticians, statisticians, econometricians, operations research specialists, actuaries) or business analysts (marketing-oriented, product-oriented, finance-oriented, etc.) we have different categories of data scientists. First, many data scientists have a job title different from *data scientist*, mine for instance is co-founder. Check the "related articles" section below to discover 400 potential job titles for data scientists.

- Those strong in **statistics**: they sometimes develop new statistical theories for big data that even traditional statisticians are not aware of. They are expert in statistical modeling, experimental design, sampling, clustering, data reduction, confidence intervals, testing, modeling, predictive modeling and other related techniques.
- Those strong in **mathematics**: NSA (national security agency) or defense/military people working on big data, astronomers, and *operations research* people doing analytic business optimization (inventory management and forecasting, pricing optimization, supply chain, quality control, yield optimization) as they collect, analyze and extract value out of data.
- Those strong in **data engineering**, Hadoop, database/memory/file systems optimization and architecture, API's, Analytics as a Service, optimization of data flows, data plumbing.
- Those strong in **machine learning** / computer science (algorithms, computational complexity)
- Those strong in **business**, ROI optimization, decision sciences, involved in some of the tasks traditionally performed by business analysts in bigger companies (dashboards design, metric mix selection and metric definitions, ROI optimization, high-level database design)
- Those strong in production code development, **software engineering** (they know a few programming languages)
- Those strong in **visualization**
- Those strong in GIS, **spatial data**, data modelled by graphs, graph databases
- Those strong in a few of the above. After 20 years of experience across many industries, big and small companies (and lots of training), I'm strong both in stats,

machine learning, business, mathematics and more than just familiar with visualization and data engineering. This could happen to you as well over time, as you build experience. I mention this because so many people still think that it is not possible to develop a strong knowledge base across multiple domains that are traditionally perceived as separated (the *silo* mentality). Indeed, that's the very reason why *data science* was created.

Most of them are familiar or expert in big data.

There are other ways to categorize data scientists, see for instance our article on Taxonomy of data scientists. A different categorization would be *creative* versus *mundane*. The "creative" category has a better future, as mundane can be outsourced (anything published in textbooks or on the web can be automated or outsourced - job security is based on how much you know that no one else know or can easily learn). Along the same lines, we have science *users* (those using science, that is, practitioners; often they do not have a PhD), *innovators* (those creating new science, called researchers), and hybrids. Most data scientists, like geologists helping predict earthquakes, or chemists designing new molecules for big pharmacy, are scientists, and they belong to the *user* category.

Implications for other IT professionals

You (engineer, business analyst) probably do already a bit of data science work, and know already some of the stuff that some data scientists do. It might be easier than you think to become a data scientist. Check out our book (listed below in "related articles"), to find out what you already know, what you need to learn, to broaden your career prospects.

Are data scientists a threat to your job/career? Again, check our book (listed below) to find out what data scientists do, if the risk for you is serious (you = the business analyst, data engineer or statistician; risk = being replaced by a data scientist who does everything) and find out how to mitigate the risk (learn some of the data scientist skills from our book, if you perceive data scientists as competitors).

According to Michael Hochster, Director of Research at Pandora:

Data Scientists are people with some mix of coding and statistical skills who work on making data useful in various ways. In my world, there are two main types:

Type A Data Scientist: The A is for Analysis. This type is primarily concerned with making sense of data or working with it in a fairly static way. The Type A Data Scientist is very similar to a statistician (and may be one) but knows all practical details of working with data that aren't taught in the statistics curriculum: data cleaning, methods for dealing with very large data sets, visualization, deep knowledge of a particular domain, writing well about data, and so on.

The Type A Data Scientist can code well enough to work with data but is not necessarily an expert. The Type A data scientist may be an expert in experimental design, forecasting, modeling, statistical inference, or other things typically taught in statistics departments. Generally speaking though, the work product of a data scientist is not "p-values and confidence intervals" as academic statistics sometimes seems to suggest (and as it sometimes is for traditional statisticians working in the pharmaceutical industry, for example). At Google, Type A Data Scientists are known variously as Statistician, Quantitative Analyst, Decision Support Engineering Analyst, or Data Scientist, and probably a few more.

Type B Data Scientist: The B is for Building. Type B Data Scientists share some statistical background with Type A, but they are also very strong coders and may be trained software engineers. The

Type B Data Scientist is mainly interested in using data "in production." They build models which interact with users, often serving recommendations (products, people you may know, ads, movies, search results).

At Google, a Type B Data Scientist would typically be called a Software Engineer. Type B Data Scientists may use the term Data Scientist to refer just to themselves, and since the definition of the field is very much in flux, they may be right. But I see the term being used most often in the general way I am proposing here.

This categorization is crude. Many Data Scientists are some mix of A and B. But this answer is long enough already.

2.5 Comparison of Data Analyst, Data Scientist and Data engineering roles

Data Analyst

A data analyst role can be found at pretty much any large corporation or government organization. From accounting, to risk analysis, to a/b testing, to working on government data, there are a lot of data analyst roles out there. A data analyst is basically a junior data scientist. It's a good place to start if you don't have a very technical background and have only taken one or two statistics classes. You won't be required to have mathematical background or a PhD/research experience, but you will be required to be diligent, strong at communication, and able to perform computer work. Once you get more experience as a data analyst, you can take more advanced courses, earn a master's degree or consider a data-science boot camp to jump into a more research-based, analytical role.

The Great White is considered to be the King of the Ocean. This is because the great White is on top of its game. Imagine if you could be on top of the game in the ocean of Big Data! Big Data is everywhere and there is almost an urgent need to collect and preserve whatever data is being generated, for the fear of missing out on something important. There is a huge amount of data floating around. What we do with it is all that matters right now. This is why Big Data Analytics is in the frontiers of IT.

Big Data Analytics has become crucial as it aids in improving business, decision makings and providing the biggest edge over the competitors. This applies for organizations as well as professionals in the Analytics domain. For professionals, who are skilled in Big Data Analytics, there is an ocean of opportunities out there.

2.6 Huge Job Opportunities & Meeting the Skill Gap

The demand for Analytics skill is going up steadily but there is a huge deficit on the supply side. This is happening globally and is not restricted to any part of geography. In spite of Big Data Analytics being a 'Hot' job, there are still a large number of unfilled jobs across the globe due to shortage of required skill. A McKinsey Global Institute study states that the US will face a shortage of about 190,000 data scientists and 1.5 million managers and analysts who can understand and make decisions using Big Data by 2018.

India currently has the highest concentration of analytics globally. In spite of this, the scarcity of data analytics talent is particularly acute and demand for talent is expected to be on the higher side as more global organizations are outsourcing their work.

According to Srikanth Velamakanni, co-founder and CEO of Fractal Analytics, there are two types of talent deficits: Data Scientists, who can perform analytics and Analytics Consultant, who can understand and use data. The talent supply for these job titles, especially Data Scientists is extremely scarce and the demand is huge.

Salary Aspects

Strong demand for Data Analytics skills is boosting the wages for qualified professionals and making Big Data pay big bucks for the right skill. This phenomenon is being seen globally where countries like Australia and the U.K are witnessing this 'Moolah Marathon'.

A look at the salary trend for Big Data Analytics indicates a positive and exponential growth.

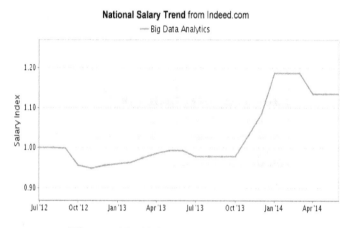

Figure 10: Salary of Data Analyst

According to the 2013 Skills and Salary Survey Report published by the Institute of Analytics Professionals of Australia (IAPA), the median salary for an analytics professional was almost twice the median Australian full-time salary.

The rising demand for analytics professionals was also reflected in IAPA's membership, which has grown to more than 3,500 members in Australia since its formation in 2006. Randstad states that the annual pay hikes for Analytics professionals in India is on an average 50% more than other IT professionals.

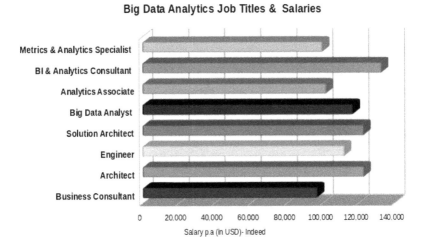

Big Data Analytics Job Titles & Salaries

Figure 11: Big Data Analytics Job Titles & Salaries

2.7   Skills Needed to Expand Big Data Career

Big data jobs typically require a *wide* range of skills – from the technical to the inferential. Many of the jobs do not require hard-core programming skills but rather require business or other job-specific knowledge, strong analytical skills, and knowledge of analytical tools.

Some specific skills that can help you expand your career in Big Data are:

I.   Data mining and machine learning techniques
II.   Data visualization tools
III.   Data warehousing
IV.   ETL (extract, translate, load)
V.   Hadoop (Hadoop is an Apache project to provide an open-source implementation of frameworks for reliable, scalable, distributed computing and data storage.)
VI.   Predictive modeling
VII.   Statistical modeling with tools such as R, SAS, or SPSS
VIII. Structured and unstructured databases.

References:

[1] https://en.wikipedia.org/wiki/Data_science#cite_note-3

[2] https://en.wikipedia.org/wiki/Data_science#cite_note-cfjwutk-6

[3] https://en.wikipedia.org/wiki/Data_science#cite_note-cfjwu01-7

[4] https://en.wikipedia.org/wiki/Data_science#cite_note-cfjwu02-8

[5] https://en.wikipedia.org/wiki/Data_science#cite_note-cleveland01-9

[6] https://en.wikipedia.org/wiki/Data_science#cite_note-dsj02-12

[7] https://en.wikipedia.org/wiki/Data_science#cite_note-jds03-13

[8] https://en.wikipedia.org/wiki/Data_science#cite_note-GilPress-16

[9] https://en.wikipedia.org/wiki/Data_science

[10] http://www.parrotanalytics.com/news/what-is-data-science-anyway/#_ftn4

[11] http://www.parrotanalytics.com/news/what-is-data-science-anyway/#_ftn5

[12] http://www.parrotanalytics.com/news/what-is-data-science-anyway/

[13] http://www.datasciencecentral.com/forum/topics/data-science-in-simple-terms

[14] http://www.huffingtonpost.com/shelly-palmer/data-science-101---defini_b_5784508.html

Chapter 3: India's Initiative in Data Science and Big Data Application

3.1 Indian Government Initiative for Big Data

In 2012, the size of the big data analytics market was estimated globally at US$ 8 billion and it was expected to grow at a compounded annual growth rate (CAGR) of 45 per cent to reach US$ 25 billion in 2015. The market for India for the same period was estimated at US$ 200 million, growing at a CAGR of 83% to reach a figure of US$ 1 billion this year. These were the finding of a study commissioned by NASSCOM, the Indian IT industry body in 2012. However, the Indian market touched revenues of US$ 1 billion in 2014 and this is expected to grow to US$ 2.3 billion by the year 2018. Not all of this is export driven as the domestic market, estimated at US$ 163 million in 2014 is expected to grow to US$ 375 million by 2018. Big data analytics accounted for some 29,000 jobs in India in 2014, of which 5000 jobs were focused on the domestic market. So big data and data analytics presents a big opportunity for IT companies in India and Bangalore is quickly becoming a hub for data science in India, as reported earlier in this blog. However, not all big data and data analytics activity in India is industry driven. The government has been a driving force in creating platforms and large datasets which will require the acquisition and manipulation of massive amounts of data. Some of these are to provide identification documents to citizens who would not other-wise have access to them easily, or to provide e-governance platforms which would simplify contacts with governmental agencies. Some of these initiatives are described below.

Figure 12: Digital India Logo

Digital India is an initiative of Government of India to integrate the government departments and the people of India. It aims at ensuring the government services are made available to citizens electronically by reducing paperwork [1].

Governmental initiatives in big data collection and usage

Figure 13: Aadhaar: Digital identity for digital India

People belonging to marginalized sections of society in India often do not have a valid proof of identity. As a result, they miss out on availing social benefits provided by the government. To overcome this Indian government launched a scheme to issue a unique 12-digit number, termed '*Aadhaar*' (meaning 'foundation' or 'support') to every resident of India. It is an identification that a person can carry for a life time and potentially use with any service provider. *Aadhaar* is the world's largest ID platform. Since the first set of *Aadhaar* numbers were issued in September 2010, 883,644,522 identification numbers have been issued (as of 15 July 2015; some 20 million enrolments take place per month) [2].

Figure 14: Digital Locker: the first step to a paper-free India

Source: http://www.linkaadharcard.com/basic-question-about-digital-locker/

It is also the largest biometric programme in the world, as biometric data of each person is recorded and stored. This unique identification is now being used by various Government agencies to ensure that services and subsidies are made available only to the people to whom they are targeted and preventing leakages in the delivery mechanisms. To learn more visit https://uidai.gov.in/

Digi Locker provides a personal storage space in the cloud to Indian citizens. Organizations that are registered with Digi Locker can push electronic copies of documents and certificates (e.g. driving license, Voter ID, School certificates) directly into citizens' lockers. Citizens can also upload scanned copies of their legacy documents in their accounts. These legacy documents can be electronically signed using the eSign facility provided in Digi Locker. A citizen can share these electronic certificates online with various agencies while applying for the services provided by them, without having to provide paper copies. Since its soft launch on 10 February 2015 (the official launch took place on 1st July 2015), over 825,000 users have registered to use the digital lockers, with over 1.5 million documents being uploaded. Over the last 30 days an average of 22,000 documents has been uploaded every day, with the highest done day number being 47,640. To learn more visit https://digitallocker.gov.in/

Figure 15: National Scholarship Portal Source: mygov.in

The portal, officially launched on 1 July 2015, is one stop solution for end to end scholarship process right from submission of student application, verification, sanction and disbursal to end beneficiary for all the scholarships provided by the Government of

India. The application process for students will be simplified as there is be a common application form for all scholarships and registration is online. Based on eligibility criteria, the system itself suggests the schemes for which a student is eligible. Transparency will be increased as duplicate applications will be eliminated and the successful applicants will have the scholarship amounts will be credited to the bank accounts for the beneficiaries. The platform is scalable and configurable. To date 11 scholarship schemes. 950 institutions and 155,000 students have registered on the portal. Almost 30,000 applications for scholarships have been made. To learn more visit https://www.scholarships.gov.in/

Figure 16: Crowd Sourcing Platform MyGov.in

The Indian government launched its crowd sourcing platform MyGov.in July 2014 to provide a citizen-centric platform which would enable citizens to connect with the Government and contribute towards good governance. The My Gov platform, which started with discussion around 7 themes, has 215 of them today, with over half a million contributions. There are more than 1 million registered users. A large professional data analytics team works behind the scenes to process and filter the data and key points emerging from the debates on the site and helps in gauging the popular mood about particular issues from social media sites. A global consultancy firm is helping in mining the data. Suggestions have been generated on various policy challenges such as expenditure reforms, job creation, energy conservation, skill development and government initiatives such as Clean India, Digital India and Clean Ganga. The suggestions generated on the platform have been sent to different ministries which have been asked to take them into consideration in their policy formulations. The first year of experience of the platform has been positive as it is action-oriented and it is expected that the number of users will increase dramatically in the near future [3].

3.2   Data related policy and initiatives: National Data Sharing and Accessibility Policy

Figure 17: Open Government Data Platform: data.gov.in

Since 2012, India has a policy of making all non-sensitive data generated through public funds by all agencies of the Indian government and which could be used for meeting scientific, economic and developmental goals accessible to all Indian citizens. Through the Open Government Data Platform government ministries and departments must publish datasets, documents, services, tools, and applications for public use. However, interoperability of these data sets is currently a problem. To learn more visit https://data.gov.in/

The Big Data Initiative of the Government of India

Researchers from India are active, amongst others, in the fields of astrophysics, materials science, earth and atmospheric observations, energy, computational biology, bioinformatics, cognitive science, statistics etc., which generate a lot of data. These challenges require the development of advanced algorithms, visualization techniques, data streaming methodologies and analytics.

Keeping in mind the momentum that big data analytics is gaining in India, the need to build a sustainable eco-system that brings in a strong partnership across the industry players, government, and academia. With this objective, the Indian government has launched a *Big Data Initiative*, with the following aims:

- Promoting and fostering big data science, technology and applications in India and developing core generic technologies, tools and algorithms for wider applications in the government.
- Understanding the present status of the industry in terms of market size, different players providing services across sectors/ functions, opportunities, SWOT of industry, policy framework (if any), present skill levels available etc.
- Carrying out market landscape surveys to assess the future opportunities and demand for skill levels in next 10 years.
- Carrying out gap analysis in terms of skills levels and policy framework.

- Evolving a strategic road map and action plan clearly defining of roles of various stakeholders – government, industry, academia, industry associations and others with clear timelines and outcome for the next 10 years.

To learn more visit http://dst.gov.in/scientific-programme/bigdatainitiative.html

The institutional connection: With the growth of the big data analytics in India, research and teaching institutions in India are also joining the bandwagon by offering courses. Business analytics has been routinely taught in management schools for some time now. Technology schools have started offering post graduate courses in data sciences. Through the Big Data Initiative mentioned above, Centers of Excellence will be created, to which academics, government agencies, industry and other stakeholders will have access.

Privacy issues: Protection of sensitive personal data and information of individuals, including passwords, financial information such as bank account or credit card details, physical, physiological and mental health condition, sexual orientation, medical records and history and biometric information is provided for in the Information Technology Act of 2000 and the Information Technology (Reasonable Security Practices and Procedures and Sensitive Personal Data or Information) Rules 2011.

While the IT Act and the IT Rules regulate the collection and use of sensitive personal information, the government has proposed to enact a specific legislation on privacy (Privacy Bill) which will override the IT Rules. The Privacy Bill recognizes an individual's right to privacy and provides that it cannot be infringed except in certain circumstances, such as for protection of India's sovereignty or integrity, national security, prevention of commission of crime and public order. Unauthorized collection, processing, storage and disclosure of personal information will be treated as infringement of privacy under the Privacy Bill. However, this bill, which was first drafted in 2013, has not yet been presented in parliament.

The debate on big data is lively. See for example an article that appeared in the Hindu (a leading newspaper) entitled Missing the Big Picture on Big Data. *The author proposes that the big data revolution that is on aims at straight jacketing everybody into a flow of data, which can then be processed for optimal value extraction (read monetization). His thesis is that while dominant consensus right now is overwhelmingly positive, if we delve deeper, the use of big data and what it would entail for the future of human lives will unravel a problematic picture. The biggest casualty would be privacy, but the graver threat would be a digital replay of colonial era exploitation, with data replacing mineral resources and raw materials as the source of value. He asks the question if analytics can find solutions to humanity's problems and responds by saying yes, but not to the problems that human beings choose not to address. He concludes by saying that big data is no different from gold — it is firstly, and ultimately, a commodity* [4 & 5].

3.3 Indian Government using Big Data to Revolutionize Democracy

Earlier this year, India's Bharatiya Janata Party (BJP) led a decisive and shocking victory in the Indian elections. Many have speculated that the party's pioneering use of big data and social media analytics played a decisive role in the BJP's and Narendra Modi's success. Now that he's in power, it would appear Modi's innovative use of big data is far from over. Yesterday it was announced that the Prime Minister's Office is using big data analytics to process citizen's ideas and sentiments through the crowd sourcing platform mygov.in, as well as continuing to mine social media to get a broader picture of citizen's thoughts and opinions on government action. As Furhaad Shah reported back in May, the BJP used a rich variety of data science techniques to track and enhance public opinion in the run-up to the election results.

Figure 18: Big Data to Revolutionize Democracy in India

"Despite the challenges of big data, the rewards as Modi has clearly demonstrated while employing this data to "drive donations, enroll volunteers, and improve the effectiveness of everything from door knocks…to social media" – are significant. BJP's website, for example, planted cookies on all computers that visited its site, and then used information about these users' further internet activity – i.e., the sites they visited after BJP's – for customized advertisements."

Now, the Modi government has enlisted the expertise of global consulting firm PwC to revolutionize their mygov.in platform. The platform was established in July, and has quickly become a treasure trove of information on how the Indian electorate is responding to government action, as well as ideas for policy augmentation. However, up until this point, dialogue on the site has been more of a monologue than a conversation.

This is about to change. As a senior official told The Economic Times, "There is a large professional data analytics team working behind the scenes to process and filter key points emerging from debates on mygov.in, gauge popular mood about particular issues from social media sites like Twitter and Face book". These key findings are then collated in special reports, with suggested actionable insights. Ministries are being urged to take these reports into account, with special regards for findings on 19 key policy challenges, including "expenditure reforms, job creation, energy conservation, skill development and government initiatives such as Clean India, Digital India and Clean Ganga".

Undoubtedly, as the platform gains traction, scale will become a key issue. India is currently the second most populous country in the world, and is expected to surpass China in population by 2050. Modi is also urging Indian communities in America and Australia to add their voices to their platform. PwC's executive director Neel Ratan believes "it is distinctly possible that 30-50 million people would be actively contributing to mygov.in over the next year and a half, given its current pace of growth."

He added that there is "a science and an art" behind the current data processing scheme. "We have people constantly looking at all ideas coming up, filtering them and after a lot of analysis, correlating it to sentiments coming through on the rest of social media."

Ratan's PwC colleague, global leader in government Jan Sturesson told The Economic Times that the scope of this project extends far beyond India. He sees the pioneering work of Prime Minister's Office as a blueprint for democracy in the 21st century.

"The biggest issue for governments today is how to be relevant. If all citizens are treated with dignity and invited to collaborate, it can be easier for administrations to have a direct finger on the pulse of the nation rather than lose it in transmission through multiple layers of bureaucracy," he said.

"The problem in the West has been that the US, Australia and UK follow a public management philosophy that treats citizens as consumers. That's ridiculous, because a consumer pays the bill and complains, while a citizen engages differently and takes responsibility."

It is reported that, data is being criminally underutilized by federal departments in the Western world. The ultimate challenge big data faces in government is that data doesn't trump ideology; and in fact, statistics can be skewed and manipulated to further boost ideologies. Yet, data can become a driving force when it pushes past correlation and into causality- show a politician exactly how data can drive his policies, and they just might listen. What crucially distinguishes the mygov.in platform is that it's not just mining the data, but turning this data into actionable insights for India's ministries.

In a world where citizens feel increasingly disenfranchised, ignored and- particularly in the case of Western countries consumeried, the Indian government's big data scheme could truly prove to be revolutionary for democracy in the 21st century.

The Promise of Big Data Analytics

Government should revolutionize policymaking by anchoring decisions on evidence. The digitization of our daily lives generates a flood of data: from our phones, credit cards, tax records, car movements, television usage. Those who have the computing abilities to trawl through this river in spate can tell your online bookseller what your reading habits are or they can help city managers plan traffic flows better. The fictional detective Sherlock Holmes was surely not thinking of big data but he captured the essence of the opportunity when he said: "Having gathered these facts, Watson, I smoked several pipes over them, trying to separate those which were crucial from others which were merely incidental".

Analysis of big data is ubiquitous today: first in companies but now increasingly in government as well. It is for this reason that we welcome the recent moves by the Indian government to use data analytics to help it design policies based on empirical evidence rather than fond hopes. The starting point should be the Aadhaar database. There are already over 700 million registered users.

This newspaper reported earlier in the week that the government is looking at ways to bring data analytics, supercomputing and the Aadhaar database together so as to design better public policies."When you have that much amount of information, you can do a lot of data analysis and figure out trends. We can thus see what are the policies needed to be defined. Therefore proactive policymaking based on previous trends is possible provided we have data," said Rajat Moona, director general of the Centre for Development of Advanced Computing in Pune.

Singapore's Land Transport Authority regularly crunches 20 million fare transactions per day to better understand the transport needs of its citizens. Based on the extensive usage data, it has been able to build more cost effective routes for cars, buses and trains, schedule the best timings and lowest fares. The remarkable aspect is that while doing so, it has also been able to reduce the cost of its revenue collection.

Similarly, according to a McKinsey & Co. report, the Bundesagentur für Arbeit (the federal labour agency in Germany), with a €54 billion annual budget and 120,000 full-time employees, not only improved its customer services by reducing the unemployed from 4.4 million to 3.2 million but also cut around €10 billion of costs between 2003-2010 using big data strategies.

However, such revolutionary ideas are largely alien to India's policymaking scenario. The ad-hoc-ism in policy choices reflects not just in India's persistently low rank in the World Bank's ease of doing business index but also in the country's grossly inefficient public sector—be it social welfare schemes or the administration of law and order.

Take the recent example of the extent of leakages in India's public distribution system (PDS). There are several competing numbers doing the rounds. The only commonality being that they are all unacceptably high. Beyond the mere numbers, there is little unanimity among researchers about the ability of PDS in improving nutritional outcomes. A big reason for this is the fact that most conclusions are based on minute sample surveys instead of the full data.

But in a country like India, big data can create its own problems. Herbert Simon, who received the Nobel Prize for economics in 1978, had once said, "A wealth of information creates a poverty of attention and a need to allocate that attention efficiently among the overabundance of information sources that might consume it."

Yet, the potential use of data analytics in evidence-based policymaking is immense. The mobile phone call data records, which proved critical in reaching out to the victims in the aftermath of Haiti's earthquake in 2010, could be used for better, even predictive, policing. Similarly, analysis of the farm related queries in Kissan Call Centers can cull out tremendous insights about the exact needs of the farmers. The government can, in turn, customize its farm support measures across fertilizers, seeds and irrigation in a far more efficient manner.

Of course, the use of big data also raises questions of right to privacy and the freedom of choice. But most Orwellian nightmares are exaggerations that can be addressed by well-designed privacy legislation.

Personal data collection

If a world governed on the basis of big data is indeed the future, then what does this bode for humanity? Why is the government so anxious to make the ownership of an Aadhaar card, which is officially voluntary, practically mandatory? Why did the online fashion store Myntra.com recently turn app-only, which means you can't shop on it through the website or mobile browser but only by downloading the app?

Why is Face book developing solar-powered drones to beam Internet from the sky? And why do both Face book and Gmail keep badgering you for your cell phone number?

What is the need for something called internet.org when there is already an Internet out there? Why does our government want to invest in 'Smart Cities' when it is unwilling to invest adequately on education? The answer to all these questions, as Bob Dylan might have said, is flowing in optic fiber cables. If not, it is definitely stored in a non-meteorological cloud somewhere. Its name: Big data.

"Big data is no different from gold; it is firstly, and ultimately, a commodity"

The UID-Aadhaar project will be the largest such citizen database on the planet. The reason Myntra wants its customers to transact only from apps is that consumer data is most valuable when tied to specific individuals, as it enables a closer tracking of user behaviour. It is also why Google, Face book, and other tech companies want your mobile number.

It is because Mark Zuckerberg does not possess a search engine like Google does which, as the entry point to the Internet for most people, is the ultimate instrument for generating consumer data that he wants to start another, smaller 'internet' for those who cannot afford the full-size one.

As for Smart Cities, it is a blatant scheme to ensure that every citizen is dragooned into a digital grid at all times, so that she secretes a non-stop data trail from birth to death. This data trail or big data would be continuously captured and processed for optimal value extraction.

If a world governed on the basis of big data is indeed the future, then what does this bode for humanity? The dominant consensus right now is overwhelmingly positive. But if we delve deeper, the use of big data and what it would entail for the future of human lives will unravel a problematic picture.

According to the optimists, big data in combination with what is described as the Internet of Things (IoT), a world where the vast majority of gadgets, machines, and humans are connected to the internet and to each other promises a future where all important decisions about business, life, and society would be taken purely and happily on the basis of data.

Human judgment, which is typically partial, flawed, and conflicted and often distorted by factors that are not measurable, and do not compute, such as moral qualms, or empathy need ever come into the picture. This, they believe, would make for greater efficiency, higher productivity, and the optimal utilization of resources for the greatest good of the greatest number.

There is a name for such decision-making driven purely by big data analytics. It's called 'evidence-based decision-making'. Its semantic twin is 'actionable information'. Evidence-based decision-making can and does pay off brilliantly in business operations— this is what enterprise software solutions do, and they were indeed the tech precursors of big data analytics. It is ideal also for, say, predicting the weather, or earthquakes, and for identifying bankable talent in team sports, as the bestselling book/ film Money ball showed.

Besides, big data already plays a major role in the management of infrastructure and industry, not to mention security, military affairs, health, and geopolitics, as the Snowden leaks made amply clear.

Purveyors of technological determinism like to argue that, with the advances in cloud and mobile computing, the non-stop generation of data on a never-before scale is bound to change how humans think, and therefore act and live.

"The graver threat is a digital replay of colonial era exploitation, with data replacing mineral resources and raw materials as the source of value"

This was the contention of Chris Andersen, the former editor-in-chief of *wired* magazine, in a widely debated piece titled *"The End of Theory: The data deluge makes the scientific method obsolete".* Andersen's logic is simple: since processing of big data can give us correlations that can predict accurately, causation is no longer relevant. So theory, or explanations of the world based on the model of cause and effect (which is how humans have traditionally made sense of the world), are now obsolete.

In other words, we no longer need to think. Collect data, feed them into the maw of analytics, and wait for solutions to emerge. In Andersen's words, "With enough data, the numbers speak for themselves."Well, this is no longer solely the chartered accountant's motto. It is the article of faith among the world's movers and shakers.

The World Economic Forum, an annual gathering of the global power elite, notes in its 2014 Global Technology Report that data is "a new form of asset class", adding, "data are now the equivalent of oil or gold. Today we are seeing a data boom rivaling the Texas oil boom of the 20th century and the San Francisco gold rush of the 1800s."

In his foreword to this very report, John Chambers, the chairman and CEO of Cisco Systems, points out that, with the number of app downloads growing from 10 billion in 2010 to 77 billion in 2014, there is "a $19 trillion global opportunity to create value over the next decade."As per industry estimates, in India alone, it is set to touch $1 billion in 2015.

Will politics surrender to analytics?

No doubt, there is overpowering business logic to the rise and rise of big data analytics. But does this mean it should get a leading role in the domain of politics and public policy?

The answer to this question may already have been decided, going by the frequency with which "evidence-based policy-making" and "actionable information" pops up in government documents and the reports of bodies such as the United Nations or the World Bank.

India, too, is well and truly on board the bandwagon. On the one hand, the large pool of English-speaking engineering/ mathematics graduates makes India an attractive destination for the off-shoring of big data analytics, which Indian tech entrepreneurs are well placed to exploit.

On the other hand, with several citizen-to-government transactions, such as passport applications and tax payments migrating online, and the state unwilling to relax its grip on Aadhaar, and plans afoot to digitize medical records, it is clear that Big Data will come to play a major role.

Besides, many examples have been cited to prove that big data can be harnessed for social good. We have been told that cell phone call logs can help locate survivors during a natural disaster. Online searches can yield data to predict a disease outbreak (the principle behind applications such as Google Flu Trends).

And given the billions of dollars the preferred term is 'value' riding on the so-called 'information economy', it is unlikely that the raw material for data manufacture also known as 'people' will have much say in the matter. We are already beginning to see this in India, with 'evidence-based decision-making' being trotted out as an argument against the precious few welfare schemes still left for India's poor, such as the public distribution system (where data show that it is leaky), or the rural jobs scheme (where data show it is riddled with corruption).A policy determined by such evidence alone would seek to scrap both schemes and replace them with cash transfers, as the incumbent government seems keen to do. But big data, by definition, is the wrong tool with which to understand the social consequences of giving cash instead of food grains a critical policy input that can come only from politics, not analytics.

Where is big data taking us?

The exponential growth of big data analytics, and its increasing utilization in government policy, is premised on many things, including growth in IT infrastructure, the digital inclusion of those hitherto excluded by poverty, and an overarching colonization of the analog universe by the digital. But what it needs above all is the erasure of the very concept of privacy. Many of us have already voluntarily surrendered our privacy, either for the sake of convenience or to save costs — by ticking the 'I accept' box when we sign on to a social media or email service. But privacy while critical for a functional democracy – is not the only casualty of big data. The graver threat is a digital replay of colonial era exploitation, with data replacing mineral resources and raw materials as the source of value.

We already have a bizarre scenario in several developing countries including India a scenario that is somehow no longer perceived as bizarre where people don't have toilets an amenity with tremendous public health consequences but own cell phones, and their mobile data is being captured for 'actionable information' on the status of their health, and for 'evidence-based' framing of health policy.

"It promises a future where decisions about business, life, and society will be taken purely on the basis of data"

It is in the context of such anomalies that a term coined by a Tanzanian health minister becomes relevant: data colonialism.

The expression gained traction when Najeeb Al Shorbaji, Director, Knowledge and Management at the World Health Organization (WHO), gave a speech in 2013, titled 'Data Colonialism'. Shorbaji used the term to describe a scenario where the West has been mining African nations for health data without the Africans benefiting in any way.

He uses the same data-as-gold metaphor used by the WEF report to draw an analogy between the flow of raw materials from the colonies to Europe, and the flow of data from the erstwhile colonies to the developed West today. The objective in both cases is the same: extraction of value.

Today, useless data or 'data exhaust' as it's called has to flow from the developing markets to the West (via Google or Amazon or their equivalent) in order to be commoditized as information. Shorbaji illustrates the social dynamic of data-driven exploitation with an example from a domain that is usually touted as a poster boy for the benefits of big data analytics: healthcare.

He describes how impoverished Africans, who are not even aware of the concept of informed consent, living as they do in countries with no legislative framework for data collection and usage, agree to become guinea pigs for risky clinical trials in exchange for a little money or free medical treatment.

The animating logic of big data

This brings us to the philosophical basis of big data, which is rooted in the abstractions of statistics. It is well known that statistics grew as a discipline to address the needs of the modern state, which had to administer populations on a big scale. In big data, the post-modern state has found a fitting collaborator for monitoring, and preemptively controlling, sections of the populations that, in circumstances of prolonged deprivation or injustice, can be prone to unseemly eruptions against those who control the levers of the state.

Typically, the 'big' of big data is construed as a reference to the sheer volume, velocity (of generation) and variety (of sources) of the datasets involved. But perhaps the real reason why 'big' data is big is that it seeks to decisively appropriate human agency and transfer it to data and algorithms.

Even the term 'actionable information', often invoked in the context of big data, suggests that it is not humans who have to decide what is to be done, and therefore take responsibility for the choices being made, but somehow the data or information itself which decides (for humanity) the action to be taken. This, finally, is the inescapable social cost of big data analytics.

Finally, we come to the big question about big data: Can analytics find solutions to humanity's problems? Yes, but not to the problems that human beings choose not to address.

Many global problems have their origins in deprivation. We don't need big data analytics to tell us this. It is common sense that if such widespread deprivation is addressed which requires solving the problem of extreme inequalities in wealth and income – a lot many problems, such as hunger and disease, can be resolved.

There already is ample data, including an OECD study, which confirms that reducing inequality boosts economic growth. But this has hardly prompted a corresponding change in government policies anywhere. While evidence-based policy-making may be good for business and the tech industry, it is only politics-driven policy-making that can make a positive difference to people's lives. For, as data evangelists never tire of pointing out, big data is no different from gold — it is firstly, and ultimately, a commodity.

3.4 PMO using Big Data techniques on mygov.in to translate popular mood into Government action

Figure 19: PMO is employing Big Data Techniques

As it is reported that The Prime Minister's Office is using Big Data techniques to process ideas thrown up by citizens on its crowd sourcing platform mygov.in, place them in context of the popular mood as reflected in trends on social media, and generate actionable reports for ministries and departments to consider and implement.

The Modi government has roped in global consulting firm PwC to assist in the data mining exercise, and now wants to elevate Mygov.in platform from a one-way flow of citizens' ideas to a dialogue where the government keeps them abreast of some of the actions that emerge from their brainstorming.

"There is a large professional data analytics team working behind the scenes to process and filter key points emerging from debates on mygov.in, gauge popular mood about particular issues from social media sites like Twitter and Face book," said a senior official aware of the development, adding that these are collated into special reports about possible action points that are shared with the PMO and line ministries. Ministries are being asked to revert with an action taken report on these ideas and policy suggestions currently being generated on 19 different policy challenges such as expenditure reforms, job creation, energy conservation, skill development and government initiatives such as Clean India, Digital India and Clean Ganga.

With the PM inviting Indian communities in America and Australia to join the online platform, which he has termed a 'mass movement towards Surajya', the traffic handling capacity of mygov.in is being scaled up consistently, the official said.

PwC executive director Neel Ratan said that the firm is 'helping the government' process the citizen inputs at Mygov.in.

"There is a science and art behind it. We have people constantly looking at all ideas coming up, filtering them and after a lot of analysis, correlating it to sentiments coming through on the rest of social media," he said, stressing this is throwing up interesting trends and action points, being relayed to ministries. "It's turning out to be fairly action-oriented. I think it is distinctly possible that 30-50 million people would be actively contributing to Mygov.in over the next year and a half, given its current pace of growth," Ratan said.

PwC's global leader in government and public services Jan Sturesson told ET the participative governance model being adopted through mygov.in could become a model for the developed world.

"The biggest issue for governments today is how to be relevant. If all citizens are treated with dignity and invited to collaborate, it can be easier for administrations to have a direct finger on the pulse of the nation rather than lose it in transmission through multiple layers of bureaucracy," he said, not ruling out the possibility of using the mygov.in for quick referendums on contemporary policy dilemmas in a couple of years.

"The problem in the West has been that the US, Australia and UK follow a public management philosophy that treats citizens as consumers. That's ridiculous, because a consumer pays the bill and complains, while a citizen engages differently and takes responsibility," said Sturesson [6].

3.5 Taking the step forward: Government Initiatives in Analytics

India is the second most populated country in the world. Thus, a mine for data analysts to research, collect and analyze data. Researchers in India are an active breed, name any upcoming field under the sun and you will find research going on in that field already!

Even though researchers in astrophysics, material sciences, cognitive sciences, energy, biology, statistics, earth and atmospheric observation, bioinformatics, biotechnology, nanotechnology and many others generate a lot of data, they require advance algorithms, visualization techniques, data streaming methodologies and analytics for further development.

Figure 20: Indian Govt. Initiative in Data Analytics

This momentum that big data analytics has gained in India has facilitated the launch of 'Big Data Initiative' by the Indian government. It will aim to:

- Promote and foster big data science, technology and application in India and developing core generic technologies, tools and algorithms

- Understand the current scenario in terms of market size, different players, SWOT, etc.

- Carryout market landscape surveys to assess the future opportunities and demand for skill levels in next 10 years

- Evolve a strategic roadmap, defining the role of various stakeholders – government, industry and academia with timelines.

Talking about the Big Data initiative will not be rendered complete without the mention of BJP's Election campaign in 2014. It was one of the most data-savvy campaigns that any country has witnessed in recent times.

The IT cell of "Elect Modi Campaign" virtually connected with about 144 million people across India through Face book, Twitter and Google plus. BJP partnered with IT and analytics firms, such as SAP, Oracle, In Modi, and PwC to get real-time updates and analysis during the elections which enabled them to react faster to any controversies in real time. Further, to drive their campaign, they planted cookies on all computers that visited the BJP website. They then extracted information about their visitors' further internet activity, for customized advertisements.

BJP had proposed to set up an Institute of Big Data and Analytics for studying the impact of Big Data across sectors for predictive science with a focus on India-specific problems, enabling businesses to invest in a wide range of issues such as national security, processing data from different languages, disseminating data to farmers about production, prices, etc.

Additionally, the Modi Government has developed various digital platforms and launched many initiatives such as MyGov.in, Digi Locker, Digital India, National Scholarship portal, Aadhaar card, Jan Dhan Yojna to connect with the citizens through websites, mobiles and smart phones and encourage citizens to be a part of discussions, suggestions and volunteering for various causes. Some of these portals, such as My Gov also keep them updated on the status of their suggestions.

Also, as a part of the "Digital India" program, common Biometric Attendance System is implemented in the government offices to collect data on the attendance of the employees.

Another example of the support of analytics is shown by the Department of Science and Technology that initiated a programme to promote Big Data Science, Technology and Applications for fostering research. They grant financial support for R&D Projects, national level Conferences/ workshops/ Seminars and for the establishment of Center for Excellence in Big Data Analytics, Predictive technologies, Cyber Security etc.

The latest to join the analytics sector is the National Payments Corporation of India with the launch of a unified payment interface that allows customers to send and receive money through smart phones without revealing their bank account details. Transactions can be done through Aadhaar number, mobile number or virtual payment address.

Further, organizations such as Swaniti and Fourth Lion are also playing an important role. While Swaniti works with politicians by focusing on data collection and analysis, creating data dashboards and synthesizing solutions to problems at grass root levels; Fourth Lion's expertise lies in understanding how national electorates behave through Insta Vaani, their quick polling tool. They may have different approaches, but both the organizations focus on analytics, building and adopting the latest technologies to provide strategies for the Indian political leaders and environment.

Even though these initiatives are encouraging, but the infrastructural bottlenecks may prove to be problematic in implementing these on ground level. However, intelligent data is the way forward and now that we have taken the first step it won't be long before we are up and ahead in the game!

3.6   Big Data Initiative: BDI: An R&D Perspective

By definition, **Big Data** is data whose scale, diversity, and complexity require new architecture, techniques, algorithms, and analytics to manage it and extract value and hidden knowledge from it. In other words, big data is characterized by volume, variety (structured and unstructured data) velocity (high rate of changing) and veracity (uncertainty and incompleteness).

In the Big Data research context, so called analytics over Big Data is playing a leading role. Analytics cover a wide family of problems mainly arising in the context of Database, Data Warehousing and Data Mining research. Analytics research is intended to develop complex procedures running over large-scale, enormous in-size data repositories with the objective of extracting useful knowledge hidden in such repositories. One of the most significant application scenarios where Big Data arise is, without doubt, scientific computing. Here, scientists and researchers produce huge amounts of data per-day via experiments (e.g., disciplines like high-energy physics, astronomy, biology, bio-medicine, and so forth). But extracting useful knowledge for decision making purposes from these massive, large-scale data repositories is almost impossible for actual DBMS-inspired analysis tools. From a methodological point of view, there are also research challenges. A new methodology is required for transforming Big Data stored in heterogeneous and different-in-nature data sources (e.g., legacy systems, Web, scientific data repositories, sensor and stream databases, social networks) into a structured, hence well-interpretable format for target data analytics. As a consequence, data-driven approaches, in biology, medicine, public policy, social sciences, and humanities, can replace the traditional hypothesis-driven research in science.

3.7 Big Data: Science & Technology - Challenges

Some of the S&T challenges that researchers across the globe and as well as in India facing are related to data deluge pertaining to Astrophysics, Materials Science, Earth & atmospheric observations, Energy, Fundamental Science, Computational Biology, Bioinformatics & Medicine, Engineering & Technology, GIS and Remote Sensing, Cognitive science and Statistical data. These challenges require development of advanced algorithms, visualization techniques, data streaming methodologies and analytics. The overall constraints that community facing are

1. **The IT Challenge:** Storage and computational power
2. **The computer science :**Algorithm design, visualization, scalability (Machine Learning, network & Graph analysis, streaming of data and text mining), distributed data, architectures, data dimension reduction and implementation
3. **The mathematical science:** Statistics, Optimization, uncertainty quantification, model development (statistical, Ab Initio, simulation) analysis and systems theory
4. **The multi-disciplinary approach:** Contextual problem solving

3.8 Big Data Analytics and the India equation

To tap the analytics momentum, India now needs to build a sustainable analytics eco-system that brings in a strong partnership across the industry players, government, and academia. Some of the key actions for analytics eco-system in India would be around.

1. **Talent Pool** - Create industry academia partnership to groom the talent pool in universities as well as develop

strong internal training curriculum to advance analytical depth.

2. **Collaborate** - Form analytics forum across organization boundaries to discuss the pain-points of the practitioner community and share best practices to scale analytics organizations.

3. **Capability Development** - Invest in long term skills and capabilities that form the basis for differentiation and value creation. There needs to be an innovation culture that will facilitate IP creation and asset development.

4. **Value Creation** - Building rigor to measure the impact of analytics deployment is very critical to earn legitimacy within the organization.

Big Data and analytics offer tremendous untapped potential to drive big business outcomes. For organizations to leverage India as a global analytics hub can be one of the key levers to move up their analytics maturity curve.

3.9   Broad contours of DST initiated BDI programme

- To promote and foster Big Data Science, Technology and Applications in the country and to develop core generic technologies, tools and algorithms for wider applications in Govt.
- To understand the present status of the industry in terms of market size, different players providing services across sectors/ functions, opportunities, SWOT of industry, policy framework (if any), present skill levels available etc.
- To carryout market landscape survey to assess the future opportunities and demand for skill levels in next 10 years
- To carryout gap analysis in terms of skills levels and policy framework.

- To evolve a strategic Road Map and micro level action plan clearly defining of roles of various stakeholders – Govt., Industry, Academia, Industry Associations and others with clear timelines and outcome for the next 10 years.

Call for Proposal under Big Data Initiative Programme (to be opened shortly).

Table2: Pro-forma for Submission of Research Projects for Financial Support

List of Proforma / Annexure

S. No.	Description	File Format
1.	Format for Submission of R&D Projects / Center for excellence	Word
2.	Format for submitting proposals for short term Training Course/Workshop/Conference under different Big Data Initiative	Word
3.	Guidelines for Implementing Research Project	Word
4.	Progress Report	Word
5.	Project Completion Report	Word
6.	Statement of Expenditure to be submitted financial year wise	Word
7.	Format for Utilization Certificate	Word
8.	Department of Science & Technology terms & condition of the grant	Word

Dr KR Murli Mohan, Head (Big Data Initiative) of the Department of Science & Technology, Technology Bhawan New Mehrauli Road New Delhi-110 016. Tel: 011-26962956, 26590319. Email: krmm [at] nic [dot] in [7].

3.10 Data Centre and Analytics Lab at the Indian Institute of Management, Bangalore

Big Data Initiative @ CSA
Department of Computer
Science and Automation
Indian Institute of Science

Today is the era of Big Data. The need to analyze vast amounts of data, being generated in different fields ranging from medicine to financial markets and from transportation to environmental modeling, is emerging as the next big challenge and opportunity. The primary objective of the Big Data Initiative is to help build a strong academic and research ecosystem that allows India to address this challenge and take a leadership position in this critical area. In order to create awareness about developments in the emerging field of Big Data including for example new algorithms and systems design for Big Data and new concepts in machine learning related to Big Data and to bring together the broader community so as to leverage existing strengths, we are initiating a series of public lectures on various aspects of Big Data, open to both academia and industry, as a platform for open exchange of ideas.

Mission: The Data Centre and Analytics Lab at the Indian Institute of Management Bangalore (DCAL@IIMB) has been set up to support interdisciplinary empirical research using data on primarily Indian and other emerging markets. The vision of this initiative is to be India's most comprehensive research data source.

Activities: IIMB offers a successful one-year certificate programme in Analytics to participants from several multi-national companies. Faculty members from the Analytics team have conducted specialized training programme for companies such as Accenture, Bank of America, Blue Ocean Market Intelligence, Fidelity, Hewlett Packard, Reserve Bank of India, etc. DCAL sponsors research programmes, doctoral dissertations and student projects.

Dissemination of research findings is carried out through journal articles, working papers, case studies, newsletters, conferences and roundtables.

One of DCAL's significant activities is the Visiting Researcher Programme, a competitive grant proposal scheme open to international researchers who spend a few months at IIMB every year on collaborative research aimed at publication in top academic journals.

The Analytics Research Team at DCAL-IIMB

A core team of cross-functional researchers - IIMB faculty specialized in Quantitative Methods and Information System, Economics, Finance, Marketing, Production and Operations Management and Public Policy - drive the research agenda [8].

3.11 Acharya Nagarjuna University (ANU) is all set to inaugurate the 'National Research Centre for Big Data Analytics'

Acharya Nagarjuna University (ANU) is all set to inaugurate the 'National Research Centre for Big Data Analytics', which is claimed to be first of its kind in the country, on November 18. The university authorities have invited Guntur MP Galla Jayadev to inaugurate the new facility that has been set up at the engineering college on the campus. The centre aims to provide training for the students as well as faculty members to help them enhance their skills. The big data analytics is the process of examining large data sets containing a variety of data types i.e., big data, to uncover hidden patterns, unknown correlations, market trends, customer preferences and other useful business information. The analytical findings can lead to more effective marketing, new revenue opportunities, better customer service, improved operational efficiency, competitive advantages over rival organizations and other business benefits. "Having knowledge in big data analytics will definitely help the students from several disciplines like mathematics, statistics, management, commerce, computers, pharmacy and all branches of the engineering to improve their employability skills. It will also assist the faculty members to improve their skills and acumen. This is a new revolution in analyzing huge data," said Prof K Viyyanna Rao, vice-chancellor of ANU. The university, which has spent Rs 15 lakh on the centre so far, is making efforts to get funding for the projects from the Department of Science and Technology (DST), (Government of India) as the latter had started Big Data Initiative (BDI) programme to promote Big Data Science, Technology and Applications.

Under this scheme, the DST will provide financial support to the academicians, scientists, technologists and other practicing researchers from recognized academic, research institutions and registered scientific societies. Since it is a new initiative, the university authorities are also seeking support from other organizations.

Principal of the University Engineering College and Coordinator of the Centre for Big Data Analytics E Srinivasa Reddy said that they were also planning to enter into a memorandum of understanding (MoU) with the Centre for Development of Advanced Computing (CDAC), Bangalore.

"As per my knowledge, no other university in the country has set up an exclusive centre for big data analytics," he said and added that they had already submitted several research topics for the BDI programme of the DST. Analysis of the crashing of the Indian shopping site 'Flipkart' is said to be one of the research topics by the faculty at the university.ANU is also planning to introduce M. Tech in Big Data Analytics from next academic year, said Prof K Viyyanna Rao, vice-chancellor of ANU. They are yet to get the nod from the executive council. It is an evening course. Source: Indian Express [9].

3.12 Government plans to use Big Data Analytics for taxation: Infosys, New Delhi

As government looks at ways to analyze huge amounts of data available on corporate as well as individual level to increase tax collections by studying various parameters like spending patterns, IT companies expect strong growth in the big data and analytics business in the coming years.

"Government is planning to use analytics to increase its revenue base," Raghu Cavale, vice president and head of India business at Infosys, India's second largest software services exporter, told PTI.He said the country's tax-payer base is just about 3 crores and the number has been inching its way slowly for the last 5-10 years, which the government would like to see growing at a faster pace.

"The economy has been expanding, which essentially means that the number of people coming in the tax rate should be more. But it is not so," Mr. Cavale added.

Big data and analytics businesses of IT firms aim at storing, sorting and analyzing vast amounts of data across various fields - finance, marketing, healthcare, utilities, climate and transaction records. According to government data, the total tax payers in the country stood at about 3.24 crores during fiscal year 2011-12 (FY12).

"As a nation, we can put together all the data. If you travel abroad, buy expensive jewellery, we can check your digital footprints on online shopping and piece together a person's lifestyle and through that create a taxable database," Mr. Cavale said.

Citing an example, he said the government in Italy follows people's lifestyle, travel and spending pattern so as to track those who could be evading taxes."So can we use this data analytics to expand out taxable database? Our total direct taxes are only 9 per cent of our GDP, whereas it should be about 18 per cent, and you cannot raise it by taxing people who you have already taxed. You are going to use analytics," he added.

On government's use of IT for collecting and utilizing income tax information, Mr. Cavale said, "We are discussing with the government many projects. Some have already been tendered, which we have won. Some other people are doing it. Government is very well aware of data warehousing and analytics. It is talking to us as well as other firms."

The Finance Ministry had collected Rs 4.73 lakh crores in indirect taxes during 2012-13. For the current fiscal, it has fixed the target of collecting Rs 5.65 lakh crores in indirect taxes, comprising customs, excise and service tax.

Total collection of indirect taxes stood at about Rs 2, 28,550 crores during the first six months of 2013-14.

Direct tax is collected from corporate and income tax payers, which was at Rs 14, 530 crores till August, surged to Rs 18,077 crores till September 15, 2013.

Mr. Cavale said Infosys is competing seriously for government deals in this area and has won some like the income tax department's online filing of returns as well as managing banking and insurance operations for India Post.

"The challenge right now is to scale this and create more efficiency, both in terms of the solutions we bring to the market, our own efficiency and, of course, how all this finally boils down to revenue stream."

Information technology can be harnessed to clearly see the position at any given point of time and help make sound financial decisions, he said, adding that it can help computerize of all government records at the central as well as state levels.

"Ideally at the end of the day our Finance Minister, like a good businessman, should be able to say what my current account deficit is for the day," Mr. Cavale added.

He said the basic aim on which Infosys has been speaking to various wings of the government is to create a medium at state government's level, so that the state treasury is computerized, state taxes are computerized and these are linked with the centre.

For the quarter ended September 30, 2013, Infosys clocked revenues of Rs 317 crore from India and a segment profit of Rs 121 crores [10].

3.13   Big Data in Government Sector

Webopedia defines "Big Data" is a buzzword, or catch-phrase, used to describe a massive volume of both structured and unstructured data that is so large that it's difficult to process using traditional database and software techniques. In most enterprise scenarios the data is too big or it moves too fast or it exceeds current processing capacity. While the term may seem to reference the volume of data, that isn't always the case.

The term big data, especially when used by vendors, may refer to the technology which includes tools and processes that an organization requires handling the large amounts of data and storage facilities.

The term big data is believed to have originated with Web search companies who had to query very large distributed aggregations of loosely-structured data. We understand how analytics can change our perception towards data. But here we are talking about how big data technologies can change the way traditional and age old processes can be made much more simple, effective and cost efficient. Let's take the case of Census in India, which is supposedly that largest exercise of its kind in the world.

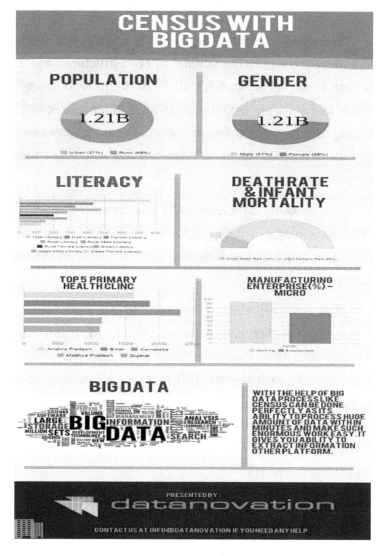

Figure 21: Census with Big Data

Let's first understand how Census in India works.

Census in India works on de facto canvasser method. " Under the 'Canvasser' method the enumerator approaches every household and records the answer on the schedules himself after ascertaining the particulars from the head of the household or other knowledgeable persons in the household. De-facto basis is counting the population at the place where a person is actually found on the reference date of the census rather than on the place of normal residence."

In the first phase of the census the enumerator visits the house hold with questionnaire for the survey. They move from house to house and collect the information manually. This practice is extended for 7 months of survey round and after that the information will go for revision round. In revision round any changes in birth, death and migration will be updated compared to the last time of visit. The survey itself has two phases' house listing and house census and population enumeration. In house listing each building related structures are updated in the survey and also other house amenities. In second phase of population enumeration every individual in the house hold will be updated through the survey.

The next phase is the data processing phase. The processing of the census data occupies a very important place in the census. Data capturing and data processing is giant phase of census as census generate large amount of data. To convert data to electronic form, it scans census schedule and extract records from it with the help of high speed duplex scanners and reading information using ICR technology. This was the advanced approach which Indian census body adopted and it did paid them enormously as it reduced their time and cost. The data size from this process can be in tetra bytes (TB).

After data processing, evaluation and analysis of results ensures that the completeness and accuracy of the published results. "The extent of error can be estimated through the use of checks of the internal consistency of the data, by examination of the reasonableness of the results and by comparison of the results with data collected in other enquiries. The publication of the census results must specify the extent of error in coverage and reporting. This will greatly help to make comparative studies and also indicate the long-term trends of certain characteristics of the population. "

The whole data processing is done in RDBMS (SQL Server – 2008) environment, where data is stored in relational tables and further queried for different summarizations.

Since this data is in TBs (tetra bytes), web scale technologies like Hadoop and NoSQL database like Cassandra makes an ideal solution for this. Hadoop with its Map Reduce framework and very high scalability will make the whole process complete in weeks and Cassandra can store this summarized data in query optimized tables which will make dissemination of results also faster.

New insights from this whole data can be generated in days. This will enable new research and analysis of data outside the census organization also faster and easier, enabling decision makers with vital data for proper planning. The whole 10 years exercise will come down to 2-3 years and the Census organization can do more frequent census as the rate of high rate of population and economic growth makes the data far from real in less than 5 years' time.

It looks Census in India is an ideal fit for a Big Data solution not only enabling quick decision making but also less costly utilizing the powerful open source alternatives [111].

3.14 3 Most Exciting Indian Data Science Initiatives

Dr Gautam Shroff, VP & Chief Scientist - TCS, in an exclusive chat with Mastufa Ahmed, talks about some of the innovative steps being taken around open data and how they will create impact in coming days.

What are your top technology predictions for 2016 and beyond?

The hype around data will die down a bit while digitization of business will remain a growing trend touching much more verticals. Data analytics and self-learning systems will move from hype (i.e., something to blog about) to capabilities that organizations will come to expect from the IT world. The startup ecosystem as well as large IT players will need to meet this demand.

What are the top data science initiatives being taken in India that will have a lasting impact in coming days?

1. **Democratization of data visual analytics** (i.e., end-user tools): to simplify data and make it accessible to everyone. Traditionally, IT departments have been the gatekeeper of analytical tools where analyzing data was a complex process for the end users. Now companies are realizing that the key to unlock the value of data is to make it accessible to its users.

2. **Public data sets** (e.g. data.gov.in): public data sets that anyone uses are going to have a lasting impact. Data.gov.in for instance is a big and lasting initiative aimed at increasing transparency in the functioning of Government which also opens up new avenues of how data can be put to use innovatively.

3. **Social sciences, NGOs, agriculture** via agro-information systems, healthcare, education, etc, where each depend on data sharing/creation and analytics thereafter.

Data and insights alone can't make any difference unless there is action in the field, which requires entrepreneurship or political will, or both, —**Dr Gautam Shroff, VP and Chief Scientist, TCS**.

How can government departments utilize 'data' to track citizen services, curb corruptions and improve healthcare?

UIDAI already has data scientists; other departments should develop their analysts into data scientists by training, MOOCs (massive open online course), etc. Agriculture and healthcare are low-hanging fruit as data is available; need of the hour is to invest in platforms that publish data and enable data sharing APIs based on which innovations will emerge from the ecosystem.

Education is equally important but in this case granular data collection has yet to begin; data from centralized examinations can be a start, appropriately anonymized of course. Peer-to-peer lending and micro-banking have already begun; these will also be data-driven ecosystems.

What are some of the initiatives from TCS around data analytics and who are the beneficiaries of the projects?

A number of socially impactful projects are data rich, ranging from agro-information systems to healthcare platforms being used in practice. Analytics can help, but data and insights alone cannot make any difference unless there is action in the field, which requires entrepreneurship or political will, or both.

How do you, as a data scientist, create impact at your current company? What are some of the areas you are working on currently at TCS?

Research – reading, doing and publishing in top venues; organizing and creating high-quality communities and events in India (e.g. India KDD and IKDD CoDS conferences series).

Creating methodologies, frameworks, and products that support our service business as well as package and deliver services is in the form of self-learning software. You can access the public details of innovation @TCS from this link: www.tcs.com/research [12 & 13].

3.15 Modi's Digital India initiative to fire up demand for Data Scientists, UI Specialists, Mobility Professionals

Figure 22: Digital India initiative

Modi's maiden budget has emphasized a strong focus on leveraging technology to drive the nation and bring in transparency within governance. The Budget allocated 500 crores for the massive

Digital India initiative, 100 crores for setting up virtual classrooms and 100 crores for promoting 'good governance' through IT, aimed at simplifying citizens' access to public services.

Modi's pet project of building 'one hundred smart cities' - which has been allocated Rs 7,060 crores - is another major project that would rely strongly on technology, calling for a robust cloud computing backend coupled with real-time surveillance and big data analytics technologies.

R. Chandrashekhar, president, NASSCOM termed the budget as pragmatic and directional and said that the announcements on a pan India digital initiative, leveraging technology for good governance coupled with initiatives on skilling and smart cities reflect the thrust on role of technology in Budget 2014.

Spike in demand for techies predicted

The direct impact of these major technology driven government projects is going to be a spike in demand for techies specializing in specific technology domains. Amar Babu, president, MAIT (Manufacturers Association for Information Technology) said, "Union Budget has many positives for the IT industry and job creation in the sector is one of them. The emphasis on creating a 'Digital India' by promoting broadband connectivity through rural areas will create new avenues of growth for the IT hardware sector, which in-turn will promote overall employment in the sector."

"Additionally, the Government is focusing on creating a cluster of 100 'smart cities' throughout the country, the step, if initiated in the right manner will boost investment in use of modern technology thereby increasing IT penetration and creating new employment opportunities in the sector," he added. Ravi Mahajan, tax partner -

Technology practice, EY also emphasized that increase in demand for employees in IT hardware and telecom sector are imminent. "Government initiatives to invest significant amounts in pan India programmes such as 'Digital India', smart cities, e-visas etc along with reduced excise duties on manufacturing of personal computer, improved broadband connectivity in rural areas, focus on SEZ revival, etc would result in increase in demand for employees in the IT hardware and telecom sector," he said.

3.16 Data Scientists, User Interface and Mobility Experts to be in demand

Industry experts highlight that in the coming quarters there is a going to be an increase in demand for specialists in the big data, cloud computing and mobility technologies. Highlighting this Mankiran Chowhan, regional VP and country manager sales, Gartner said, "With a large chunk of capital being set aside for tech led initiatives such as good governance, smart cities, e-Visa and across various industries, there is going to be as spike in demand of tech professionals possessing skills in social, mobile, cloud and analytics (SMAC) which is generally referred to as nexus of forces."

Sakaar Anand, VP - HR, CA Technologies says that the smart cities project is based strongly on Internet of Things (IoT) and big data analytics technologies. "Such data driven projects would not only drive demand for not only data scientists who can write intelligent algorithms to cull out relevant trends but also create a demand for User Interface (UI) professionals who can represent these data in a consumable format," he adds [14].

3.17 Bangalore is fast becoming the Data Science Hub of India

Interview with *Prof. Pulak Ghosh*, member of the UN's Big Data Group and Professor at IIM Bangalore - by Maitree Dasgupta, swissnex India.

The Federal Council of Switzerland recently launched a National Research Programme devoted to the development of Big Data solutions, with a budget of CHF 25 million. We looked at a similar trend arising in India – where Bangalore, the Silicon Valley of India is witnessing the rise of Big Data analytics as a sector in itself. Here's what Prof. Pulak Ghosh – member of the UN's Big Data Group and Professor at IIM Bangalore – had to say about the new developments and the future of Big Data in India.

Dr. Pulak Ghosh is a Professor at the Indian Institute of Management Bangalore (IIMB) and formerly a Professor at the Georgia State University and Emory University, Atlanta, USA. He also serves in the Advisory group of Big data at the United Nations (UN) Global Pulse, a big data initiative by UN.

Prof. Pulak Ghosh - Professor at the Indian Institute of Management Bangalore (IIMB) / IIM Bangalore

How would you describe the growth pattern of India's Big Data analytics ventures?

Well, the entire Big Data world is moving from a www. to vvv world! Big Data is supposed to be a $25 billion industry and India has the great opportunity to take a large share from it. However, Big Data is in a nascent stage in general and more so in India, and many believe that this technology is about large volume of data. While this is true and has always been there, what compounds its intricacy is the nature of data which is mostly 'unstructured'. The real value of Big Data is combining off-line (structured) and on-line (unstructured) and making the inference real-time. Firms in India are yet to combine the two in this real-time fashion. I see two big avenues of Big Data growth in India - Commercial and government. While the Commercial part of Big Data is mainly concentrating on the volume, the government part is mainly concentrating on mining the unstructured data for filling what we call the "data gap". Particularly for a country like India, where good and timely data in a panel structure is not available in abundance, Big Data can be very helpful. For example, Big Data can be used for regular employment generation, infrastructure development, etc. It can also be used in the tracking of public service projects in a real-time fashion.

Which sectors are the front-runners of Big Data and analytics in India? Please elaborate some of the data driven initiatives of these sectors in India.

Before commenting on the commercial use of analytics, let me shed some light on the silent revolution happening in the use of Big Data and analytics in the Govt. of India. One of the major issues of the government is timely tracking of projects for public good, monitoring and tracking the direct benefit transfer for poor people. There is a silent revolution happening in this side in the government's approach to deal with these burning issues. Using Big Data one can analyze the satellite picture to find the truth about the progress of projects. By mapping the mobile phone usage across the districts one can figure out the effect of direct benefit transfer. Mobile phone usage is an unstructured data which has tremendous use in the government projects.

Coming back to the commercial part, main front runners are banks and internet e-commerce companies. Post 2008, banks started realizing the potential of the humongous customer data they already had stored. This eventually led them doing more business with the existing customers by betting on customer preferences and addressing their pain points. The new data-driven business model gave them a fillip to their new initiatives of doing more business with the on-board customers, given that banking data is more reliable than the data from other business verticals such as retail. Indian banking giants like State Bank of India, HDFC, and ICICI are front runners in using analytics for better service and better business.

The next big players for use of Big Data analytics are e-commerce companies - Flipkart, Amazon etc. They are mostly using unstructured and structured data in a combined way also. For example, e-commerce companies also need to develop algorithm for cross-sell / up-sale. However, with nearly 1.5 lakh product on display how does one develop the algorithm in real-time. Added with that, the problem of sparseness in the data as not every product get sold frequently and there is an inherent minimum time before a customer buys the same product again.

What role Indian start-ups are playing in the Big Data ventures? Do you observe any particular trends?

Yes, I see Bangalore becoming the data science hub of India both from new startup clusters as well as established analytics firm opening their shop in Bangalore. I think because of the IT boom the entrepreneurial environment was already existent in Bangalore and the ease of finding correct talent also helped in these new startup clusters on analytics. Also presence of institutes like Indian Institute of management Bangalore, Indian Institute of Science, Indian statistical Institute and many more helps the clusters.

Are the Indian start ups equipped to deliver / manage the demands of the industry?

Since the analytics in India is very nascent stage, startups are doing ok. Also, most startups are service based and thus doing fine. However, companies that are a bit more advanced are definitely short of right talent. We neither have plenty computer engineers with solid and deep learning understanding, nor we have enough statistician. So the startups are struggling a bit.

Considering the rising demand from the business sectors, what are the implications of Big Data on research and education in India?

I see more and more business schools in India are opening programmes on analytics which will help in meeting the demand. However, we need more structure and depth in the research and education on analytics in India. The tide is yet to come!

How do we leverage this potential for growth?

I see a similar era as we saw back in early 1990s for IT boom. Potential for growth is definitely there. However, need push from government to facilitate the analytics industry and academic institutions need to come up with more courses.

How are the Indian Businesses positioning themselves in the Big Data boom for both domestic and international markets?

There are clearly two aspects to it. Big companies are opening their own analytics vertical. Like Banks and internet companies (to whom data is the most intelligent advantage over others) are in this league. Then there are lots of companies which are service-oriented and a few startups that are product-oriented. Innovation is must for analytics industry to survive and that way the product-oriented startup is our best bet [15].

3.18 Science and Technology in India – Key Govt. initiative

Latest update: February, 2016

Key Government Initiatives

	Key focal points include:
12th Five-Year Plan (2012–17)	Creation of major national facilities under partnerships Programmes for centre-state technology partnership Building educators for science teaching Investments into mega science for creation of R&D infrastructure within India and abroad under partnerships
National knowledge network	A state-of-the-art multi-gigabit (multiples of 10 Gbps) pan-India network is planned to link some 5,000 nodes in India It will be the sole vehicle for international connectivity in future
National Innovation Council	2010–2020 has been declared the Decade of Innovation to stimulate innovations and produce solutions for societal needs such as healthcare, energy, infrastructure, water and transportation
Improving Academia	Innovation universities would be set up as public private partnerships to develop new hubs of education, research and innovation The Educational market in India has the potential of reaching US$ 110 billion by FY15 with the increasing demand for quality education

Source: News articles, Government websites, swissnex India

Modern India has had a strong focus on science and technology, realizing that it is a key element of economic growth. India is among the topmost countries in the world in the field of scientific research, positioned as one of the top five nations in the field of space exploration. The country has regularly undertaken space missions, including missions to the moon and the famed Polar Satellite Launch Vehicle (PSLV). On 16 October 2014, Indian Space Research Organization (ISRO)'s PSLV-C26 successfully launched IRNSS-1C, the third satellite in the Indian Regional Navigation Satellite System (IRNSS), from Satish Dhawan Space Centre, Sriharikota. This is PSLV's 27th consecutive successful mission.

Currently@, 27 satellites including 11 that facilitate the communication network to the country are operational, establishing India's progress in the space technology domain. India is likely to take a leading role in launching satellites for the SAARC nations, generating revenue by offering its space facilities for use to other countries.

There has been considerable emphasis on encouraging scientific temperament among India's youth through numerous technical universities and institutes, both in the private and government sectors. At present, the country has a total of 17 Indian Institutes of Technology (IITs), 31 National Institutes of Technology (NITs), 677# universities awarding about 29,000 doctorate degrees, and about 40 research laboratories run by the Council of Scientific and Industrial Research (CSIR).

Market size

India is among the world's top 10 nations in the number of scientific publications. Position-wise, it is ranked 17th in the number of citations received and 34th in the number of citations per paper across the field of science and technology (among nations publishing 50,000 or more papers). The country is ranked ninth globally in the number of scientific publications and 12th in the number of patents filed.

With support from the government, considerable investment and development has incurred in different sectors such as agriculture, healthcare, space research, and nuclear power through scientific research. For instance, India is gradually becoming self-reliant in nuclear technology. Recently, the Kudankulam Nuclear Power Project Unit-1 (KKNPP 1) with 1,000 MW capacities was commissioned, while the Kudankulam Nuclear Power Project Unit-2 (KKNPP-2) with 1,000 MW capacities is under commissioning.

Recent developments

Some of the recent developments in the field of science and technology in India are as follows:

- Indian Space Research Organization (ISRO) is taking steps towards developing its own reusable rocket using a Winged Reusable Launch Vehicle Technology Demonstrator (RLV-TD), whose tech demo is expected to be conducted in February 2016.
- Indian Space Research Organization (ISRO) has launched six satellites of Singapore aboard the Polar Satellite Launch Vehicle (PSLV-C29) from Satish Dhawan Space Centre in Sriharikota, marking the completion 50 launches from Sriharikota since 1979.
- The National Institution for Transforming India Aayog (NITI Aayog) plans to release a blueprint for various technological interventions which need to be incorporated by the Indian manufacturing economy.

- The Indian Institute of Science (II Sc), Bangalore has become the first Indian institution to enter the Top 100 universities ranking in engineering and technology*.
- The Union Minister for Science & Technology and Earth Sciences Dr Harsh Vardhan and the German Federal Minister for Education and Research Ms Johanna Wanka have signed an agreement for increased cooperation between India and Germany in the field of science and technology.
- A team of scientists from India and Bangladesh will conduct for the first time, joint marine research within Bangladesh's Exclusive Economic Zone (EEZ), which is expected to help in understanding climate change and monsoon patterns in India.

Investment Scenario

The Government aims to invest 2 per cent of the country's GDP on research and development (R&D) in its 12th Five-Year Plan period (2013–17). Accordingly, the Government has undertaken various measures for promoting growth of scientific research, such as:

- Sustained increase in plan allocations for scientific departments
- Setting up of new institutions for science education and research
- Launch of new Science, Technology and Innovation Policy 2013
- Creation of centers of excellence for research and facilities in emerging and frontline science and technology areas in academic and national institutes
- Establishment of new and attractive fellowships

- Strengthening infrastructure for R&D in universities
- Encouraging public-private R&D partnerships
- Recognition of R&D units
- Fiscal incentives and support measures for enhancing industry participation in R&D
- Several recent developments indicate the progress made in R&D.
- A project to build India's largest underground laboratory for advanced research on the smallest particle known to man has been cleared by the prime minister's office. This is a move that could make India a major nuclear physics research hub.
- Antrix Corporation Limited, the commercial arm of ISRO, has finalized contracts to launch 16 satellites of six countries in the coming years.
- India-based Neutrino Observatory (INO) aims to study the properties of atmospheric neutrinos, which are subatomic particles produced by the decay of radioactive elements. An initiative Marine Advanced Simulation Training (MAST) centre is among the world's most advanced simulation centers, and would be a part of the ongoing efforts of MOL and its partner Synergy Group, a ship management firm with over 100 vessels under its management, to step up recruitment of seafarers from India.
- Dr Jitendra Singh, Union Minister of State, Science & Technology and Earth Sciences, MoS PMO, Personnel, Public Grievances & Pensions, Atomic Energy and Space, has launched a joint Indo-Canadian science programme focusing on clean water technologies. According to Dr

Singh, the new programme would be pursued through a joint collaboration between the Department of Science & Technology under the ministry and the National Science and Engineering Council of Canada.

- Saama Technologies Incorporation, the Big Data analytics solutions and services company, headquartered in the Silicon Valley, plans to invest US$ 2 million to create the largest pure play data science and analytics hub in India.

Government Initiatives

The central government plans to soon institute a nation-wide consultation process with a view to develop the first publicly accessible Science and Technology policy. The policy 'Vision S&T 2020' would articulate the country's future towards self-reliance and technological independence in the 21st century.

The Department of Information and Technology plans to create a separate online portal for inviting ideas from technology innovators, with the objective to provide them with assistance including finance (bankrolling), and thus help to boost initiatives like Startup India and Digital India.

Ms Nirmala Sitharaman, Minister of State (Independent Charge) for Commerce and Industry, has launched the Technology Acquisition and Development Fund (TADF) under the National Manufacturing Policy (NMP) to facilitate acquisition of Clean, Green and Energy Efficient Technologies, by Micro, Small & Medium Enterprises (MSMEs).

National Council of Science Museums (NCSM), an autonomous organization under the Union Ministry of Culture, is engaged in the establishment of Science Centers across the country. NCSM is developing a Science City at Guwahati, Assam, which would be handed over to the Government of Assam for future operations and maintenance. The organization has received proposals from various state governments for setting up of such Science Cities. NCSM has undertaken the Science Centers / Cities projects in a phased manner depending on the availability of resources, project handling capacity of NCSM, and existing level of science centre activities in a particular state.

In the Union Budget 2015–16, the following initiatives have been taken in the field of science and technology:

- The space budget includes funds for Aditya-1, India's first satellite to study the Sun, and is intended to launch after 2017.
- Finance Minister Arun Jaitley announced funds for two more IIT centers and five more medical schools in the All India Institutes of Medical Sciences (AIIMS) system.
- Overall, the Ministry of Science and Technology, which is India's main agency for disbursing research grants, received Rs 95 billion (US$ 1.42 billion) in the Union Budget 2015–16.
- Some other government initiatives undertaken recently are as follows:
- The Ministry of Science and Technology and Ministry of New and Renewable Energy Resources collaborated through joint expert committee meetings, inter-ministerial consultations, and delegations to clarify R&D priorities to develop energy-efficient and environment-friendly technologies. Thus far, three multi-institutional networked virtual Joint Clean Energy Research and Development Centers on solar energy, second-generation bio-fuels, and

building energy efficiency have been set up. The research carried so far has resulted in 72 publications in peer reviewed journals and filing of one patent.

- India's leading research centers are seeking more scientific partnerships for the country's remote areas, particularly the northeastern states while working with the Indo-French Centre for the Promotion of Advanced Research (CEFIPRA). CEFIPRA is India's first and France's sole bilateral organization, committed to promoting collaboration between the scientific communities of the two countries across the knowledge innovation chain. Established in 1987, the centre receives financial support from the Department of Science and Technology under the central government, and the foreign affairs ministry of France.

- Mr. Y S Chowdary, Union Minister of State for Science & Technology and Earth Sciences, said the ministry plans to establish an Indian Innovation Centre (IIC) and all states of the country will be its members. He also expressed the need to establish a science city in every state of the country.

- The Department of Atomic Energy (DAE) has developed and deployed technologies for the use of atomic energy in the areas of electricity generation, nuclear power, agriculture, food preservation, healthcare, isotope hydrology, R&D and deployment in areas pertaining to national security.

The Road Ahead

India is aggressively working towards establishing itself as a leader in industrialization and technological development. Significant developments in the nuclear energy sector are likely as India looks to expand its nuclear capacity. Moreover, nanotechnology is expected to transform the Indian pharmaceutical industry. The agriculture sector is also likely to undergo a major revamp, with the government investing heavily for the technology-driven Green Revolution. The Government of India, through the Science, Technology and Innovation (STI) Policy-2013, among other things, aspires to position India among the world's top five scientific powers.

References – Media reports, Press Releases, Press Information Bureau (PIB)

Notes - @ - As per information provided in Lok Sabha, # - In 2014, as per Ministry of Human Resources and Development, * - as per The Times Higher Education of London [16].

3.19 Open-Access Publishing Initiatives in India

Open-Access Publishing In Developing Countries: Open-access publishing is the provision of free online access to quality scholarly material that can be defined as "open domain," meaning publicly supported research information, and "open access," so that it is copyrighted to be freely available scholarly material. Several enablers have motivated the development of open-access publishing. These include global movement and initiatives for open access like the Open Archives Initiative, the Budapest Open Access Initiative, Scholarly Publishing and Resources Coalition, and Free Online Scholarship, as well as the initiatives undertaken by ICSU, UNESCO, and CODATA.

Other important enablers are availability of free online publishing and digital repository management software and protocols for metadata standards. Using these standard protocols for metadata allows interoperability among the repositories for sharing information and providing centralized services.

Much has been said about the value of open-access publishing in developing countries. Open-access publishing enables researchers in developing countries to establish priority for their research, which they could use later to defend their intellectual property. It removes excess barriers in terms of both price and permission, enhances national research capacity, and improves visibility for developing-country research. Open access thus enables a global platform for this research and collaboration and reciprocates the information flow from South to North among all countries. It is hoped this also leads to improved economy.

Open-Access Initiatives in India: In India, there is a large opportunity for open-access publishing. There are many noncommercial research and development institutions, both academic and research laboratories. For example, there are approximately 300 universities that offer both graduate and research programs. There are also many R&D laboratories operating within government science agencies, which cover domains like industrial research, defense research, agricultural research, medicine, ecology, environment, information technology, space, energy, and ocean development. These institutions, which produce research work, could potentially convert their data into online accessible material. Many of these institutions, and also several professional societies, publish science journals. Tools like the Open Journal Systems could help many of these journals to come online in an open-access environment.

Technical reports produced by many R&D projects, laboratories, and other institutions would also be candidates for providing open access. Theses and dissertations at universities, conferences, research papers—whether preprints or post-prints, unpublished research findings, data, or standards are candidates for open-access publishing in India and in other countries.

The following examples of open-access initiatives in India are drawn from scholarly science journals, theses, institutional archives, books, data and open access at the metadata level, and open access at portal and gateway services.

One example is the Indian Academy of Sciences, established in 1934. The Indian Academy of Sciences is one of three science academies in India. Apart from various other activities it publishes 11 science journals reporting research work both in India and outside. These journals, mainly in print, are freely accessible on the Web. The Indian Academy of Sciences is currently digitizing all the archival issues and expects to post them online very soon. The managing editor of these journals noted that offering these journals on the Web has increased subscriptions to the print journals from foreign countries, because more researchers and libraries outside India are learning about them.

The Indian National Science Academy publishes journals, proceedings, and monographs and provides these online. Vidyanidhi, meaning the "treasure of knowledge" in Sanskrit, is another open-access initiative that is trying to digitize and host theses and dissertations. It operates from the University of Mysore and is part of the global electronic thesis and dissertation initiative. The Vidyanidhi project is also developing workflows and definitions and addresses multilingual support issues. Other institutions are putting their theses online as well, including the Indian Institute of Technology in Delhi.

The E-print archives of the Indian Institute of Science is an online digital repository of research papers, both preprints and post-prints, technical reports, unpublished findings, and journal articles of the faculty. It was set up using eprint.org open-source software, and is registered in the e-prints registry. Eprints@iisc is now part of the worldwide institutional e-print archives. The E-prints archives allow the faculty and students to submit their publications electronically to the campus network. Although depositing is not allowed from outside the campus, access is allowed from anywhere on the Internet. The eprints@iisc Web site also supports metadata for browsing and searching. It is also integrated with the Greenstone Digital Library software, which enables full-text searching of the e-prints.

The Universal Library is another interesting project. It is funded by the Office of the Principal Scientific Advisor to the Government of India and is hosted by the Indian Institute of Science in collaboration with the Carnegie Mellon University in the United States. The goal of this project is to provide a free, searchable collection of 1 million books that are no longer copyrighted. The collection is also expected to act as a test bed for research in language processing, indexing, and retrieval.

There are some examples of initiatives that provide open access to data as well. The National Chemical Laboratory is a national research lab in India that provides free access to their data, including data from the National Collection of Industrial Micro-organisms and the National Centre for Biodiversity Informatics. There are also open-access initiatives at the metadata level. INDMED, at the National Informatics Centre in Delhi, is a bibliographic database of Indian biomedical literature and indexes 75 Indian journals. There is also a backup document delivery service associated with this. The University Grants Commission is the body that coordinates all Indian university education. It supports an information library network program INFLIBNET that makes Meta databases related to R&D projects available on the Web.

There are other major open-access initiatives as well. For example, the World Health Organization and the Indian Council for Medical Research are working together on the National Health Information Collaboration. The project provides a portal for Indian health data and information and free open software, which enables people to use it for other purposes. The Council of Scientific and Industrial Research is responsible for scientific industrial research in India and has a unit for R&D for information that aims to provide open access to Indian patents and medicinal plants information.

There are also interesting gateway services that integrate access to other open-access resources on the Internet. SciGate at the Indian Institute of Science is a science information portal that integrates a variety of science information sources on the Web. Another example is Aero-Info at the National Aerospace Laboratory, which provides an aerospace virtual library.

3.20   An Open-Access Publishing Model for India

How can these examples of open access be replicated and adapted in an organized manner across India? One proposal is a national network of distributed, interoperable, open-access digital repositories of research material, both at the institutional level and across the institutions in open-access science journals and conferences. The motivation for this network is the strong support for open-source software in India and the increasing interest to use digital library software, such as the Greenstone library software developed by the

New Zealand Digital Library Group. This software has been used innovatively to publish content, both on the Web and on CD. There is an emerging model provided by the E-print archives, using the Open Archives Initiative interoperability framework, which makes this software compliant with that initiative.

How do we realize this model? Academic institutions can set up institutional repositories of their research output. Science journals can adopt open-access publishing that is compliant with the Open Archives Initiative. New online open-access journals that focus on areas of local strength, such as agriculture and medicine, and graduate student journals could also is established.

A key issue is the incorporation of peer review and quality control in such an open-access publishing environment. Peer review must be employed at the institutional level or across the institutions to ensure that we put quality materials on these repositories. As of now, however, there appears to be no consensus on an effective mechanism for establishing quality control in such systems.

How do we operate this model? These repositories at the institutional levels act as data providers and provide metadata for harvesting. This is possible because of the availability of software that is compliant with the Open Archives Initiative (e.g., eprints.org, DSpace, CERN CDSWare, and Open Journal Systems). Some of these institutions themselves could act as the service providers by harvesting the metadata from different repositories and offering a variety of national level services. One such service could be a central metadata index service, wherein a user could identify papers, and then go to the actual research paper hosted on an institutional repository.

Libraries have a major role to play in this. For example, they could lead the way in establishing and operating an institutional repository and supporting researchers with open-access publishing activities. Libraries are best suited to provide document preparation and content management expertise.

A national-level mechanism is essential to promote and coordinate open-access publishing systems and to improve awareness for open access. Training is also very important, in terms of tools, processes, and standards (http://web.inflibnet.ac.in).

There should be wide support for setting up working models and services. National resource centers for open-access publishing in developing countries could lead the way in setting up a working model. Once the system starts evolving, it could run on its own.

It is also very important to have the support of organizations like UNESCO, ICSTI, ICSU, and CODATA to promote and support these initiatives [17].

3.21 NASSCOM Big Data Summit redefining analytics landscape in India

a. *NASSCOM 10,000 Startups showcased 6 promising big data startups on the sidelines*

b. *Launched a report on "Institutionalization of Analytics in India: Big Opportunity, Big Outcome"*

To address the growing business opportunities in the Analytics and Big Data space, National Association of Software and Services Companies (NASSCOM) today held the 2nd edition of the NASSCOM Big Data & Analytics Summit 2014 in Hyderabad. With the theme of "Industrialization of Analytics", the focus of the summit was to share thought leadership on how to build analytically-mature organizations with analytics embedded at the business core & across the business value chain. The summit witnessed industry leaders share best practices on processes, tools, technology, technique and applications used in the context of analytics and also insights upon how to build India's Analytics talent strength.

Key Highlights

- Total Revenues in FY2014 ~USD 1 billion; to grow >2X and reach USD 2.3 billion by 2018
- Domestic market at USD 163 million; to double in size and reach USD 375 million by 2018
- Total analytics employees: ~29,000; domestic market focused: ~5,000
- 900 million telecom subscribers with 40 million+ smart phones, 243 million internet users, 170 million social media users in India

Other Highlights:

- Global Analytics to grow at 12 per cent CAGR from USD 96 billion in 2014 to USD 121 billion in 2016
- Analytics services outsourcing: CAGR 14.3% from USD 42 billion in 2012 to USD 71 billion in 2016
- Analytics Software: CAGR 10% from USD 35 billion in 2012 to USD 51 billion in 2016.

Big Data start-ups showcased:

Flutura
Germin8
DataWeave
Formcept
Nanobi
Veda Semantics

Analytics today has proven to be the crucial ingredient of success for organizations across industries. With the combination of networking, big data and advanced analytics, the industry is working on big ideas and a renewed vision to help businesses transform to being digital enterprises. It is also increasingly becoming the vital business dimension which offers customer solutions and improves operations. Interestingly, over the years a large number of start-up companies are looking at analytics to drive innovation and transform business processes and operations. To showcase some of the cutting edge work being done, the NASSCOM 10,000 Startups program also presented six promising big data startups on the sidelines of the summit which hold tremendous potential for the future.

Speaking at the occasion, Mr. R. Chandrashekhar, President, NASSCOM, said, "Big data offers a unique suite of advanced analytics and helps derive meaningful insights from customer data to increase sales, better target customers, improve reach and gain competitive advantage. The Indian market is still in early stages of adoption of analytics and there is a need to industrialize use of analytics to derive long term value. However, with surplus talent, established infrastructure, and a mature ecosystem, India is on its way to become a global hub for analytics. Going forward, industry stakeholders will need to work on a 6 point agenda which involves raising awareness, creating talent, variabilizing cost of offerings, standardizing tools and technologies, setting up cross functional analytics teams and getting C-level buy in, to drive industrialization of analytics in India. At the summit we aim to share perspective on the agenda to redefine analytics landscape of India and the importance of industrialization of analytics among enterprises in India."

NASSCOM also launched a report in partnership with Blue ocean Market Intelligence, titled "Institutionalization of Analytics in India: Big Opportunity, Big Outcome" on the sidelines of the summit. The report analyses the current scenario, trends in the India market, factors driving adoption, challenges faced by both users and suppliers. The report additionally showcases global and India examples of how firms have implemented analytics and the benefits gained. Further, it sets out a roadmap on what needs to be done by stakeholders involved, to industrialize this technology within enterprises in India [18].

3.22 Urban Sciences, Big Data and India's Smart City Initiative

Cities are repositioning themselves to play a pivotal role in the development of humanity; though because of rapid population growth and nonstop urban expansion; cities are stressed with a variety of challenges related to urban life such as urban planning and management, environmental management, urban safety, resource mobilization and utilization, urban health, energy efficiency, traffic management, social activities, recreation and entertainment. Letting down to cope with any of the aforesaid challenges might be a threat to the city's prosperity[1]and quality of life affecting its residents adversely hence 'Smart City' concept has been materialized as a problem-solving technological instrument to real urban world problems. Smart cities are also recognized as lively cities which can respond to resident's basic needs and aspirations in 'real time's [19].

3.23 How is Open Data changing India?

Recently I attended an India Open Data Community meeting organized by the World Bank in New Delhi that brought together government officials, academics, corporate, developers and a few development sector professionals to discuss social and economic Open Data opportunities in India and the emerging partnerships forming around them.

Organized at the highly regarded Indian Institute of Technology, the meeting was focused on three key areas; experiences of institutions using open data around the world, how organizations need to prepare to tap into the growing potential of Open Data, and how to build and strengthen the community of data users and providers. The aim was to help assess the challenges and opportunities for extracting and using open government data in India, and to then communicate these at a subsequent National Conference on Open Data and Open API.

India – Open Data opportunity

One of the key speakers at the meeting was Professor Jeanne Holm, a senior Open Data consultant at the World Bank and former evangelist for Data.gov in the US. In a brief presentation, she summarized the key reasons for governments' willingness to open their data. These include improved internal efficiency and effectiveness, transparency, innovation, economic growth and better communication with citizens and other stakeholders.

She highlighted some key observations about the opportunities for Open Data in India: the availability of a vast resource of data; a stable, open source platform for open government data; rich technological expertise and knowledge; and opportunities to design specific data sciences programmes in educational institutions. A rapidly growing community of open data enthusiasts in India, DataMeet, is also shaping the discourse on data and its civic uses and exploring engagement opportunities with a wide spectrum of Open Data users.

Barriers to Open Data in India

However, there are certain challenges that are currently preventing these opportunities from being tapped. The infrastructure to support efficient data collection, processing and management needs to be strengthened. Issues of privacy and data anonymisation are a concern. There is also a lack of standardization of data collection formats that make it difficult to aggregate and make sense of data.

Recently I stumbled across a detailed, informative report by the Centre for Internet and Society that backs up this view, observing "Open Government Data (OGD) in India must be looked at differently from what it has so far been understood as in countries like the UK and the US."

Global trends

Oleg Petrov, Senior Program Manager at the World Bank talked about two significant global trends in the Open Data movement. The first was the data revolution, which is set to put data at the heart of the way the post-2015 Sustainable Development Goals are evaluated. Secondly, he discussed Smart Digital Government, which "focuses on doing more with less" and is inherently characterized as being digital and open in design, data-driven and easy to integrate with other systems.

Data is the new oil

Open Data is increasingly seen as the raw material for entrepreneurial activity, innovation and economic growth. A McKinsey report on Open Data, published in 2013, estimates its annual potential value to be more than US$3 trillion. The legendary investor Ann Winblad has described data as the "new oil."

Laura Manley, project manager at Open Data 500, shared insights on the private sector trend in the US of innovative businesses and products delivering commercial value from open government data. Some small and medium enterprises use Open Data to improve their decision-making and efficiency. Others are capitalizing on new opportunities to create saleable products and services. One example is Enigma, which cleans, visualizes and aggregates large amounts of public data produced by governments and other organizations for wider usage.

How are open government data initiatives taking shape in India?

India was one of the first countries to join the Open Data movement after the US and UK. Since then, more than 20 countries have opted for open government data (OGD) and released their datasets online.

The idea of OGD in India evolved over a period of time before it took the shape of a formal, robust National Data Sharing and Accessibility Policy (NDSAP) in March 2012. Some of the key milestones that created a conducive environment for the open government data policy in India were the widespread usage of computers by the central government from 1975 and the creation of the National Informatics Centre (NIC) for launching e-governance initiatives to move from manual, paper-based systems to automated processes.

This was followed by landmark legislation, The Right to Information Act in 2005 that transformed the citizen-government relationship with the agenda to promote transparency and accountability within government. Due to the changing global financial climate, many prominent Indian technology firms like Infosys started collaborating with the government to develop e-governance systems geared towards Open Data.

In 2012, the Indian government approved NDSAP, declaring a proactive disclosure of "all sharable, non-sensitive datasets in open formats by various ministries, departments, subordinate offices, organizations and government agencies as well as individual states."

The NIC, in collaboration with the US government, has created the Open Government Data Platform India as an open source portal, data.gov.in, for Indian government departments and ministries to publish their datasets for easy and open access by citizens.

Digital India, a recent initiative of the newly formed government in India, plans to prepare the country for a knowledge future by increasing efficiency and improving interactions between government departments and citizens. It aims to ensure government services are made available electronically to reduce paperwork. It is structured on nine pillars of which Pillar Six (Information for All) is of prominence with respect to Open Data in India. It entails the online hosting of information and documents and the proactive engagement and interaction of government and citizens through social media, online messaging, etc.

Currently 85 government ministries, departments and agencies have contributed more than 12,000 datasets across segments such as population census, water and sanitation, health and family welfare, transportation and agriculture to data.gov.in. One of the unique features of the Open Data portal in India is that citizens or users can demand a specific dataset from the government and others looking for similar data can endorse these requests. It then becomes mandatory for a department to release that data if 100 such endorsements are raised for a particular dataset.

Limitations and reliability concerns

However, a large volume of existing government data is still not accessible in digital formats. NDASP is still a policy, but not a mandatory policy. As a result, a lot of departments are reluctant or slow to share their respective datasets. Issues of capacity, attitude, lack of demand, confidence to release the data, and the existing state of data (in paper-based formats) explain this reluctance. Even when data is made available in a machine-readable format, in most cases the reliability is questionable; the raw data needs to go through rigorous editing and aggregation before it can be used. Different departments collect and collate information in their respective silos using diverse formats and terminology, making it tough to use that data effectively. Adoption of data sharing at the state level has also been slow with only four out of 29 Indian states contributing data to the national portal.

The granularity of open government data in India has been a concern, as it fails to satisfy the users to access and use only micro-level data. There is also serious demand for geospatial data for visualizing and communicating issues as they exist on the ground. The unavailability of official map data due to the conservative map policy of the government and lack of interoperability in sharing this data has discouraged a discourse about better planning, tracking progress in the 'real space' and pushing government to take remedial steps.

Where are the NGOs?

The discussions around Open Data also highlight the absence of non-profit organizations among the technology-focused groups, entrepreneurs and businesses. There is a need for such organizations to be more visible in Open Data circles and proactively get up to speed with the technological trends set to define the next steps forward. Observing this need, Akvo facilitates the use of open source technology tools in helping development aid organizations move towards a more collaborative and effective way of working. We help organizations working in diverse fields of activity to build their capacity to collect, manage and disseminate their data and enhance their overall data literacy, usage and practices. As Thomas Bjelkeman, one of our founders, has said, 'Going open has huge benefits.'

This post first appeared on The World Bank's Information and Communications for Development *Blog. Publication does not imply endorsement of views by the World Economic Forum* [20].

3.24 Big Data Analytics and Indian Healthcare

In the ancient times India had family healers that were called upon to combat disease and improve the standards of care. These medicine men of the old not only had knowledge of fields like Ayurveda, Siddha and Unani but also had knowledge of family history that used to help in their diagnosis. After the coming of the British though traditional medicine got supplanted by modern allopathic treatment the role of the family physician continued. So your family history and your own medical history were known to these physicians. In a sense we had an efficient system for Big Data and Analytics though it was not system driven. But healthcare till then was the privilege of a few and not easily available to all.

With the breakdown of the joint family system and the mass migration to the cities since independence, we see that the family physicians are hard to come by. While healthcare is more available in the cities, most patients prefer specialists and as a result, the medical history is lost. For example you have an eye irritation so you would go to an ophthalmologist, who would prescribe a few medicines and solve the problem. Subsequently a couple of years later if you have the same eye irritation you might not have saved the previous prescription or scanned it on, to create a digitized copy as a result the new doctor would not know your history. Also each doctor sees so many patients that paper records and memory does not serve the cause.

As a result of this issue, the west has embraced Big Data and Analytics in a big way. In the US for example most hospital systems would have your medical history and even if you switch physicians, your health insurance firm would have your history. In the UK the NHS has health records on all your ailments and also has records on your family history if they lived in the UK. In both these scenarios the adoption of technology has also led to increased investments in areas like Big Data and Analytics. Hospitals are able to predict patterns for re admission for other patients and are able to institute preventive measures to ensure against it. Also use of analytics helps them understand disease patterns n the community and focus on population health initiatives against to improve the health standards of a community.

But in India with technology adoption in the hospitals just at the inception, what is the future for adoption of big data and analytics? To find answers to these questions, a high powered panel met at the Philips Digital Health Conclave in Bangalore to explore if Indian healthcare was ready for big data and analytics. The panel members were Sandeep Singhal, Managing Director Nexus Venture Partners, Unni Nair VP &head of Information Management, Philips, Dr. Ranjan Shetty, Professor & Head of Cardiology Department, KMC- Manipal,

Tushar Vashisht Founder, Healthify Me, Gopal Devanahalli COO Manipal health enterprise.

I had the opportunity to moderate this panel and set the tone by setting the context on big data and analytics and how it impacts the Indian healthcare. We started the discussion by asking each of the panel members on what were their impressions of the adoption of big data and analytics in healthcare.

Dr Shetty kicked things off my discussing how it was very difficult to get any kind of analysis going with the hospital systems today. Paper records take time to be digitized and by the time they can get any analysis going for patient readmission or population health it is almost 6 months. Also Dr Shetty emphasized that while most people felt doctors did not like digital or adopt them faster, the truth is far from it. Interestingly he said improved digital form factors could definitely enhance the adoption of big data among medical professionals.

Sandeep chipped in that most doctors would like to look at the patient while they are writing prescriptions, an art most doctors have perfected over the years, but the same cannot be said about typing into the device. So, while deciding the form factor of the devices and systems used in healthcare set up, innovation must come in. Clearly it is up to the UX and design community to help doctors adopt analytics and big data and improve its adoption in Indian healthcare set up.

The discussion took a turn to understand whether we actually needed Big Data and analytics. And the consensus was that we needed it badly, managing a population of this size was not going to be possible without the use of analytics. On Big Data the opinion was split while some panelists felt it was necessary the others felt it was too early to take that call.

Very interesting insights came from Gopal on the adoption of big data and analytics in the Manipal hospitals. He talked about their patient satisfaction surveys which were taken a few days into admission of the patient and if any concerns found were acted upon almost immediately. When the surveys were re-administered, both patients and their party polled higher on satisfaction. So analytics in a way had helped the hospital to respond to feedback real time unlike the traditional model where it would have taken days or even weeks to act upon surveys. He also spoke about the new EMR system that the hospital had developed and which had gone live just last week and in implementing that the hospital chain had clearly demonstrated how important analytics was to healthcare.

Now I have been using Healthily Me for a while and in my opinion it on one of the best nutrition apps in the country. But behind the app is an analytics engine that has been running thanks to the vision and efforts of Tushar Vashist, a former Wall Street Banker who was also associated with the UID program. Healthily Me worked with the department of nutrition, government of India to classify more than 10 million Indian food items, that was a mammoth task by itself and a huge Big Data project, but since then they have users creating content and the speed and agility of user created content has been phenomenal.

Also the Indian big data and analytics issues can be divided into two parts, dealing with legacy data and the new age user created data. The two need different systems to deal with.

Unni Nair from Philips spoke about the care continuum and what Philips has been doing in that space, looking at technology from a patient perspective has given those options to partner with organizations to deliver improved care on the backbone of analytics and big data. Incidentally Manipal Health Ventures, Philips Healthcare and Healthily Me have joined hands to work on a wellness program for the employees.

But the toughest responses came from Sandeep who did not mince his words while describing the scenario today. When a young entrepreneur from the audience asked him if hospitals should open their healthcare data to entrepreneurs, he wanted to know what these start-ups would do with the data. Simply asking hospitals for the data would not work and there has to be compelling reason for the hospital to do so.

At the end of the discussion we took a poll to understand if Indian healthcare was ready for Big Data and Analytics and the answer was a yes but only narrowly, winning 3-2.

In my opinion I don't think we are ready in the current form. Yes we need these insights and they have to come from the medical history but the way we are structured I don't think it will be anytime soon that we would be able to leverage the full benefits of big data and analytics on the Indian healthcare scenario

In conclusion we had some interesting insights

- Form factor was an important consideration for adoption of Big Data and Analytics by the doctors
- Analytics was definitely required but on Big data the opinion was split
- Hospitals had started adoption these technologies on the patient satisfaction front and organizations were coming together to engage on employee wellness initiatives
- The future of adoption belongs to start ups and how they can think innovatively and introduce new ideas that would use these technologies to improve the car models in India

[21]

Rationale for big data analytics in healthcare is cogent, however implementation is one of the biggest hurdles providers face along with data security. To ride this new wave of business intelligence, Indian healthcare providers must realize that big data is a necessity and not a luxury **By M Neelam Kachhap**

If you have a social media account, chances are that you would have encountered a wishful debate/ discussion on big data analytics in recent times. Big data is the current buzzword and by all means, it is going to affect healthcare. But if you are not from the IT domain it's difficult to gauge and keep track of the conversation on big data. In the present healthcare business environment, providers need to understand that big data analytics is a necessity and not a luxury and so is the understanding of big data analytics.

Arvind Sivaramakrishnan

Big data analytics has enormous potential to impact healthcare positively by improving quality of care, saving lives and lowering costs. "Fundamentally, big data is helping organizations become more productive, efficient and reduce costs. Like many other industries, healthcare has adapted to data analytics not only for its financial returns but also for improving patients' quality of life," says Arvind Sivaramakrishnan, CIO, Apollo Hospital Enterprise, and Chennai.

So, what is big data?

Professor Wullianallur Raghupathi from Fordham Graduate School of Business New York, US describes big data in healthcare as 'electronic health data sets so large and complex that they are not difficult to manage with traditional software or hardware; nor can they be easily managed with traditional or common data management tools and methods.'

Niranjan Ramakrishnan

For some time now, Indian providers have been using electronic health records (EHR) and hospital information systems (HIS) to make their organization productive and profitable. These technologies collectively generate a lot of data. "Indian healthcare industry is engaged in generating zetta bytes (1021 gigabytes) of data every day by capturing patient care records, prescriptions, diagnostic tests, insurance claims, equipment generated data for monitoring vital signs and most importantly the medical research. Growth of the digital data would be exponential and explosive in the next two years," explains Niranjan Ramakrishnan, CIO, Sir Ganga Ram Hospital, Delhi. According to an industry report, California-based managed care consortium Kaiser Permanente is believed to have between 26.5 – 44 peta bytes (1,000,000 gigabytes) of potentially rich data from EHRs.

Ashokkan VRS

"Organization like us has data close to 500 terabyte of information," informs Ashokkan VRS, Group CIO, Columbia Asia Group. "Healthcare as an industry should definitely have data in exabytes," he adds.

However, 'big' in big data analytics not only defines the size but also the quality and complexity of data. "Big data could be defined as the total comprehensive data about an entity encompassing all sources. To better understand big data, it is important to understand what data is and how it differs from information, which is quite often thought of as one and the same. Data should be considered as raw information with or without filter, duplication, or structure that forms the building block for information. Transformation of data to information happens when one adds some logic to present a particular fact or view point. Information gathered from big data is often more substantial and unique, hence its value," explains Sumit Singh, CIO, Wockhardt Hospitals, Mumbai.

Big data is also defined as large volumes of high velocity, complex and variable data that require advanced techniques and technologies to enable the capture, storage, distribution, management and analysis of information.

Ravi Ramaswamy

"Big data is a term which describes the exponential growth and availability of structured and unstructured data," says Ravi Ramaswamy, Sr. Director & Head – Healthcare, Philips Innovation Campus. He further describes the characteristics of big data by the 4Vs: volume, velocity, veracity and variety. (As described by the research and advisory firm Gartner)

Volume: It's the quantity of data which gets generated and denoted in peta/ exa/ zeta bytes of data.

Velocity: Data is streaming in at an unprecedented speed and must be dealt with in a timely manner. RFID tags, sensors and smart metering are driving the need to deal with torrents of data in near-real time.

Variety: Data today comes in all types of formats - Structured, numeric data in traditional databases. Information created from line-of-business applications. Unstructured text documents are email, video, audio, stock ticker data and financial transactions. Managing, merging and governing different varieties of data are something many organizations still grapple with.

Veracity: In addition to increasing velocities and varieties of data, data flows can be highly inconsistent with periodic peaks. Is something trending on social media? Daily, seasonal and event-triggered peak data loads can be challenging to manage. Even more so with unstructured data involved.

"As per SAS Institute, a fifth element is also to be considered, which is complexity," says Ramaswamy. "Today's data comes from multiple sources. And it is still an undertaking to link, match, cleanse and transform data across systems. However, it is necessary to connect and correlate relationships, hierarchies and multiple data linkages or your data can quickly spiral out of control," he explains.

Sources and ownership of big data

Data in healthcare comes from many sources like machine-to-machine data, transaction data, biometric data, human generated data as well as web and social media data. This data has to be pooled, cleansed and readied for the purpose of big data analytics. "As big data is all the data about an entity, say for example healthcare, the existence of it is distributed across multiple sources and hence housed in a distributed fashion all over.

Figure 23: Sources of big data

The data may not be all electronic or digital either. Hence, it is likely it will not be under any specific control either and will have multiple sources or ownership. Much of it would be on social sites so popular today and a lot of intelligence could be harnessed out of it if one could get to them," says Singh.

In the US and other developed countries, national registries and state departments collect health related data and aggregate it over the years. Thus makes big data available for scientist to work on. However, in India health records are aggregated and stored by individual health organizations. There is a fair chance that this data may be in duplicates and is difficult to access. Having said that, some health organizations, for the larger benefit of the patients, may agree to share the data but even then it is a herculean task to get all similar data on one platform.

3.25   Scope for Big Data Analytics in India

According to a report 'Big Data Vendor Revenue and Market Forecast 2011-2026' by Wikibon the US Big Data market reached $27.36 billion in 2014 and is slated to grow to $84 billion in 2026 . According to the report, one of the factors driving growth of the big data market was the increasing establishment of big data-driven decision making as a key strategic priority in board rooms and C-suites across vertical markets but particularly in the financial services, retail, healthcare and telecommunications industries.

3.26   Use of Big Data in Healthcare

Clinical Operations

Comparative effectiveness research to determine more clinically relevant and cost-effective ways to diagnose and treat patients

Research & Development

- Predictive modeling to lower attrition and produce a leaner, faster, more targeted R&D pipeline in drugs and devices
- Statistical tools and algorithms to improve clinical trial design and patient recruitment to better match treatments to individual patients, thus reducing trial failures and speeding new treatments to market
- Analyzing clinical trials and patient records to identify follow-on indications and discover adverse effects before products reach the market

Public Health

- Analyzing disease patterns and tracking disease outbreaks and transmission to improve public health surveillance and speed response
- Faster development of more accurately targeted vaccines, e.g., choosing the annual influenza strains
- Turning large amounts of data into actionable information that can be used to identify needs, provide services, and predict and prevent crises, especially for the benefit of populations

Evidence-based Medicine

- Combine and analyze a variety of structured and unstructured data-EMRs, financial and operational data, clinical data, and genomic data to match treatments with outcomes, predict patients at risk for disease or readmission and provide more efficient care;

Genomic analytics: Execute gene sequencing more efficiently and cost effectively and make genomic analysis a part of the regular medical care decision process and the growing patient medical record

Device/ remote monitoring: Capture and analyze in real-time large volumes of fast-moving data from in-hospital and in-home devices, for safety monitoring and adverse event prediction;

Patient profile analytics: Apply advanced analytics to patient profiles (e.g., segmentation and predictive modeling) to identify individuals who would benefit from proactive care or lifestyle changes, for example, those patients at risk of developing a specific disease (e.g., diabetes) who would benefit from preventive care

On the other hand, Indian business intelligence (BI) software revenue is forecast to reach $150 million in 2015, a 15 per cent increase over 2014 revenue of $133.8 million, according to Gartner. "Anecdotal studies indicate that the Indian healthcare sector is expected to contribute around 12 per cent of the big data generated in India. It is expected that this number will grow to 25 per cent of the overall data generated by 2017," predicts Ramaswamy.

Advantages

Big data analytics generate actionable insights which can be used to predict disease outcomes, plan treatment protocols and for strategic organizational planning. By digitizing, combining and effectively using big data, healthcare organizations ranging from single doctors practice to small and large hospitals to national hospital networks stand to benefit.

"Data analytics can help hospitals in financial planning, supply chain management, human resource management and quality care delivery," says Sivaramakrishnan. "Decrease in re-admission rates, predictive algorithms for diagnostics, real-time monitoring of ICU vacancies are some of the practical applications of big data in hospitals," he adds.

Big Data in Healthcare

- **Clinical data:** Doctor's notes, prescriptions, machine generated data, large format of images, cine sequences, scanned documents which are generated during clinical care and are not analyzed as normal text data analysis
- **Genomic data:** Data acquired from gene analysis and sequencing
- **Health tracker data:** Data acquired from various devices, sensors, home monitoring and tele health
- **Web and social media:** Health related data tweets, posts and publishers
- **Health publications and clinical reference data:** Clinical research, drug information, disease information, ministry and health body reports
- **Other related data:** Personal preferences, behaviours etc. Administrative, commercial, socio economic, population etc.

According to Prof Raghupathi, potential for big data analytics in healthcare to lead to better outcomes exists across many scenarios. For example; applying advanced analytics to patient profiles to proactively identify individuals who would benefit from preventive care or lifestyle change; or creating new revenue streams by aggregating and synthesizing patient clinical records to provide data and service to third parties like licensing data to assist pharmacy companies in identifying patients for inclusion in clinical trials.

In the public health domain, big data helps to analyze disease patterns to improve public health surveillance and speed response. "Big data analysis can help public health department to understand disease trends, help control sudden breakouts, lastly, helps in building awareness with facts and data," says Ashokkan.

Cases in point

There are examples across the globe where big data analytics has benefitted healthcare organizations. The Institute for Health Technology Transformation, US cites a famous example of Kaiser Permanente which associated clinical data with cost data to generate a key data set, the analytics of which led to the discovery of adverse drug effects and subsequent withdrawal of Vioxx from the market in US. An IBM report cites the example of North York General Hospital, a 450-bed community teaching hospital in Toronto, Canada, which uses real-time analytics to improve patient outcomes and gain greater insight into the operations of healthcare delivery. North York is reported to have implemented a scalable real-time analytics application to provide multiple perspectives, including clinical, administrative, and financial. The Rizzoli Orthopedic Institute in Bologna, Italy, is reportedly using advanced analytics to gain a more 'granular understanding' of the clinical variations within families whereby individual patients display extreme differences in the severity of their symptoms. This insight is reported to have reduced annual hospitalizations by 30 per cent and the number of imaging tests by 60 per cent. In the long-term, the Institute expects to gain insight into the role of genetic factors to develop treatments.

The Hospital for Sick Children (Sick Kids) in Toronto is using analytics to improve the outcomes for infants prone to life-threatening nosocomial infections. It is reported that Sick Kids applies advanced analytics to vital-sign data gathered from bedside monitoring devices to identify potential signs infection as early as 24 hours prior to previous methods.

Back home, Sivaramakrishnan describes infection control using data analytics at Apollo Hospital.

"Microbiology department has important roles to play in any potential outbreak situation, including early recognition of possible clusters and outbreaks, rapid notification of and collaboration with the infection control team, which requires maintenance of an organism bank," says Sivaramakrishnan. "The microbiology laboratory should also act in a consultative capacity with the infection control team to help determine whether an outbreak is 'real' or a potential pseudo-outbreak due to contamination of specimens outside or within the laboratory," he adds.

"The current process is laborious with manual statistical analysis by the Microbiology department and by the infection control team to get this output. Apollo Hospitals has developed in house analytical tools for use on our HIS. The system was created using Microsoft Business Intelligence tool and utilized Excel front end dashboard. Both Microbiology department and infection control team was granted access to the analytical tool. Since it's an Excel front end dashboard training the staff was easy on the use of the analytical tool," he further adds.

"Dengue seems to rear its ugly head in many part of the country regularly and affects many citizens and their families. With the availability of big data, many factors that help in its formation are identified and then alerts are sent ahead of time to prepare to handle the outbreak," explains Singh.

Talking about examples of the benefits of big data analytics in India, Ashokkan says, "Very little is being done today, as the information technology adoption in healthcare industry needs a large revolution and standardization in the Indian sub-continent." Some examples of application in Columbia Asia are; determining the accuracy of diagnostic investigation reporting with cross match of data sets which vary from diagnostic images, culture reports, clinical notes, diagnosis identification etc. And customizing health check packages for customer segments," he adds.

Sharing examples from Philips, Ramaswamy says, "A study over five years examined the impact of Philips' remote intensive care unit (eICU) programme on nearly 120,000 critical care patients. The programme enables healthcare professionals from a centralized eICU centre to provide round-the-clock care for critically ill patients using bi-directional audio/ video technology, and a clinical decision support system. The study found that eICU patients, compared to patients receiving usual ICU care, were 26 per cent more likely to survive the ICU, and were discharged from the ICU 20 per cent faster."

Philips is now extending these initiatives by building an open digital platform that can link to all kinds of devices, allow doctors to feed information about patients, allow patients, relatives and doctors to be connected to each other, and do large scale analytics. "Any doctor anywhere will be able to look into the entire history of a patient to do better diagnosis. Relatives and professional care folks can get immediate alerts if something goes wrong. And the vast amounts of data collected on the platform can lead to algorithms that can improve diagnoses, figure out what works for what kind of patient," explains Ramaswamy.

Challenges

According to Prof Raghupathi, "Healthcare data is rarely standardized, often fragmented, or generated in legacy IT systems with incompatible formats." This is one of the biggest challenges in India. "Over a period of time, India will build a staggering amount of healthcare data but it would be spread among hospitals, primary care providers, researchers, health insurers, and state and central governments—just to name a few. Each of these acts as a silo, preventing data transparency across the healthcare system," says Ramaswamy.Another challenge would be veracity of data. "Different types of data from different systems, adherence to standard formats, inter-operability issues and homogeneity would also pose a great challenge," says Ramaswamy. In addition to aggregating a massive amount of data, there's the challenge of maintaining patient privacy. According to Dwayne Spradlin, CEO of the non-profit Health Data Consortium, private healthcare data is critical to big data's success, it doesn't mean that private data will become public. Figuring out how to leverage information to deliver better quality care to patients, while keeping it secure, is a major challenge.

Policies related to privacy, security, intellectual property, and even liability will need to be addressed in a big data world. Organizations need to not only put the right talent and technology in place but also structure workflows and incentives to optimize the use of big data.

Healthcare in India is witnessing a new wave of competition with foreign investments and disruptive technology and this will further intensify as the turf gets structured. The organizations that are looking at big data now are the ones with lowest-hanging fruit, and their success stories will help other providers see how they can make their own ventures, fruitful [22, 23 & 24].

3.27 Are Indian Companies making enough sense of Big Data?

Though some big companies have made a start, most Indian companies are still simply learning to store Big Data, and are yet to exploit its full potential. The market potential is huge for vendors of Big Data analytics services. It's no exaggeration to say that Big Data analytics, the process of capturing, managing and analyzing massive amounts of data to generate useful information, was in part responsible in helping the Bharatiya Janata Party (BJP) and its allies secure the biggest election victory in more than three decades.

Taking a leaf from US President **Barack Obama**'s 2012 campaign that took recourse to analytics to garner votes, the BJP moved beyond just having a presence on social media websites such as **Face book**, **Twitter** or **Google Hangouts** to holding workshops to educate candidates about social media practices, employed reputation management and analysis tools to identify and nurture social media influencers and enhance its brand.

While governments and politicians have historically been early adopters of newer technologies like Big Data analytics—the US National Security Agency's much-criticized use of analytics to pry on conversations being a case in point—big companies the world over are following suit and are using sophisticated software to analyze the mountains of semi-structured and unstructured data, looking for hidden patterns, trends or other insights to help them better tailor their products and services to customers, anticipate demand and improve performance.

Companies are using analytics for everything from driving growth, reducing cost, improving operational excellence, recruiting better people to completely transform their business strategy, according to a September 2013 report by consulting firm **KPMG** and lobby group Confederation of Indian Industry (CII).

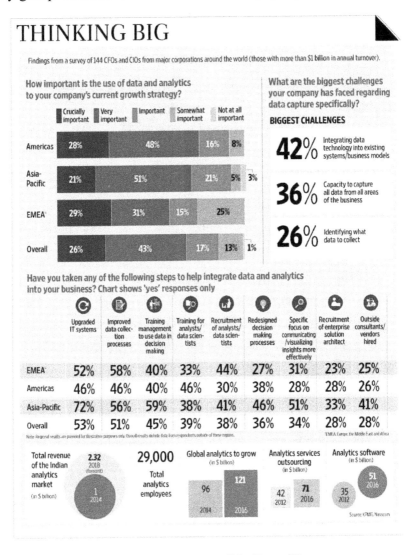

Figure 24: Survey on Big Data Usage

In Singapore, for instance, **Citigroup Inc.** keeps an eye on customers' credit card transactions for opportunities to recommend those discounts in restaurants. **Santander Bank** in Spain, the report said, uses analytics to send out weekly lists of customers who it thinks may be attracted to particular offers from the bank, such as insurance, to its branches.

Tesco PLC applies sophisticated analytics tools to its supply chain data to cut waste, optimize promotions and stock fluctuations, helping it save £100 million in annual supply-chain costs. **WalmartLabs**, the technology arm of Wal-Mart, acquired predictive analytics firm **Inkiru** in June 2013 to bolster its ability to create better customer experiences through data, the report said.

In India, though, Big Data analytics is in its infancy, according to **Amit Khanna**, partner, analytics at **KPMG** India, with most companies just learning to store data, known as data warehousing.

Big Data broadly involves three steps—storing data with master data management solutions and frameworks like **Apache Hadoop** (an open-source software framework for storage and large-scale processing of data-sets on clusters of commodity hardware) and **Google Inc.**'s **BigQuery**.

Next comes processing the data with tools like customer relationship management, business intelligence and statistical tools, and finally companies have to use, or apply, the insights culled from the data in their respective sectors.

3.28 Are Indian Companies investing in Big Data Analytics capabilities?

From what I know, Indian Big Data industry is more catered around offering outsourcing solutions to markets in US and Europe.

Also, MNCs are investing in building offshore Big Data capabilities. But what is about Indian companies?

Harshit Mishra thinks the question being asked here can be broken down into two parts: *'Are Indian public sector companies investing in Big Data? Why?'* [eg: *Indian Railways, Delhi Metro, Power Grid, BHEL, NTPC, EIL, SBI, RBI, and SEBI]*

The simple answer to this is "**No**". There are several reasons:

1. The public sector companies have a very tight budget and the expenditures (which reflect the business model) have to be kept transparent. In the current economic situation where curtailing the fiscal deficit is of foremost importance, any deviation from the conventional business models (models which might have been successful in 70s-80s but are completely obsolete now) is bound to meet with resistance.

2. This reason is somewhat related to the first. There is almost negligible room for R&D and innovation. Big Data analytics is a relatively new concept and quite a few benefits are still speculative. In fact, compared to the amount of data we are generating now, there was barely any data a decade ago. It would be just to expect a public company to gamble in the given scenario.

[Remember, the reason for establishing a public sector company is not just to provide quality goods/services but also to secure livelihoods of thousands of families. You and I may say that it is *"none of a government's business to do business"* but the government does not think so]

In short, while the policy makers are often mulling over plans to *"disinvest"*, we are talking about *"investing"* in Big Data. At best,

PSUs will embrace Big Data Analytics after it has worked successfully in the private sector for 10-12 years.

'Are Indian private sector companies investing in Big Data? Why?' [e. g. Jet Airways, Reliance, Indigo, L&T, Tata, Maruti, Godrej, Mahindra, Bajaj, Sahara]

The answer to this is **"quite positive"**. Juxtaposing these companies with their foreign counterparts at this point of time would be unfair. The main reasons why private sector is driven to employ Big Data--

1. Being globalized market, there is cut-throat competition between companies in the same segment. For instance, Jet has to compete with Indigo (and even Emirates & Lufthansa on the international routes); Godrej home products (says soaps & air fresheners) have to compete with Unilever and Proctor & Gamble. In a scenario like this, Indian companies cannot afford to ignore market trends and hence, have to delve into Big Data.

2. Investors are sanguine about returns from a constantly growing Indian economy & see an emerging middle class as major consumer to their goods and services. Moreover, a manufacturing sector that presently occupies only 18% of the GDP appears to be a highly lucrative venture. Thus, the Indian companies receive sumptuous investments. More importantly, and thanks to leadership of visionaries like Azim Premji, Anand Mahindra, Kumar Mangalam Birla etc., the companies infuse a good proportion of their revenues into R&D and innovation.

On the other hand, there are some pieces missing from the puzzle. For instance, it may be easy to analyze consumer behavior from Wal-Mart but how would you know the selling trends from a *Kirana* store [In India, a large segment of population even in urban areas buys grocery from such stores, let alone the 70% population living in villages] Another example, how would you know that a typical mason who works under MNREGA (employment guarantee scheme of Govt. of India prefers ACC cement or L&T cement? The answer to most of such issues is pervasive implementation of information technology.

Nevertheless, at one point of time, we were skeptical about use of Information technology at Indian workplaces & the situation now is that direct cash transfer to people BPL (Below Poverty Line) has been initiated. It is reasonable to expect that there would be a giant pool of Big Data emanating from India within a few year depending on the rate at which technology penetrates. It is only after we begin to have Big Data. Can we imagine how willing companies are to invest in it.

Jonathan Fernandez, Big Data Analytics, Sustainability, Technology, construction. Answer requested by Shreevant Tiwari

We are living in a digital age where tons of gigs of data are being produced every second. This data when analyzed and processed can provide a great deal of informative insights. These insights can then be used to avoid risks and take proper business decisions. This information can also be used to satisfy customers by understanding their wants and needs. Customer sentiments are also fished out through big data analytics. Now the main aim of any organization is to satisfy its customers and no other source than big data analytics can come to your rescue when it comes to customer satisfaction. So yes I definitely think that big data analytics is the obvious choice for Indian companies so that they can provide what its customer needs. Big data analytics is soon growing in India and there are many big data companies that provide such services. I came across one such website whose big data services are pretty amazing. Check it out!!

Big Data Analytics Platform - Aureus

"Big Data" is that cool kid in the town which each of these companies want in their houses but none of them knows how much investment, it will require. They also, somehow don't know that he has been around for long enough and this new cool avatar is just a makeover of what they already do in a not-so-cool way.

These companies are already working on huge datasets (descriptive analytics on huge datasets is common in most of Indian Analytics companies) but they are mostly using SAS, which is sort of not that cool any more. Everyone wants to work on R, Hadoop, Hive, Pig, Mongodb, etc but no one knows how to. Each of these companies is trying to hire few individuals to start off with this and see the way forward [25].

3.29 National Digital Library

Libraries are the storehouse of knowledge as they maintain the book and other knowledge resource available - mostly in printed form. However, with the advent of digital technology and Internet connectivity, the library scenario is changing fast. Digital technology, Internet connectivity and physical content can be dovetailed resulting in Digital Library. Data available in physical form has been preserved digitally in Digital Library. Digital Libraries have the ability to enhance access to information and knowledge. They also Bridge barriers of time and space.

In the past initiatives have been taken by different Ministries / Departments / organizations for digitizing and preserving data available in physical form. However, this activity has been restricted mostly in the area of the work / interest of the organization. Department of Electronics and Information Technology (DeitY) too has in the past, supported projects in the area of Digital Library Initiatives. The initiatives have been essentially of two types:

- Setting up of Mega Centers and Scanning Centers in coordination with Indian Institute of Science, Bangalore and in collaboration with Carnegie Melon University, USA. Under the collaborative management, scanners for these centers were provided by Carnegie Melon University, USA, under its Million Book Universal Digital Library Programme. Indian Institute of Science, Bangalore is coordinating this Programme under the guidance of Professor N. Balakrishnan, Associate Director. DeitY provided financial support for computers, training, manpower, tariff etc.

- Digitization with the full financial support from Department of Electronics and Information Technology

The digital data generated by these scanning centers under this activity is web enabled on "Digital Library of India "web site http://www.dli.ernet.in *. A mirror site* www.dli.gov.in *of this data has been also developed.*

The details of the projects are given below:

Table3: List of Projects and Current Status including Achievements of National Digital Library

Sl. No.	Name of Project and Implementing Agency	Objectives and deliverables of the Project	Status of the Project
1	Establishment of Digital Library of India by ERNET India	Make Collaborative arrangement between institutions in India and US to digitize around a million books Contain different type of content both of technical literature and art Facilitate easy access and optimize the bandwidth (both domestic and International) Set up servers at 13 nodal centers and Link the nodal centers on the ERNET India's backbone for making available digital books accessible for anyone on the net.	Project Completed. Installed servers at 13 Nodal centers. Provided the connectivity to 6 nodal centers i.e. internet bandwidth of 2 Mbps to SERC, IISc. Bangalore, IIIT, Hyderabad, I Mbps to IIIT, Allahabad , 512 Kbps to C-DAC, Noida & Rashtrapati Bhawan and 128 Kbps to Sri Jagadguru Shankracharya Sharada Peetham, Sringeri.
2	Setting up of Scanning Centers in	To digitize books of common interest to	Project completed. Scanned data web

Sl. No.	Name of Project and Implementing Agency	Objectives and deliverables of the Project	Status of the Project
	Uttar Pradesh for participation in the Million Book Universal Digital Library Project of Carnegie Mellon University of USA by IIIT Allahabad	the communities and make them available in a location and time independent way	enabled http://www.dli.ernet.in and www.dli.gov.in
3	Setting up of Scanning Centers in Maharashtra for participation in the Million Book Universal Digital Library Project, by MIDC, Mumbai	Conversion of rare books of common interest in digital form and make it available on the web,	Project completed. Scanned data web enabled http://www.dli.ernet.in and www.dli.gov.in
4	Setting up of Scanning Centers at Hyderabad for participation in Million Book Universal Digital Library Project by Central Library Hyderabad and State Central Library Hyderabad	Conversion of rare books of common interest in Telugu and Sanskrit in digital form and make it available on the web	Project completed. Scanned data web enabled http://www.dli.ernet.in and www.dli.gov.in
5	Digitization of ancient manuscripts	Digitization of ancient manuscripts	Project completed. Scanned data web

Sl. No.	Name of Project and Implementing Agency	Objectives and deliverables of the Project	Status of the Project
	and other in south Indian Languages pertaining to the vedas, vedangus, Upanishad and other sastric studies by Sri Sri Jagadguru Shankaracharya Mahasamsthanam Dakshinamanga Sri Sharada Peetham, Sringeri		enabled http://www.dli.ernet .in and www.dli.gov.in
6	Digital Archiving for preservation of rare manuscripts and old magazines from mid 19th century to 1960 available with Nagri Pracharni Sabha, Varanasi by C-DAC Noida	Digital Archiving for preservation of rare manuscripts and old magazines from mid 19th Century to 1950 available with 'Nagri Pracharini Sabha, Varanasi.	Project completed. Scanned data web enabled http://www.dli.ernet .in and www.dli.gov.in
7	"KALASAMPADA " Digital Library - Resource of Indian Cultural Heritage (DL-RICH)- by	To enhance the access to cultural resources using digital technology. Digital resources	Project completed. Scanned data web enabled http://www.dli.ernet .in and

Sl. No.	Name of Project and Implementing Agency	Objectives and deliverables of the Project	Status of the Project
	IGNCA; New Delhi	made accessible to the students, Scholars, researchers and scientific community.	www.dli.gov.in
8	Digital Archiving for Preservation of Rare Manu-scripts and Folios Available with Namgyal Institute of Tibetology – Sikkim by Namgyal Institute of Tibetology – Sikkim with technical support of C-DAC Kolkata	• Digital Archiving for preservation of rare manuscripts and folios available with Namgyal Institute of Tibetology, Sikkim. • Digitization of Hymns reactions	Project completed. Scanned data web enabled http://www.dli.ernet.in and www.dli.gov.in
9	Setting up of scanning center at Sringeri, Karnataka for participation in Million book universal Digital library project of Carnegie Melon University of USA by Sringeri Math , Sringeri Karnataka	• Heritage Collection & Digitization/ OCR of Palm Leaf Manuscripts, Kaditas, Paper Manuscripts and printed books on Vedas • Video recording of Shastrartha deliberations	Project completed. Scanned data web enabled http://www.dli.ernet.in and www.dli.gov.in

Sl. No.	Name of Project and Implementing Agency	Objectives and deliverables of the Project	Status of the Project
		• Transcriptions of Vaidik, Sanskrit Manuscripts and Books • Development of indexing using self learning mechanism of DB2 content manager for manuscripts	
10	Setting up of scanning centre at Goa for participation in Million book universal Digital library project of Carnegie Melon University of USA by University of Goa	Digitization/OCR of rare books in Portuguese, Marathi and Konkani in the Digital forms and make them available to public and also on the web	Project completed. Scanned data web enabled http://www.dli.ernet .in and www.dli.gov.in
11	Setting up of scanning centre at Hyderabad, for participation in Million book universal Digital	Digitization/OCR of rare books in Telgu, Sanskrit, Hindi and English & Indian History, etc.	Project completed. Scanned data web enabled http://www.dli.ernet .in and www.dli.gov.in

Sl. No.	Name of Project and Implementing Agency	Objectives and deliverables of the Project	Status of the Project
	library project of Carnegie Melon University of USA by University of Hyderabad		
12	Setting up of scanning centre at Bharatiya Jnanpith for participation in Million book universal Digital library project of Carnegie Melon University of USA by Bharatiya Jnanpith, Lodhi Road, New Delhi	Digitization/OCR of rare books and manuscripts etc. of Jain Heritage culture in the digital forms and make them available to public and also on the web.	Project completed. Scanned data web enabled http://www.dli.ernet.in and www.dli.gov.in
13	Setting up of Scanning Canters in Maharashtra for participations in the Million Book Universal Digital Library Project by University of Pune	Conversion of rare books of common interest in Marathi and Sanskrit in digital form and make it available on the web	Project completed. Scanned data web enabled http://www.dli.ernet.in and www.dli.gov.in
14	Print your own book -Mobile Digital Library by C-DAC Noida	Mobile Digital Library is to bring 1 million digitized books Expanding	Project Completed. Books scanned, printed and distributed in

Sl. No.	Name of Project and Implementing Agency	Objectives and deliverables of the Project	Status of the Project
		access to Information and Knowledge in schools, library and hospitals etc. Updating digital library with available contents	schools.
15	Creation of Digital Library of Books in President House by C-DAC Noida	To create a free-to-read, searchable collection of data in the form of images in the first phase and then conversion of data into text format in English and Indian languages by scanning the books and indexing the images through keywords.	Project completed. Scanned data web enabled http://www.dli.ernet .in and www.dli.gov.in
16	Establishing Centers for Digital Archiving and creation of rare knowledge pertaining to Ayurvedic Medicine,	Digitize Manuscripts & Information related to Ayurvedic and forestry	Project completed. Scanned data web enabled http://www.dli.ernet .in and www.dli.gov.in

Sl. No.	Name of Project and Implementing Agency	Objectives and deliverables of the Project	Status of the Project
	integrating & show casing of the content created through Digital Library outlet for Uttaranchal State Govt. by C-DAC Noida		
17	Development of National Databank on Indian Art and Culture (A pilot project)" by IGNCA	Digitize Copy right free books, Visuals Recording of Audi/Video Walkthrough historical Monuments	Project completed. Scanned data web enabled http://www.dli.ernet.in and www.dli.gov.in
18	"Digital Library of India 2 : Creating a large collection of Wide National Interest" at IIIT, Hyderabad	"Digitize (IPR Free) books	Project completed. Scanned data web enabled http://www.dli.ernet.in and www.dli.gov.in
19	"Coordination, Web Hosting & Maintenance of Digital Library of India" BY IISc., Bangalore	Hosting the DLI web site for accessing the digitized data and maintaining the web site	Project in Completed. Activity is continuing. http://www.dli.ernet.in
20	"Digitize copyright free books and	Digitize copyright free books and	Project completed. Scanned data web

Sl. No.	Name of Project and Implementing Agency	Objectives and deliverables of the Project	Status of the Project
	Conducting the programs on Digital Literacy / Competency for faculty, students and researchers at University of Delhi" by Delhi University	Conducting the programs on Digital Literacy / Competency for faculty, students and researchers	enabled http://www.dli.ernet .in and \www.dli.gov.in
21	Mega Center Digital Library of India –2nd Phase: Content Creation (in East Indian Languages as well as in English) and Storage and Access" by C-DAC, Kolkata	"Digitize (IPR Free) books	Project completed. Scanned data web enabled http://www.dli.ernet .in and www.dli.gov.in
22	"Rajasthan Heritage: Digitization of Rare Books" at Bansthali Vidyapith, Bansthali (Rajasthan)	"Digitize (IPR Free) books	Project completed. Scanned data web enabled http://www.dli.ernet .in and www.dli.gov.in
23	"Digitization of Libraries" by C-	"Digitize (IPR Free) books	Project completed. Scanned data web

Sl. No.	Name of Project and Implementing Agency	Objectives and deliverables of the Project	Status of the Project
	DAC, Noida		enabled http://www.dli.ernet.in and www.dli.gov.in
24	Digitization copy right free books available at Gujarat Vidyapith and Mahatma Gandhi Museum, New Delhi by C-DAC, Noida	Digitize books and documents available at Gujarat Vidyapith, Ahmadabad and Mahatma Gandhi Museum, New Delhi	Project completed. Scanned data web enabled http://www.dli.ernet.in and www.dli.gov.in
25	Digital Archiving for preservation of rare manuscripts at various monasteries in Sikkim by NIT Sikkim	Digital Archiving rare manuscripts at various monasteries	Project completed. Scanned data web enabled http://www.dli.ernet.in and www.dli.gov.in
26	"Digital Library Mega Center: Content Creation in Tibetan, Sanskrit and English" at IIIT, Allahabad	Digitizing of rare books within IPR Limits and web enable the same	Project completed. Scanned data web enabled http://www.dli.ernet.in and www.dli.gov.in
27	"Setting up Repository of digitized data, providing	Setting up Repository of digitized data, providing connectivity and hosting of	Project is Completed: Repository at AUCCA, Pune has

Sl. No.	Name of Project and Implementing Agency	Objectives and deliverables of the Project	Status of the Project
	connectivity Nodal Centers and hosting of digitized data" at ERNET India	digitized data	been set up. Data has been transferred at this repository and web hosted at www.dli.gov.in
28	"Rajasthan Heritage: digitization of Rare Books- 2nd Phase" by Banasthali Vidyapith, (Rajasthan)	Digitize, Preserve and web enable copy right free books available in Rajasthan.	Project completed. Scanned data web enabled http://www.dli.ernet.in and www.dli.gov.in
29	"Digital Library for North Eastern States (Content Creation, Storage and Access)" by C-DAC, Kolkata	Digitize, Preserve and web enable copy right free books available in North Eastern States.	Project is ongoing. Digitization work has been started at Assam Tripura and Manipur. A digital Library portal was created in Tripura and data is being hosted at http://www.dli.ernet.in
30	"Digitization of Rare Books available in Jammu and Kashmir" at University of Kashmir by Alma Iqbal Library, University of	Digitize, Preserve and web enable copy right free books available in Jammu and Kashmir.	Project is ongoing. Data is being hosted at http://www.dli.gov.in

Sl. No.	Name of Project and Implementing Agency	Objectives and deliverables of the Project	Status of the Project
	Kashmir.		
31	"Rajasthan and Gujarat Heritage: digitization of Rare Books- 3 rdPhase" by Banasthali Vidyapith, Banasthali (Rajasthan)	Digitize, Preserve and web enable copy right free books available in Rajasthan and Gujarat.	Project completed. Scanned data web enabled http://www.dli.ernet.in and www.dli.gov.in
32.	"Digitization of Documents available at Gujarat Vidyapith, Ahmadabad and Aligarh Muslim University, Aligarh" by C-DAC, Noida	Digitize, Preserve and web enable copy right free books available in Gujarat Vidyapith, Ahmadabad and Aligarh Muslim University, Aligarh	Project is ongoing. Data is being hosted at http://www.dli.gov.in
33.	"Digital Library accessibility of data digitized in phase-I& II" by C-DAC, Noida	Convert the data from TIFF to PDF, OCR and make searchable.	Project is ongoing. Data is being converted

|26|

3.30 Overview of Analytics Industry in India (notes and views)

One of the most common questions I get asked around is '*What is your view about Analytics industry in India?*'

And it comes in various shapes and sizes. From the curious ones asking finer details about the industry, the optimists confirming that data science would be the fastest growing field in the next decade to pessimists asking whether data scientists would even be required 5 years from now.

To be honest, **I myself don't know answers to a lot of these questions** (and that is the reason it is exciting to be working in this domain!) and at times I discuss these questions with various thought leaders in industry. **But, I do have my views on these questions**. These views are mostly based on my work experience and interaction with people in industry across the globe over last 9 years.

Since I get these questions very frequently, I hope that a lot of people would be interested in knowing these views. Hence, I thought I would share my notes and views on the industry through this article. I hope this helps those thousands of people trying to answer these questions for making their own decisions.

Overview of Analytics / Data Science industry

Before we proceed any further, let us understand the setup of analytics industry today. As you can see, the industry can be looked as a summation of three different verticals – Data Science products, the in house analytics happening in various companies and the third party services / consultancy provided by companies. Among the three, it is very difficult to size the in house analytics setup. How do you put a value to the contribution of data science in the products and services provided by Google? Hence, whenever you hear any metric related to size of data science industry, it would mostly be focused on either products or services. Also, there are a few additional industries associated with data science which are not covered in this framework. These would include data science training institutes, placement agencies and even Analytics Vidhya! We will touch upon these associated industries later in the article.

How big is analytics industry and how fast is it growing?

Size of analytics services market: According to Avendus Capital (in 2012), the data analytics market in India is expected to reach $1.15 billion by 2015, and will account for a fifth of India's knowledge process is outsourcing (KPO) market of $5.6 billion. Further, as per recent report published by NASSCOM (2014), this is further expected to double up and become $2.3 billion by 2017-18. Bulk of this revenue would be driven by the top companies like Mu-Sigma, Fractal, Absolute Data, and Latent View etc. According to a research from Everest Group, the size of global analytics services is between $2 – 2.5 billion in 2013. This essentially means that India holds 35% – 50% of global analytics services market.

The Analytics Products market: If you thought, the numbers quoted above were big, there are bigger numbers coming ahead. And if you thought that the numbers above were not so big, continue reading. The global Data Science / analytics marketplace today stands at $100 billion and is growing at 30% year on year. So, the services industry mentioned above is actually a small portion in overall scheme of things. However, for some reason the focus of data science industry in India has been services and not products – possibly because of presence of the employers.

3.31 Which sectors are using / benefiting from analytics?

In terms of penetration, different sectors have seen different penetration and adaption of analytics. Here is the distribution of services revenues (globally) by various sectors from the study done by Everest research in 2013.

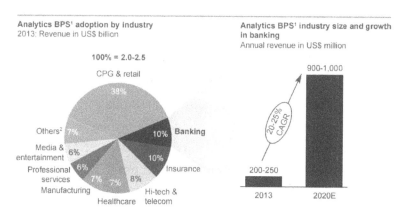

Figure 25: Distribution of Services Revenues Globally by Various Sectors

As you can see, the sectors with highest revenues are CPG & Retail, BFSI, Telecom and Healthcare. Similar trend holds true for India as well. I would think that BFSI & telecom would be a larger share in India as opposed to global revenues based on my interaction with people in industry, but that is a view.

3.32 Rise of Analytics Start-ups globally & in India

This is probably one of the most exciting times to be in a startup, more so for a data science startup. In general, people are more open to taking risk than ever before. Big Data and Data Science projects have received a very favorable response from the venture capital. Today data science is directly or indirectly impacting every major start-up. A while back, we also saw an increase in data science based start-ups in Y Combinatory. Just for context, here is a list of top 10 most funded analytics / Big Data startups in Jan 2015 (Source: Gill Press on Forbes):

Table 4: Rise of Analytics Start-ups globally & in India

Start-up Name	Amount of Funding	What are they doing?
Cloudera	$1040	Hadoop-based software, services and training
Palantir Technologies	$950	Analytics applications
MongoDB	$311	Document-oriented database
Domo	$250	Cloud-based Business intelligence
Mu Sigma	$195	Data-Science-as-a-Service
DataStax	$190	Apache Cassandra-based platform
MapR	$174	Hadoop-based software services and training
Opera Solutions	$122.2	Data-Science-as-a-Service
Guavus	$107	Operations intelligence platform
[Tie] Adaptive Insights	$101.3	Cloud-based Business Intelligence
[Tie] GoodData	$101.2	Cloud-based Business Intelligence

Data Science Start-ups in India

Until few years back, analytics market in India was primarily being driven by Blue Chip companies and Consulting Firms. But, the situations have started to change now. The ferocious wave of startups striking every possible industry also entered the analytics market.

While it may be too early to comment on success / failure of these startups right now, what I like is the fact that some of these start-ups are aimed towards creating products rather than the services market. For example, Gramener is creating software for visualizing data. Here is a list of some exciting startups in India. As would be evident from the list above, Opera Solutions and Mu Sigma would be the most funded start-ups from India.

3.33   A few other trends in analytics industry in India

- While Bengaluru & Delhi NCR have traditionally been the hub of analytics in India, there are new cities like Pune, Hyderabad and Chennai coming up fast on the heat map.
- In terms of tools, SAS would still dominate the market share as most of the banks, telecom players and CPG players rely on SAS. However, the start-ups and consultancies have clearly started focusing on R and Python. So, this might be up for a change, especially given the trend in the U.S.
- Currently, there are only a limited set of companies working on real Big Data analytics problem. While Big Data has generated a lot of buzz, most of the job openings today are focused towards developers as opposed to analysts.

- The industry is going through really tough competition in recruiting the top talent directly from colleges. This has resulted in a very healthy increase in pay packages to the best talent from premier institutes.

- In coming times, I expect a lot of action in analytics in the heated e-commerce space in the country. With the likes of Flipkart and Snapdeal setting up their own analytics units and Amazon being Amazon, data assets are expected to create a differentiation in coming times [27].

3.34 Big Data Market - Global Scenario, Trends, Industry Analysis, Size, Share and Forecast 2012 - 2018

The humungous amount of data generated across various sectors is termed as big data. The exponential growth in the quantum of big data is leading to the development of advanced technology and tools that can manage and analyze this data. Hadoop technology is used by Yahoo, Face book, LinkedIn and eBay among others to manage and analyze the big data. This study will provide complete insights of the Big Data market and explain about the current trends and factors responsible for driving market growth. The analysis will prove helpful for emerging players to know about the growth strategies implemented by existing players and help existing players in strategic planning.

The report includes segmentation of the big data market by components, by applications and by geography. The different components included are software and services, hardware and storage. Software and services segment dominates the components market whereas storage segment will be the fastest growing segment for the next 5 years owing to the perpetual growth in the data generated. We have covered eight applications namely financial services, manufacturing, healthcare, telecommunication, government, retail and media & entertainment and others in the application segment. Financial Services, healthcare and the government sector are the top three contributors of the big data market and together held more than 55% of the big data market in 2012. Media and Entertainment and the healthcare sectors will grow at high CAGR of nearly 42% from 2012 to 2018. The growth in data in the form of video, images, and games is driving the media and entertainment segment.

The multiple and varied stakeholders including the medical and pharmaceutical product industries, providers and patients, all generate pools of data. A major portion of the clinical data is not yet digitized and so big data tools are helping these stakeholders to use the pool of data effectively. The cross-sectional analysis based on geographic segments has also been covered in this report and the major four geographies covered are North America, Europe, Asia Pacific and RoW. North America is the largest market and held nearly 55% of the total big data market in 2012. This region will continue to dominate the big data market in future but Asia Pacific region will prove to be the fastest growing market and will grow at a CAGR of 42.6% from 2012 to 2018. The shortage of talented personnel to analyze the big data will limit the growth of this market in North America.

The key drivers, restraints and opportunities are a part of this study along with the impact analysis of the drivers and restraints, which would serve as a strategic tool for players of the market to take corporate decisions. Porter's five forces analysis covered will further help the reader to understand the intensity of competition among the different players in the market. The market share analysis of the players of this market will give a holistic picture of the intensity of competition prevalent in the market. In addition to this; the research also includes an overview of the big data market by product requirements consisting of existing Database Management Systems (DBMS), Relational Database Management Systems (RDBMS), Structured Query Language (SQL) and Hadoop. The comparison between SQL databases and Hadoop would provide a better idea about the benefits of Hadoop over SQL.

We have used secondary research for deriving our market numbers for each segment of the research report and further validated our analysis with C-level executives of major companies operating in the big data market as well as the users of big data tools through means of primary research to finally come up with our results [28].

3.35 How Big Data & Analytics can help Government agencies run better?

Over the past decade or so, analytics has undergone a rapid transformation. During its initial stages, analytics was used more as a reactionary measure i.e., to observe the business trends of the past. So, there was a significant time lapse between the pain points and the corresponding course correction. But over the years, analytics bridged this time gap and is currently helping businesses take real-time decisions. Not just that, it is opening up avenues to predict future outcomes so that decision making is more proactive. This paved way for analytics being the backbone of "Strategy" and thus we saw the role of Chief Data/Analytics Officer joining the C-suite. Now with business organizations across the globe embracing Analytics like they did never before, the important question to be asked is "Do citizens have the right to expect their governments to be run on par with the best business organizations?" The answer to this question is a resounding **Yes** and this was precisely the vision of Mr. Bloomberg,

Mayor of New York city(more on this later in the article), who had setup an Analytics division which helped in making

New York a model city in terms of governance

Government agencies have huge volumes of data and more often there would be little / no dialogue happening between departments. This essentially makes them work in silos which curb the possibility of decision making using collective information. The insights that can be derived out of having a common data warehouse and tapping into the collective knowledge of various departments are left to one's imagination. It would generate outcomes more than sum of its parts. Now let's look at some of the **Why, What** and **How** of a typical city government's problems and then we will look at how Analytics, with its arsenal of tools, helps tackle these problems.

- How can a government reduce/eliminate financial leakages from social welfare schemes?
- What are the most crime-prone areas in a city?
- Why can't we eliminate Fraud and waste in government agencies?
- What are the best practices that governments can adopt from private banking/financial sector companies in dealing with Fraud?
- How can we improve emergency services like 108(or 911 in US) by using predictive analytics?
- How can we deal with disaster response using predictive analytics?
- How can we better allocate resources to various departments be it monetary, human or other kind of resources?
- How can amendments to laws and policies be data driven?

These are just a few ways that Governments, at least in the developed countries, can utilize the potential of analytics and big data to help serve people better. As is the case with business organizations, it would take some time for governments of developing countries to catch up with their developed counterparts. Now let's look at some of the case studies and real world examples of how Governments addressed some of the issues mentioned above and how they tapped into an ocean of data to discover pearls of insights.

MODA: Formally instituted by Michael Bloomberg, Mayor of NYC, at the beginning of 2013, the Mayor's Office of Data Analytics (MODA) had a clear vision of using data analytics for a more effective and transparent government. MODA represents a paradigm shift in how government works – one that is guided primarily by data and the expertise of the people behind it. MODA created a data warehouse by the name **Data Bridge**, a common platform to facilitate inter-agency data handshake. The following are some of the major achievements of MODA

1. **911:** Emergency response is a very crucial service offered by city governments and in some cases a split second is all that stands between life and death. With an average of 25,000 calls to the emergency 911, it is imperative for the administration to provide the best-possible service in the shortest possible amount of time. While it is difficult to reduce the time taken by making police cars race even faster through NYC streets, the city is taking action to reduce the time to respond, including shortening the initial operator script, improving the relay between agencies, and more effectively routing services to the location. The information provided by the 911 end-to-end analysis lead to a better understanding of emergency services, and decision

making that leads to faster responses at the most critical times for New Yorkers. When a New Yorker dials 911, they receive one, integrated experience. From the initial routing of the call through Verizon to NYPD telephone operator fielding the call until emergency services are on the scene, the caller is served by a staff of trained professionals who are collecting the vital information quickly and efficiently.

2. **FDNY:** Based on decades of historical data on fire breakouts in various parts of the city, MODA has developed a statistical model to predict future fire risks. During this exercise, they took key inputs from veteran fire-fighters to refine and improve the model. Focused group discussions were conducted and risk inputs were appropriately weighed in to build the fire risk model. Thus, MODA was able to identify high-risk zones in Harlem, Downtown Manhattan, and the Rockaway.

3. **Hurricane Sandy:** The disruption that Sandy caused to NYC was unprecedented in terms of magnitude. It displaced one-eighth of the city's population and left many more without basic amenities. During these testing times, MODA played a paramount role in the recovery process. Working closely with Deputy Mayor for Operations and his staff, and the leadership of the Office of Emergency Management (OEM), MODA integrated from City agencies, National Guard surveys of affected residents, and daily outages from Consolidated Edison (ConEd), the Long Island Power Authority (LIPA), and National Grid. The day-to-day progress was delivered to City Hall through the

"Recovery Report," a two-page summary of recovery efforts that was used to allocate disaster response resources, and ensure that vulnerable populations received needed attention.

4. **Legislation:** Generally, legislative deliberations do not take into complete consideration the potential impact of the changes. This would jeopardize the idea/intent behind the legislation and sometimes they would also run the risk of being counter-productive. This is precisely where MODA comes into the picture. It would give the council members, a first-hand experience of the possible outcomes of a particular policy change. MODA developed a statistical model to factor in the potential impact and thus helped predict the outcome at a near-granular level.

   o   To put things into perspective, let us take an example of a policy change in current budget by the Govt. of India. The excise duty on Gutka (and chewing tobacco) was increased from 60 to 70%.Now let us see how Predictive Modeling helps answer some pertinent questions. How would these policy impact sales of Gutka companies? Is this a hike that the end-consumer can bear, or will it lead to lower sales? Now, if the intent of the government is to bring down the sales (in lieu of a healthy society), is the hike steep enough to discourage consumers from buying? On the flipside, if the policy does indeed lead to a decline in sales (and if it is sharp) are we providing other avenues for Gutka companies to save money and stay afloat? Is there another policy in which we can bake in this impact and thus reduce the impact on these companies? These and a plethora of subsequent questions can be satisfactorily (if not comprehensively) answered using the power of analytics [29].

3.36   9 Big Data Trends Impacting Enterprises in 2016

According to a recent Nasscom report, the Indian IT and BPM sector is estimated to have generated revenue of USD 150 billion in 2015, marking an increase of about USD 17 billion over the last year. Exports in this sector accounts for about 67% share in the total revenue and reports show the clear unprecedented growth that the sector has been witnessing in the recent times.

Sunil Jose, Managing Director, Tera data India said "Data is what exists at the core of all innovations and technological advancements today. As India continues to consolidate its position as the global hub for IT BPM services, it is big data, the analysis of the same along with the related technologies for analysis which is the harbinger for bringing about digital transformation across the country. With the increase in the volume of data, the ways in which data is being used along with the insights that it provides, the need for real time analysis of the same becomes critical for organizations across sectors".

In 2015, new data-driven and analytics-driven business markets were further consolidated and organizations were constantly seeking big data opportunities in the context of a rapidly shifting technological landscape and disruptive forces that produce and demand new data types and new kinds of information processing. "Data liberation led to new technologies and new approaches to data, which opened up new business scenarios by extracting insights for decision-making and operational efficiency that were not previously available. Organizations began to recognize that technology is their business advantage and they must look for opportunities sustained by big data and its analysis," he said.

The Big Data analytics and related technology market is predicted by IDC to grow at a 26.4% compound annual growth rate to $41.5 billion through 2018. In fact by 2020 IDC believes that analytics will be one of the key drivers for the economic growth of any nation worldwide.

This huge opportunity brings in the need for new tools, solutions, frameworks, hardware, software and services to make the most of it. Good big data toolsets provide scalable, high-performance analytics at the lowest cost and in near-real time as business users increasingly demand continuous access to data. India currently stands at between the first and the second stage i.e. while it has embraced traditional analytics; it is yet to implement big data analytics effectively. In 2015, analytics started making an appearance with regard to customers, finance, risk management and operations; 2016 will see a major focus with regard to analytics in these areas.

This new generation of organizations will drive the need for predictive, real time analytics and cognitive-intelligence applications. Jose highlights some of the current trends in the Big Data market that will impact the enterprise big time.

1. Big Data Analytics in the Cloud: Analysts have predicted that given the large amount of data that is being churned and collected along with the growing demand for the same across various organizations and departments within the organization, the future state of big data will be a hybrid of on-premises and cloud. This will provide organizations with a cost effective, robust and scalable model to adopt analytics.

2. Big Data Analysis to drive Datafication: The process that makes a business, data driven is by collecting huge data from various sources and storing them in centralized places to find new insights that lead to better opportunities - can be termed as Datafication. Datafication will take big data analysis to new heights - into real insights, future predictions and intelligent decisions. Datafication is what happens when technology reveals previously invisible processes—which can then be tracked and optimized.

3. Predictive analytics: This includes using big data to recognize events before they occur. With newer and sophisticated big data analytics, extracting information from data and using it to predict trends and behaviour pattern is becoming the game changer for organizations.

4. Renewed Rise of Open Source such as Hadoop: Open source is regaining popularity in the big data analytics space. Open source solutions are often free or inexpensive and the communities around them can enable rapid development and iteration. This is makes it the choice of solutions platform for many new and emerging organizations world over especially for start-ups that have limited financial resources at their disposal.

5. Data Security: Analytics have an increasingly important role to play in data security. Analytics are transforming intrusion detection, differential privacy, digital watermarking and malware countermeasures. Strong security practices, including the use of advanced analytics capabilities to manage privacy and security challenges, can set businesses apart from the competition and create comfort and confidence with customers and consumers.

6. Internet of Things (IoT): Internet of Things is probably the most popular buzzword with regard to data analytics today. Globally, from less than 5 billion devices in 2009, it is predicted to grow to over 25 billion devices by 2020. It has slowly but gradually penetrated into a wide variety of sectors with BFSI, Manufacturing, Healthcare, Retail, Government and Transportation being the ones which it has seen maximum penetration. According to Gartner, it is expected to have a total economic value add of $1.9 trillion by 2020.

7. Mobile BI and analytics: The increasing adoption of mobile devices has opened up new platforms from which users can access data and both initiate and consume analytics. Executives on the go can apply analytics to gain deeper insight into business performance metrics, while frontline sales and service personnel can improve customer engagements by consuming data visualizations that integrate relevant data about warranty claims, customer preferences, and more.

8. Storytelling: As analytics and advanced analytics becomes more main stream, being able to tell the story with analytics is becoming an important skill. A data story—a narrative that includes analysis—can move beyond recounting of facts to weave together pieces of analysis that make an impact and move people to action. 2016 will see a lot of big data analytics, a combination of big data and advance analytics which will definitely prove to a game changer for organizations irrespective of its size and the sector in which it operates.

9. Multi-polar Analytics: The process by which data is collected and analyzed in multiple places, according to the type of data and analysis required. This will involve both regular data feeds between poles and federated analysis to provide a connected view across the enterprise.

"India is currently at the stage of getting used to Big Data and Analytics Technology. In this scenario, along with the solutions, it is essential for organizations to understand the detailed application of the same to generate the results and insights that it is looking for. Proper intelligence and the strategies derived from the same is what will give companies the competitive edge," concluded Jose.

References:

[1]   https://fusion.werindia.com/hot-from-the-oven/digital-india-integrates-citizens-records

[2]   http://www.linkaadharcard.com/basic-question-about-digital-locker/

[3]   https://mygov.in/

[4]   http://www.thehindu.com/news/national/the-big-data-conundrum/article7224734.ece

[5]   https://globalstatement2015.wordpress.com/2015/08/12/big-data-in-india-the-governmental-intervention/

[6]   http://articles.economictimes.indiatimes.com/2014-11-26/news/56490626_1_mygov-digital-india-modi-government

[7]   http://www.dst.gov.in/big-data-initiative-1

[8]   http://www.iimb.ernet.in/initiatives/data-centre-analytics-lab

[9] http://analyticsindiamag.com/anu-open-big-data-analytics-centre-soon/

[10] http://profit.ndtv.com/news/industries/article-government-plans-to-use-big-data-analytics-for-taxation-infosys-371321

[11] http://datanovation.com/blog-page/5

[12] http://bwcio.com/3-data-science-developments-that-will-create-huge-impact-in-india/#sthash.LqkfZfSA.dpuf

[13] http://bwcio.com/3-data-science-developments-that-will-create-huge-impact-in-india/

[14] http://articles.economictimes.indiatimes.com/2014-07-11/news/51354820_1_smart-cities-telecom-sector-good-governance

[15] http://www.swissnexindia.org/2015/07/24/bangalore-is-fast-becoming-the-data-science-hub-of-india/#sthash.2CZoNLIY.dpuf

[16] http://www.ibef.org/industry/science-and-technology.aspx

[17] http://www.nap.edu/read/11030/chapter/35

[18] http://www.nasscom.in/nasscom-big-data-summit-redefining-analytics-landscape-india

[19] http://www.gjms.co.in/index.php/gjms/article/view/478

[20] https://www.weforum.org/agenda/2015/02/how-is-open-data-changing-india/?pk_campaign=open%20india

[21] http://www.healthcare-in-india.net/healthcare-technology/is-indian-healthcare-ready-for-big-data-and-analytics/

[22] *Raghupathi, W., Raghupathi, V.: Big data analytics in healthcare: promise and potential. Health Inf. Sci. Syst. 2, 1, 3 (2014).*

[23] mneelam.kachhap@expressindia.com

[24] http://www.financialexpress.com/article/healthcare/cover-story-healthcare/big-data-analytics-and-indian-healthcare/162330/

[25] https://www.quora.com/Are-Indian-companies-investing-in-Big-Data-analytics-capabilities

[26] http://deity.gov.in/content/national-digital-library

[27] http://www.analyticsvidhya.com/blog/2015/07/overview-analytics-industry-india/

[28] http://www.transparencymarketresearch.com/big-data-market.html

[29] http://www.analyticsvidhya.com/blog/2014/08/big-data-analytics-government-agencies-run-better/

Chapter 4:   Skill Development for Data Science Jobs

4.1   What is Data Scientist: Popular Definitions by thought Leaders

Data scientist is a person who has the knowledge and skills to conduct sophisticated and systematic analyses of data. A data scientist extracts insights from data sets for product development, and evaluates and identifies strategic opportunities.

1. "There's a joke running around on Twitter that the definition of a data scientist is "a data analyst who lives in California," — Malcolm Chisholm

2. "A data scientist is that unique blend of skills that can both unlock the insights of data and tell a fantastic story via the data," — DJ Patil

3. "Data scientists are involved with gathering data, massaging it into a tractable form, making it tell its story, and presenting that story to others," — Mike Loukides

4. "A data scientist is a rare hybrid, a computer scientist with the programming abilities to build software to scrape, combine, and manage data from a variety of sources and a statistician who knows how to derive insights from the information within. S/he combines the skills to create new prototypes with the creativity and thoroughness to ask and answer the deepest questions about the data and what secrets it holds," — Jake Porway

5. Data scientists are "analytically-minded, statistically and mathematically sophisticated data engineers who can infer insights into business and other complex systems out of large quantities of data," — Steve Hillion

6. "A data scientist is someone who blends, math, algorithms, and an understanding of human behaviour with the ability to hack systems together to get answers to interesting human questions from data," — Hilary Mason

7. Data scientist is a "change agent." "A data scientist is part digital trends potter and part storyteller stitching various pieces of information together." — Anjul Bhambhri

8. "The definition of "data scientist" could be broadened to cover almost everyone who works with data in an organization. At the most basic level, you are a data scientist if you have the analytical skills and the tools to 'get' data, manipulate it and make decisions with it." — Pat Hanrahan

9. "By definition all scientists are data scientists. In my opinion, they are half hacker, half analyst, they use data to build products and find insights. It's Columbus meet Colombo – starry eyed explorers and skeptical detectives." — Monica Rogati.

10. "A data scientist is someone who can obtain, scrub, explore, model and interpret data, blending hacking, statistics and machine learning. Data scientists not only are adept at working with data, but appreciate data itself as a first-class product." — Daniel Tunkelang

11. An ideal data scientist is "someone who has the both the engineering skills to acquire and manage large data sets, and also has the statistician's skills to extract value from the large data sets and present that data to a large audience." — John Rauser

12. Data scientist is "someone who can bridge the raw data and the analysis – and make it accessible. It's a democratising role; by bringing the data to the people, you make the world just a little bit better," — Simon Rogers

13. "A data scientist is an engineer who employs the scientific method and applies data-discovery tools to find new insights in data. The scientific method—the formulation of a hypothesis, the testing, the careful design of experiments, the verification by others—is something they take from their knowledge of statistics and their training in scientific disciplines. The application (and tweaking) of tools comes from their engineering, or more specifically, computer science and programming background. The best data scientists are product and process innovators and sometimes, developers of new data-discovery tools," — Gil Press

14. "A data scientist represents an evolution from the business or data analyst role. The formal training is similar, with a solid foundation typically in computer science and applications, modelling, statistics, analytics and math. What sets the data scientist apart is strong business acumen, coupled with the ability to communicate findings to both business and IT leaders in a way that can influence how an organization approaches a business challenge. Good data scientists will not just address business problems; they will pick the right problems that have the most value to the organization," — IBM researchers [1].

4.2 Data Scientist Skills & Responsibilities

Typical day-to-day activities and in-demand skill sets for Data Scientists include:

> ➤ Perform data-mining, modeling and hypothesis generation in support of high-level business goals.

➢ Stay current with emerging tools and techniques in machine learning, statistical modeling & analytics.

➢ Successful data scientists often have strong aptitudes for business, technology, mathematics & statistics.

➢ Need strong oral & written communication skills to present data as a concise story for diverse audiences.

➢ Big data scientists develop customized algorithms to solve analytical problems with incomplete data sets.

➢ Big data scientists often use data visualizations, e.g., heat maps, to analyze and present complex trends.

➢ Many data scientists use Hadoop - an open-source Apache framework - to analyze & mine big data sets.

➢ Some data scientists have computer programming skills – such as SQL, Python, UNIX, PHP, R and Java – which they use to modify or develop custom analytical solutions.

➢ Data scientists often work in a team setting, with managers, IT administrators, programmers, statisticians, graphic designers, and experts in the company's products or services.

4.3   Data Scientist Education Requirements

The education requirements for data scientists are among the steepest of all IT occupations. Approximately 40% of data scientist positions require an advanced degree, such as a Master's, MBA or PhD. Others companies will accept data scientists with undergraduate diplomas in an analytical concentration, such as Computer Science, Math & Statistics, Management Information Systems, Economics, Engineering and Hard Sciences. Schools also offer career-focused courses, degrees and certificates in analytical disciplines like database management, predictive analytics, business intelligence, big data analysis and data mining, all of which provide a solid base for a data scientist career. Targeted training programs like these also present a great way for current business and IT professionals to learn the skills required to break into this red-hot field.

Research and compare the top-reviewed *data scientist education programs* below.

4.4   Skills Required Becoming a Big Data Scientist

A Data Scientist must have a set of technical skills, visualization skills and business domain expertise. A data scientist should also posses' strong analytical and problem solving skills.

1. *Technical Skills*:

I.   Knowledge of at least one big data technology such as **Hadoop**.

II.   Knowledge of programming and scripting languages like **Java** and **Python**.

III.   Knowledge of database management and **SQL**.

IV.   Knowledge of data modeling and relational databases.

V.   Knowledge of statistical tools like SAS and Excel

2. *Visualization Skills*:

These include presentation skills and knowledge of tools like Powerpoint, Google Visualization API, **Tableau**, MS Paint etc.

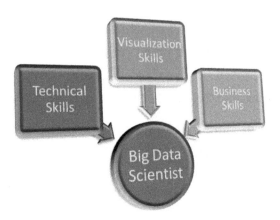

Figure 26: Skill Requirement (technical skills, visualization skills and business domain expertise) for a Data Scientist

3. Business Skills:

These include knowledge of the business domain where you're going to work, understanding and meeting the business needs, knowledge of risk analysis etc.

4.5   Big Data Analytics: A Top Priority in a lot of Organizations

According to the 'Peer Research – Big Data Analytics' survey, it was concluded that Big Data Analytics is one of the top priorities of the organizations participating in the survey as they believe that it improves the performances of their organizations.

Based on the responses, it was found that approximately 45% of the surveyed believe that Big Data analytics will enable much more precise business insights, 38% are looking to use Analytics to recognize sales and market opportunities. More than 60% of the respondents are depending on Big Data Analytics to boost the organization's social media marketing abilities. The Quin Street research based on their survey also backs the fact that Analytics is the need of the hour, where 77% of the respondents consider Big Data Analytics a top priority.

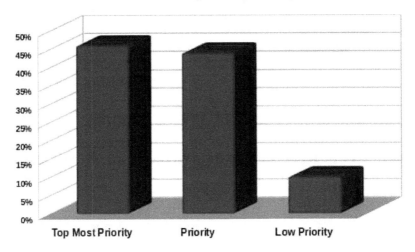

Big Data Analytics - Priority in Organizations
Peer Research – Big Data Analytics Survey

Figure 27: Priority of Big data in Organizations

A survey by Deloitte, Technology in the Mid-Market; Perspectives and Priorities, reports that executives clearly see the value of analytics. Based on the survey, 65.2% of respondents are using some form of analytics that is helping their business needs. The image below clearly depicts their attitude and belief towards Big Data Analytics.

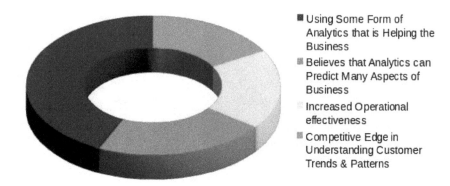

Figure 28: Value of Analytics

4.6 The Rise of Unstructured and Semi Structured Data Analytics

The 'Peer Research – Big Data Analytics' survey clearly reports that there is a huge growth when it comes to unstructured and semi structured data analytics.

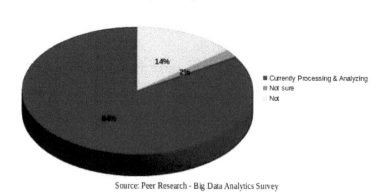

Figure 29: Analyzing Unstructured Data

Eighty four percent of the respondents have mentioned that the organization they work for are currently processing and analyzing unstructured data sources, including weblogs, social media, e-mail, photos, and video. The remaining respondents have indicated that steps are being taken to implement them in the next 12 to 18 months.

4.7   Analytics: A Key Factor in Decision Making

Analytics is a key competitive resource for many companies. There is no doubt about that. According to the 'Analytics Advantage' survey overseen by Tom Davenport, ninety six percent of respondents feel that analytics will become more important to their organizations in the next three years. This is because there is a huge amount of data that is not being used and at this point, only rudimentary analytics is being done. About forty nine percent of the respondents strongly believe that analytics is a key factor in better decision-making capabilities. Another sixteen percent like it for its superior key strategic initiatives.

Analytics – Key Benefits

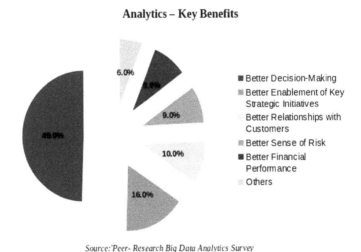

Source:'Peer- Research Big Data Analytics Survey

Figure 30: Key Benefits of Analytics

Even though there is a fight for the title of 'Greatest Benefit of Big Data Analytics', one thing is undeniable and stands out the most: Analytics play an important role in driving business strategy and making effective business decisions.

Seventy Four percent of the respondents of the 'Peer-Research Big Data Analytics Survey' have agreed that Big Data Analytics is adding value to their organization and allows vital information for making timely and effective business decisions of great importance. This is a clear indicator than Big Data Analytics is here to stay and a career in it is the wisest decision one can make.

References:

[1]   http://bigdata-madesimple.com/what-is-a-data-scientist-14-definitions-of-a-data-scientist/#sthash.xA22pUlp.dpuf

Chapter 5: Data Science and Big Data Courses Offered in India

5.1   How do I become Data Scientist?

In this era of "Big data", more and more businesses are relying on people who can make sense of the vast amounts of information generated around us – people who can use sophisticated tools and complex-sounding statistical techniques to derive insights from larger and larger mounds of data.

Businesses have started to understand the power of data. They realize they can use it to make better and faster decisions, outwit their competitors and be more successful. More and more, they are reaching out for people who have the skills to do this.

It is no wonder that there is a huge demand for trained analytics professionals. A recent report suggested there will be a shortfall of over 150000 analytics resources in the US; another study suggested a similar shortfall in India as well.

The gap between demand and supply is increasing rapidly and this is reflected in the increasing salaries data scientists can command. In the US, data scientists are already commanding higher salaries than MBAs. In India, starting salaries range from 4 lakhs to 8 lakhs.

Data scientists are the new astronauts. Everyone wants to become one. And it is not difficult to understand the reason for this. So how does one go about becoming a data scientist? What are the skills required to succeed in this field?

Well, there is no simple answer to this. Data scientists are a curious breed. They need to possess not just one skill but a combination of multiple skills. Let us examine the skill set requirement in more detail.

Technical Skills

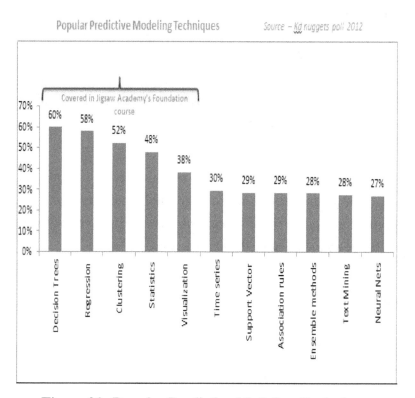

Figure 31: Popular Predictive Modeling Techniques

Understanding of Statistics– Data scientists need to have a good understanding of basic and advanced statistical concepts. These concepts form the basis for most predictive modeling techniques and therefore one need to understand them well. Knowledge of concepts like measures of central tendency and dispersion, probability distributions, hypothesis testing and probability are essential for most sophisticated analyses.

Knowledge of predictive modeling techniques– Predictive modeling techniques like regression, clustering and decision trees are applied on historical data to predict the future.

It is these predictions that guide a business's strategy. Thus knowledge of common predictive modeling techniques, their application, best practices involving their use etc. is a must in this field.

Proficiency on analytic tools – Analytic tools are specialized tools that are used to analyze large amounts of data. These tools allow the data scientists to perform descriptive as well as predictive analytics. A data scientist needs to be proficient in one or more analytic tools in order to do her job effectively. Microsoft Excel is the most popular analytic tool in the world. It does an excellent job of performing descriptive analytics on limited amounts of data. SAS is also an extremely powerful and popular tool. It allows users to build many kinds of predictive models on huge amounts of data.

For a more detailed discussion on various analytic tools available in the market, click here. To find out which is the best tool for you, click here.

Inherent Qualities

Quantitative aptitude – Data scientists need to have a strong quantitative aptitude. They should be comfortable dealing with numbers, large excel sheets or even larger databases.

Inquisitive Nature – Call it thirst for knowledge, intellectual curiosity or inquisitive nature – a data scientist needs to work like an investigator. She has to sift through mounds of data to find useful things. She needs to know where to look and what to look for. She needs to have the ability to ask the right questions and the persistence to find the answers.

Stakeholder Management – Analytics is always applied in the context of a business situation – usually a problem or an opportunity. A data scientist cannot work in isolation. She has to work with multiple business stakeholders. A good data scientist will have the ability to explain the results of an analysis in non-technical terms in order to build consensus amongst the business stakeholders.

These are all the skills and qualities that are needed in order to succeed in the exciting and high growth field of analytics. If you feel you have the inherent traits to become a data scientist, you should seriously think about equipping yourself with the requisite technical knowledge as well.

At Jigsaw Academy, our Foundation course has been designed by industry veterans and covers all the 3 required technical skills. Our course has helped thousands of people move into analytics. Learn more about analytics training [1, 2 & 3].

5.2   Definition of Big Data

We've often heard this term Big Data, but still there is confusion and a huge gap in people's understanding of what actually does Big Data Means. Let's understand this to remove the confusion. What we've known till now is that *"Big Data is something which is so big & complex that it cannot be handled by traditional data processing infrastructure and architecture"*. There is plenty of definition all over the internet which signifies the same above mentioned thing. But, what does that actually mean? Let's study this with an example. For instance let's say you run a small business and data infrastructure of your company handles all your sales transaction, let's say 30,000 transaction per month and your system is designed to handle up to 40,000 transaction per month. Now what if you get more than 40,000 transactions per month? Will your system still handle those transactions? Answer is no. Suppose if you get 3,000,000 transactions in a month, so this data is big data for you as your system can handle this data, but not for those which handles 10,000,000 transactions in a month. So, Big Data is essentially a relative term in comparison to your architecture. Also, what might look Big today may not be Big any more in future.

5.3   Why you should Learn Big Data?

Here are some facts which show the scenario of Big Data growth which might encourage you to learn this technology.

- ✓ In 2015, there were about 1.9 million Big Data jobs in the U.S.

- ✓ As per the information, in upcoming years India would need at least 1, 00,000 data scientists to fill the Big Data space.
- ✓ In upcoming years India will be the most preferred destination to harbor analytics outsourcing compared to Philippines and China
- ✓ The annual salary of data analytics professional could be as high as Rs 6-9 lakhs or more depending on experience and skills.

5.4   Jobs after Learning Big Data

There are plenty of Jobs available for various position and companies are desperately ready to pay to big bucks to qualified and skilled people. According to the reports, in 2015 there were about 1.9 million Big Data jobs in the U.S. This number isn't gonna come down any time sooner, the scope of big data is on the way up and this field is considered as a life changing career option. Here we've shared different positions that you can pursue after Big Data course.

- Chief Data Officer
- Big Data Scientists
- Big Data Analyst
- Big Data Solutions Architecture
- Big Data Engineer
- Big Data Researcher

Indeed Big Data is a big opportunity for job aspirants around the world. So, if you are ready to make an exceptional career, move to the field of Big Data [4].

5.5   Big Data Analytics Training in Noida

Big Data Training in Noida: Big Data analytics is not a small thing. As long as we rely on the internet to get things done, the scope data science does not cease. But it's not an overnight thing to step into.

You have to have thorough knowledge. Most of the companies require some sort of experience also. Also, you should make sure that the institute you study is the best in class.

If you are a person looking forward to getting training on big data, and you are from Noida, this post is very useful for you. You don't have to research a lot to find the course that suits you the best anymore.

Not everyone realized that big data is a gold mine of opportunities. Tons of websites are making use data science. Even the

Automatic Teller Machine aka ATM works on the basis of data science engineering.

Check the list given below to choose the right course for you.

#1. Techaltum Training

Techaltum is a platform of a bunch of courses like big data. Here, you will get training for Apache Big Data Hadoop.

Daily hell lots of data are produced. Mainly the data can be classified as structured, unstructured and semi- structured. Producing data in high velocity is referred to as big data.

Hadoop is a broad topic. You can easily get proper training on the same in Noida with Techaltum training. Mr. I. Malhotra, having a long five years experience as a software developer is the trainer. His phone number and social media profiles are displayed on the page itself.

You can use them to have clearer information from the trainer himself. He has taught more than 200+ students and working professionals till now.

The website has a placement page, which can easily fetch you some good opportunities. Make sure to compare your requirements and this course's offerings before joining.

#2. I Class Training

Noida is prosperous of big data courses. So, you should learn to differentiate gold from coal. Not everything is good.

I Class Training provides you the best in class training on Big data and Hadoop analysis. Their website features a handful of promises for the students, which include,

Real Time Trainers

100% Placement

Small Training Batch

Flexible Timings

Practical Guidance

Excellent Lab Facility

Big Data Resume Preparation

Hands- on Experience

Big data Certification Support

You can also find a link to Student Reviews on their webpage. 90% of students gave 4 or 5 stars. I don't know about the remaining 10%.The course fees link shown as a floating button on the right portion of the screen. You can also avail discounts. You get three batch options to get trained (Regular, Weekend and Fast Training batch). Only five students are allowed in each batch.

#3. Croma Campus Training Institute

I found this while researching for some good data training courses in Noida. All the reviews written here are breathtakingly positive.

The complete address is given on the web page. Though they have no dedicated website, the entire information is available for you on the above link. The main trainer (Sharma) has about eight years of expertise. Apart from him, more than 25 other trainers are there to teach you.

Croma has three placement cells.

#1. Croma Campus has dedicated team for placement (Croma Campus Placement Cell)

#2. Croma Campus is having tie up's with 28 software companies in NCR

#3. Croma Campus is having our own job portal. (http://cromacampusjobportal.blogspot.in/)

The complete syllabus is available for reference on the link I have provided you at the beginning of this section. If you want to start the training right away or want to get all the details, use the phone number or email address.

#4. Ducat India Hadoop Training

Ducat is one of the prestigious big data Hadoop training centers in North India. It has mainly six branches (Noida, Ghaziabad, Faridabad, Gurgaon, Greater Noida and Jaipur).

Ducat India Hadoop Training offers you offline courses only.

The training is divided into eight different categories. And, for each category, there are a handful of subcategories. Use it as a reference to the syllabus.

On the right sidebar, you can see an Enquiry form. Choose every option according to your convenience and then, submit your query. That's all about it.

On the footer, you can see links to all the six branches. For getting more details, click on any of the places.

An online registration form is provided on the website.

Ducat India provides many technology training courses. Have an official chat with their executives making use of the contact information, so that you can decide to go with them or not [5].

5.6   How to learn Big Data Analytics?

With the involvement of Big Data Technologies in almost every sector of business, there are anticipated to be millions of Big Data jobs vacancies in government and other sector of business. That's the reason why everyone is intrigued to learn Big Data as there are lot of unfilled vacancies and a lucrative career ahead. Now the question is "How to Learn Big Data Analytic?" Obviously you can't go to back to the college to get a degree and relevant experience, but there are alternatives.

Keeping the scope of this industry in mind, many universities and colleges have started to put their Big Data courses online for the convenience of aspirants. However, these courses aren't completely free, one has to pay a particular amount depending on the course. There are few different prerequisites for different courses that a person should have knowledge of before grabbing the insight details of the course. Firstly let's understand what actually Big Data is?

5.7   Data Science Courses Training & Certification in Kolkata and Noida, India

Join the data revolution. Companies are searching for data scientists. This specialized field demands multiple skills not easy to obtain through conventional curricula.

Data Science is an emerging multidisciplinary field that incorporates techniques and theories from mathematics, statistics and computer programming. The focus of our data science course is on generating business critical and analytical insights from staggering amount of data that is being generated at an ever increasing pace, including both structured and unstructured data from non-traditional sources, including text, images, and social interaction.

Certification options from:

- Data Brio Academy
- Centre of Excellence of IT/ITES Training, Dept. of IT initiative, Government of West Bengal (CEIAT)
- WROX Wiley

Course Coverage – Data Science

- **BIG DATA ANALYTICS AND THE DATA SCIENTIST ROLE**

  - The characteristics of Big Data
  - The practice of analytics
  - The role and required skills of a Data Scientist

- **DATA ANALYTICS LIFECYCLE**

  - Discovery
  - Data preparation
  - Model planning and building
  - Communicating results
  - Operationalizing a data analytics project

- **INITIAL ANALYSIS OF THE DATA**

  - Using basic R commands to analyze data
  - Using statistical measures and visualization (Box, Scatter, Histogram, Bubble Charts) to understand data
  - The theory, process, and analysis of results to evaluate a model

- **ADVANCED ANALYTICS – THEORY AND METHODS**

  - Hypothesis Tests (ANOVA, T Test, , Chi-Sq, Logistic, Median tests)
  - Linear regression

- Machine Learning
- Classification using Nearest Neighbours
- K-means clustering
- Market Basket Analysis using Association rules
- Naïve Bayesian classifiers
- Decision trees
- Random Forest
- Neural Networks and Support Vector Machines
- Time Series Analysis
- Re-sampling Method
- Discriminate Analysis
- Text Analytics
  - Vector Space model
  - Term-Document Matrix
  - Word Cloud
  - Stop Word Removal
  - Latent Semantic Indexing
  - Hierarchical Agglomerative Clustering
  - Sentiment Analysis

- **ADVANCED ANALYTICS FOR BIG DATA – TECHNOLOGY AND TOOLS**

  - Hadoop Ecosystems, HDFS
  - MapReduce, PIG, HIVE
  - RHadoop for Advanced Analytics

DURATION – 120 HOURS

Why Data BRIO?

- Learn directly from industry practitioners with more than 22 years of corporate experience with companies like Dell R&D, Infosys, Perot System, Tectonics etc.

- Certificate directly from Centre of Excellence of IT/ITES Training, Dept. of IT initiative, Government of West Bengal (CEIAT) in collaboration with Data Brio Academy and compliant to National Skill Development Council (NSDC), Govt. of India's sector skill council NASSCOM's Qualification Pack

- Get the business perspective – more importantly develop the mindset to 'see and work with data' the right way instead of learning just the tools & theories

- Unique training methodology with real-time case studies, assignments with data sets and projects with end-to-end life cycle

- Only academy to offer hands-on workshop and Data Science training. Participants work on systems along with faculty. This enables participants to be more versatile and confident during project/interview opportunities.

- End-to-end life cycle experience of real-time project. Internship provision in our parent company Business Brio. Business Brio is NASSCOM and CII (Confederation of Indian Industry) Member Company and provides projects and consulting services in Big Data and Analytics.

- Authorized training partner of Wrox Wiley (for global certification programs)

- 100% Placement assistance through dedicated placement cell (offers resume workshop, interview guidance and placement opportunities [6].

5.8   Top Data Science Certification Programmes in India

The field of data science has taken the world by storm. From being a niche field of study to its adoption as a mainstream business practice, it has topped the lists of best paid and sought after jobs. With the commercialization and utilization of Big Data on a massive scale, it makes sense that professionals from different sectors want to jump on the bandwagon and take up one of the most promising careers today.

The first big question is what do I learn and where do I learn it? To help you take your first step, we've come up with a list of some of the best Data Science courses available in India. The list includes both online and offline certification and training programmes.

1.   International School of Engineering (INSOFE)

INSOFE is an institute, which is training students and working professionals in Applied Engineering with current focus area in Data science/Big data analytics. They offer a Certificate in Big Data Analytics and Optimization for students and Custom Data Science training for corporate.

2.   National Institute of Securities Market

The Post Graduate Certificate in Data Science is collaboration between NISM, an educational initiative by Securities and Exchange Board of India (SEBI) and Department of Economics (DOE) of The University of Mumbai. This course's main aim is to create practitioners in the field of Data Science (Big Data), mainly for India and the Indian sub-continent, empowering the students with the current methods of practice in western countries.

3. <u>Jigsaw Academy</u>

Jigsaw Academy is a leading online school of analytics that offers certification courses on Data Science (Big Data, SAS, R) and Analytics (Finance, HR, Retail, Fraud, Web). It categorizes its courses as beginner, intermediate and advanced levels and equips their students with the data analytics skills that are in demand in today's workplace. Jigsaw also trains corporates and universities to enable them in becoming analytics ready.

4. <u>EduPristine</u>

EduPristine is a training provider for international certifications in Finance (like CFA®, FRM® and PRM®), Accounting (CPA and CMA) and Analytics. They have conducted more than 500,000 man-hours of quality training in finance. It has conducted trainings for J. P. Morgan, Bank of America, E&Y, ING Vysya, NUS Singapore, and others. Their virtual classes include Big Data/Hadoop and Business Analytics, with their classroom training offering Data Science and Data Visualization in addition to the classroom versions of the ones offered online.

5. <u>Edureka</u>

Edureka began as an alternative learning platform that offers online courses and certifications in 15 different categories such as Big Data Analytics, Mobile Development, Finance, Marketing Project Management, etc. The courses relevant to data include Data Science, Data Analytics with R, SAS, and Big Data & Hadoop among others.

6. <u>Simplilearn</u>

Simplilearn is a professional certifications and online training company with courses across Business and Technology domains. Their Big Data and Analytics category offers courses on Data Science,

R, SAS, and Hadoop etc. They also provide a Master's Program Certificate when a student successfully completes three of the specified courses that are eligible for this.

Introduction to Python for Data Science by EdX

Microsoft is launching an introductory course on **Python for Data Science on edX**. The course looks promising and we are sure that being from Microsoft it would be full of useful information for beginners in Python. For all those, who are starting out on Data Science this is a must course and its **absolutely free! The course is starting on 19th January 2016.**

The course is of 4 weeks of duration and would take around 10 to 12 hours of total effort by students who are willing to complete the course and the assignments during the course [7].

About This Course

Master the basics of Python using fun videos and interactive in-browser coding challenges on the Data Camp platform.

Python is a very powerful programming language, used for many different applications. Throughout time, the huge community around this open-source language has created many tools to efficiently work with Python. In recent years, many tools specifically for data science have been built. Analyzing data with Python has never been easier.

Starting from the true basics, such as basic arithmetic and variables, you will learn how to handle data structures such as Python lists, Numpy arrays and Pandas Data Frames. Along the way, you will be introduced to Python functions and control flow. You will also take a first dive into the world of data visualization with Python and create your own stunning visualizations on real data.

Fun tutorial videos will explain the concepts and you will continuously practice your newly acquired skills through interactive in-browser coding challenges on the Data Camp platform. You'll solve real data problems while receiving instant and personalized feedback that guides you to the solution. This learn-by-doing approach combined with a focus specific for Data Science makes this Python course unique.

1. Certified Program in Business Analytics (CBA) – Indian School of Business

The offering from Indian School of Business (ISB) continues to retain the top spot in this year rankings as well. The course covers several topics and is run in a format where the students have to attend class rooms every alternate month. The course uses technology aided platform during the months of no classroom. There is ample industry interaction and a 3 – 6 month project at the end of the course. With the ISB brand and tie-up with SAS, the course provides almost everything a person would have wished for! I say almost because the only thing which goes against the course is considerably higher fees compared to other courses. Add the expense of travelling to Hyderabad every alternate month and you might end up thinking twice, even if you get selected for the program.

2. PGPBA – Great Lakes Institute of Management, Chennai and Gurgaon

Great Lakes arrived with its analytics programme slightly late into the game, but when it came – it came in style! It comes closest to challenge ISB with its focus on structured thinking and business application. The format is again a mix of classroom and tech aided platform. Significant industry interaction, tie-up with Jigsaw Academy to deliver online content and option to choose from 2 destinations are some of the reasons why this course makes it to this spot.

My discontent with this course is mainly the lack of focus on a particular tool. While tool is only a means to an end, depth on at least one tool would make the offering very compelling. You can read detailed review about the program here.

3. Certificate program in business analytics for executives (CPBAE) IIM Lucknow

This course is taught jointly by faculty from IIM Lucknow and Kelley School of Business. The course is divided in 4 modules and requires a residency in each module. In addition, there is a tie-up with SAS for E-Miner training at the end. The positives for the course include 2 (or 3 if you take up SAS training) big brands backing it up with a wide range of topics.

The main discontent with the past participants of the programme has been the gap between what is taught in the classroom and what is required on the job. As per discussions with one of past participants (with 6 years of experience in IT before taking this course) *"The focus on practical aspects and applications needs to be higher."*

4. Executive Programme in Business Analytics – IIM Kolkata

The course is spread over a year and is divided in 10 modules. With only 2 visits on the campus, majority of the course is delivered through Hughes Education. While the programme has lower work experience requirement compared to some of the counter parts, relatively lower class room interactions make it a less desired choice. Again, the focus is on covering a range of topics and the theory behind them as opposed to practical applications on the job.

5. Business analytics and Intelligence – IIM Bangalore

IIM Bangalore was probably the pioneer in starting the one year executive programme in Analytics. This course is again a mix of classroom and online platform, with an optional module to cover SAS E-Miner at the end. The positives include a course which covers wide range of algorithms and topics and is backed by the brand of an IIM.

Special mentions

I have not ranked these courses in the list because of different nature of offering they have to offer:

Post Graduate Programme, Praxis Business School, Kolkata: Praxis gets brownie points for taking a different approach to solving the talent gap. A full time programme which is open to fresher's as well as professionals with experience and is probably the only one which takes ownership to solve for placements of students by its industry tie-ups. So, if you have relatively low work experience and can afford to take a break, this might be a good choice.

CPEE- Big Data Analytics & Optimization-International School of Engineering (INSOFE)

INSOFE has not only crafted a niche by focusing on Big Data and Optimization. It also has tie-ups with universities in the United States. A few students are sent to these universities as part of their tie-up. So, if you want to learn Big Data Analytics or aim to settle down in the US, this might be the preferred route.

Ranked these programs based on the following four parameters?

- **Coverage of the course:** Coverage refers to the breadth of material covered during the program. Do the programmes cover aspects like structured thinking? Advanced topics like Big Data? Data Visualization tools and methods. The broader the coverage, the higher the score on this attribute.

- **Quality of the content:** Quality of content refers to depth of the core topics in the program. In takes into account factors like industry interaction, pedigree of the faculty, time spent on class room interaction etc.
- **Industry Recognition:** This refers to the recognition a program has earned in the analytics industry – it is somewhat synonymous with the brand value of the course. Since we are looking at long duration courses, this recognition would reflect in placements of the candidates.
- **Value for money:** Once we have the score on all these parameters, we weigh them up and compute overall score [8].

Hadoop Tutorial for beginners You tube Videos: Hadoop is an Apache open source framework written in java and handles the challenges faced by Big Data. The Big data in a distributed environment is divided into small clusters using simple programming models. Designed in such a way that it scales up from a single server to thousand of machines, each machine offers the data storage and computation. So basically this open source framework for distributed storage, processes large sets of data on commodity Hardware.

Hadoop is a framework of tools and the objective is to support running of applications on big data. It helps businesses to have quick insight about their structured and unstructured data. Before beginning with the Hadoop you must have a clear understanding of What is Big Data?

Learning how to code to a program and developing it for the Hadoop Platform can lead to lucrative career. The brief video tutorials will provide a quick introduction to Hadoop.

What is Hadoop?

This video explains what is apache Hadoop, Big Data, Apache, Big Data Challenging points, Traditional Architecture, Hadoop Architecture ,Components of Hadoop, Pillars of Hadoop: Map Reduce & HDFS , Projects, Usage area of Hadoop, Example of Applications and Hadoop's future Outlook in brief. Hadoop is a framework of tools and their objective is to support running of Applications on Big data.

Hadoop for Beginners Youtube Videos Tutorials

Tutorial – Challenges produced by Big Data

So in this video, we will discuss the challenges produced by Big Data and how Hadoop is addressing them. In this, you will learn why traditional enterprise data fails to address challenges created by Big data and why the creation of Hadoop became a necessity.

Tutorial – History behind creation of Hadoop

Here in this video, we will discuss very briefly the history of Hadoop. How Google invented its technology, and how Hadoop come in need. Let see how Doug Cutting and Michael Cafarella created Hadoop and how it went to Apache.

Tutorial – Overview of Hadoop Projects

So previously we discussed about two main components of Hadoop: MapReduce and HDFS. These are also called Pillars of Hadoop. However there are few projects managed by Apache that also fall under the umbrella of Hadoop. These projects add a certain value to the core functionality at multiple levels.

Here is a brief introduction to Hadoop Projects:

1. **Apache Hive**: A data warehouse infrastructure build on top of Hadoop for providing data summarization, query and analysis.

2. **Apache Scoop**: This tool to transfer bulk data between Apache Hadoop and Relational Databases.

3. **Apache Pig:** In order to make the programming easy a higher level of language was created called Pig Latin which falls under the umbrella of Apache Pig and this do same job as SQL is doing.

4. **Apache Flume:** A distributed service for collecting, aggregating and moving large amount of log data. This is robust and fault Tolerant.

5. **Apache Mahout**: It's a distributed and scalable machine learning algorithms on the Hadoop Platform.

6. **Apache HBase:** An Open source, non relational, distributed database. This is written in java and runs on the top of HDFS.

7. **Apache Oozie:** This is a java based application that is responsible for scheduling the jobs and Hadoop systems.

How to Install Hadoop on Computer / Laptop (Windows/OS X)

This video will explain you how to install Hadoop on your personal computer running operating system Windows or OS X.

Your education can take you to different routes. Hadoop is a very powerful technology; just make sure you get the essential and basics from the above videos. The best way to learn Hadoop is by enrolling yourself in a real world task. As you will grow in Hadoop you will appreciate the power of Hadoop. Whatever tasks to decide to tackle in Hadoop, you will find the walk though codes online. I hope these videos will help you clear the basics of Hadoop, its origin and its relation with Big Data [9].

5.9 Top Business Analytics Programmes in India (2015 – 16)

Introduction: December stands out for us for multiple reasons – we are planning for 2016 & reflecting back on the fabulous year 2015 has been. It is also the time of the year, when we release our rankings for analytics programs in India. But before that, let us look at the changes, which happened in the landscape of Analytics Programs in India.

2015 – The year of new programs

Since we did our last round of rankings, there are some notable changes in landscape of analytics programs. Some of the best institutes in the country have come up with their analytics programs – most notable being the nexus between IIT Kharagpur, ISI Kolkata and IIM Calcutta, S.P. Jain Institute of Management & MISB Bocconi.

Institutes have tried creating different programs in different formats (ranging from 6 month full time course to 2 year full time courses) focusing on needs of different audience.

On the other hand, we have seen industry become more open to candidates from these programs as well. We have seen transitions happening through these programs and the placements across the programs (either officially supported or not) have gone up.

So, here are the rankings for long duration courses on the parameters we chose (explained below). We hope that these rankings will help our audience make better career decisions.

Which programs are covered in these rankings?

In these rankings, we have covered business analytics programs with duration more than 1 year. We haven't covered the short term courses & training certifications here. Further, we have ranked these programs in two categories: **Programs for Working Professional (with experience) & Program for Fresher's (less experience).**

Please see that these rankings are based on our interactions with various stakeholders from these institutes. We have done a comprehensive study and included all the institutes in India offering long term programs as part of our study. Also, the purpose behind releasing these rankings is to help our audience with their queries. This is by no means a judgment on the courses run by these institutes. Each program has its own set of pros and cons and you should look at the fit before taking an important career decision.

Rankings (Executives / Experienced Professionals)

1. Indian School of Business (ISB), Hyderabad

ISB retains the No. 1 Ranking this year as well (from the last 2

years). This program accepts candidates with 4-6 years of work experience. Interestingly, freshers are also welcome, if someone turns out to be extraordinary (analytical thinking, business knowledge). This course comprises of alternate month classroom session. In other half, the classes are held online. There is ample industry interaction and a 3 – 6 month project at the end of the course.

The only downside of this program is expense in a part time program through the year (especially so, if you are a Non-Hyderabad resident). For an additional payment, you can also get a SAS certification from this program.

Fees: INR 600,000 + taxes

2. Great Lakes Institute of Management, Gurgaon / Chennai / Pune / Bangalore

On the surface, it might look like Great Lakes retained its position at No. 2. But, the actual story is much more than that. Great  Lakes are fast catching up on the gap between them and ISB. They have launched two new campuses at Bangalore and Pune. With this expansion, they are now available in 4 cities in India including Delhi NCR (Gurgaon) and Chennai. This program is well supported by industry leaders and leading companies. The enrollment in this program happens through a written test followed by personal interview.

It would be interesting to see how this program from Great Lakes will fair in 2016.

Fees: INR 355,000 (Gurgaon, Pune, Bangalore) / INR 425,000 (Chennai) + taxes

3. Indian Institute of Management (IIM), Bangalore

 As compared to last year, IIM Bangalore has secured its position in our list. With a renowned brand name and wide coverage of analytics tools & techniques, this is one of the favorite courses in business analytics in India. This is a 1 year program. The course curriculum covers EMiner, SPSS, R, Qlikview, SAS etc.

Needless to say, students passed out of this program have managed to do well. This program is yet to introduce Big Data related technologies in their curriculum.

Fees: INR 425,000 + taxes

4. MISB Bocconi, Mumbai

This program is jointly delivered by SDA Boconni and Jigsaw Academy. Their faculty team is supported by international faculties from Bocconi. This program requires minimum 2 years of work experience. It is a blend of online and offline learning which help working professionals in routine adjustments.

Their endless effortless on ensuring placements and industry exposure, have helped many students securing a successful career.

We think that the program is supported by high quality faculty and it is only a matter of time before brand Bocconi becomes a more familiar name among Indian corporate.

Fees: INR 390,000 + taxes

5. SP Jain School of Global Management, Mumbai

This is a 1 year executive program. Classes are held on weekends. The program is designed such that students receive in depth knowledge of data science & analytics related concepts. This institute has a well established international presence. Students in the program are being taught by international faculties. Their enrollment process includes a written test and personal interview. The first batch of this program will roll out this year. It would be interesting to see the actual placement statistics and success.

Fees: INR 620,000 + taxes

Rankings (For Less Experienced)

These programs are best suited for people looking for full time program in business analytics. The programs ranked below provide comprehensive knowledge in analytics and data science, with an exceptional focus on practical learning.

1. Indian Institute of Technology (IIT), Kharagpur

This program is being offered jointly by top 3 institutions of India namely IIT Kharagpur, IIM Calcutta and ISI Kolkata. You can expect abundance of knowledge sharing in this 2 year course. This is a full time program. If you manage to get into this course, consider your future secured (assuming you'd work hard).

This course is being taught in all these three campuses. You get to learn management from IIM, technology from IIT and data science from ISI. What better could you ask? To enroll in this program, you written test and personal interview need to be cleared.

Fees: INR 1,600,000

2. Praxis Business School, Kolkata

This is a 1 year Full Time program. This institute has delivered exemplary results in terms of placements & quality of knowledge delivered. With over 500 hours of classes, this institute is known for depth of analytics topics (tools & techniques) covered in the program. It covers tools such as SAS, R, Python, Big Data, Data Visualization and intensive industry projects. For people new to analytics, this could be a great place to start your career.

It is indeed a value for money program. With their brand

growth over time, this program could become the top choice for people determined to build a successful career in analytics & data science.

Fees: INR 425,000

3. SP Jain School of Global Management, Mumbai

This is 6 months Full Time Program. It is suited for fresher's and people with less than 5 years of experience. Over 400 hours of study, this program covers a wide range of subjects such as big data, machine learning, Python, R, SQL, data visualization and much other related expertise. Its first batch started in October 2015 of 30 students.

Fees: INR 620,000 + taxes

4. Narsee Monjee School of Management (NMIMS), Bangalore

With their exceptional placement figures, this program has ensured that students' learning is in sync with industry skills demand. This is a Full Time Course. This course has lowest fee structure. The duration of this course is 1 year. With 390+ hours of class lectures, the program is designed to provide analytics knowledge pertaining to various domains (Marketing, Finance, Supply Chain, and HR).This could become one of the best programs, if they emphasized equally on in detail machine learning algorithms and data visualization.

Fees: INR 250,000 + taxes

5. Aegis School of Data Science, Mumbai

This is a 1 year Full Time program in association with IBM. This program MTNL's world class campus with state of art "IBM Business Analytics Lab" and "IBM Cloud Computing Lab" at Powai in Mumbai. This course would introduce you with various tools such as SAS, R, Tableau, Spark, IBM Cognos, Hadoop etc. The course is designed to provide comprehensive knowledge on business analytics and big data. The pedagogy involves 5 days classroom session and weekend online sessions. It would be interesting to see the placement statistics of this course once the batch passes out. If they continue to gain momentum, this program could help many companies with well educated candidates.

Fees: INR 350,000 + taxes

[10]

5.10 Executive Programme in Business Analytics by MISB Bocconi

MISB Bocconi recently announced the launch of their new Executive Program in Business Analytics (EBPA) in partnership with **Jigsaw Academy**. The program focuses on giving participants an understanding of predictive modeling, data mining, big data analytics, marketing, operations and risk analytics, among other analytics areas. On program completion, participants will be capable of data driven decision making and leadership in industries such as retail, finance, telecommunications, healthcare and manufacturing.

"The USP of the Course Is That It Includes Renowned International Faculty from SDA Bocconi in Milan, Italy, Together With Analytics and Big Data Experts from Jigsaw Academy,"

The program involves 120 hours of in-person training to be held over six (6) three-day modules at the MISB Bocconi campus in Powai, Mumbai. In the interim, Jigsaw Academy will also conduct twenty (20) live online classes of three (3) hours each for a total of 60 hours which participants can attend from their home, office or any other convenient location using an Internet connection. In addition to the live online and in-person classes, participants will also have access to over 100 hours of pre-recorded video lectures on data science and Big Data analytics for a period of 12 months.

Learning hours are supplemented by round-the-clock, unrestricted access to the Jigsaw Lab, a cloud-based analytics tool and content library that allows participants to gain hands-on competence with the most in-demand analytics tools and technologies in the industry, including SAS, R and Hadoop. The corresponding data science toolkit is designed to augment participants' practical exposure to these tools [11].

5.11   Wipro Launches WiSTA: Data Scientist Academic Programme for fresh Graduate hires

Integrated Masters' Program by Vellore Institute of Technology (VIT) for 2014 batch of graduates, hired by Wipro

Bangalore, India and East Brunswick, New Jersey, USA - September 10, 2014: Wipro Ltd. (NYSE:WIT), a leading global information technology, consulting and business process services company today announced the launch of its 'WiSTA – Data Scientist' program in India, an integrated post graduate program in Analytics for the 2014 batch of engineering and Science graduates hired by Wipro as full-time employees. The Vellore Institute of Technology (VIT) will conduct the program and award the Master of Technology and Master of Science degrees in analytics.

With the rise of digital economy, data explosion, changing face of competition and unprecedented pace of innovation, it is imperative that organizations use analytical insights to make informed business decisions. According to industry estimates, organizations in the United States alone face a shortage of 140,000 to 190,000 employees with deep analytical skills. The US also requires 1.5 million managers and analysts who can analyze big data and make decisions based on the findings.

The WiSTA – Data Scientist program is an initiative aimed at creating an industry ready cadre of Data Scientists within Wipro in the information management and analytics space. These Data Scientists will work with Wipro's customers in the US and in various other international locations.

"Capturing new opportunities in the digital world hinges on our ability to have the best people in the industry. This will be achieved by offering the "talent pool" projects which excite and stimulate their intelligent minds. We believe investing in creating the frameworks to nurture the resources of the future will be in the best interests of our clients and the industries we operate in. It is an exciting program." said **Jeff Heenan Jalil, Senior Vice President and Global Head, Advanced Technologies & Solutions, Wipro Ltd.**

This course, taught over weekends at Wipro's corporate headquarters in Bangalore, comprises of various modules on analytics and is a two year program for the engineering graduates and a four year program for the Science graduates. Students are shortlisted for this program based on their previous academic performance and college ranking. The course content has been jointly created by Wipro and VIT and also includes modules prescribed and taught by professors from Massachusetts Institute of Technology (MIT) and University of Michigan. Along with a Masters' degree from VIT on completion of this course, the graduates will also receive program completion certificates from MIT and the University of Michigan for the modules covered by them.

"The WiSTA - Data Scientist program is designed to train fresh graduate employees in analytics, business processes, communication skills and relevant technologies, to help them become industry ready and chart out a career in the Data Analytics space. This program has been designed keeping in mind the current industry requirements and to build a cadre of data driven business leaders for the future. We believe that continuous learning expedites success and innovation." said **Rajeev Kumar, Global Head, Campus Hiring, Wipro Ltd.**

About Wipro Ltd. Wipro Ltd. (NYSE:WIT) is a leading Information Technology, Consulting and Business Process Services company that delivers solutions to enable its clients do business better. Wipro delivers winning business outcomes through its deep industry experience and a 360 degree view of "Business through Technology" - helping clients create successful and adaptive businesses. A company recognized globally for its comprehensive portfolio of services, a practitioner's approach to delivering innovation, and an organization wide commitment to sustainability, Wipro has a workforce of over 140,000, serving clients in 175+ cities across 6 continents. For more information, please visit www.wipro.com.

Forward-looking and Cautionary Statements: Certain statements in this release concerning our future growth prospects are forward-looking statements, which involve a number of risks, and uncertainties that could cause actual results to differ materially from those in such forward-looking statements. The risks and uncertainties relating to these statements include, but are not limited to, risks and uncertainties regarding fluctuations in our earnings, revenue and profits, our ability to generate and manage growth, intense competition in IT services, our ability to maintain our cost advantage, wage increases in India, our ability to attract and retain highly skilled professionals, time and cost overruns on fixed-price, fixed-time frame contracts, client concentration, restrictions on immigration, our ability to manage our international operations, reduced demand for technology in our key focus areas, disruptions in telecommunication networks, our ability to successfully complete and integrate potential acquisitions, liability for damages on our service contracts, the success of the companies in which we make strategic investments, withdrawal of fiscal governmental incentives, political instability, war, legal restrictions on raising capital or acquiring companies outside India, unauthorized use of our intellectual property, and general economic conditions affecting our business and industry. Additional risks that could affect our future operating results are more fully described in our filings with the United States Securities and Exchange Commission. These filings are available at www.sec.gov. We may, from time to time, make additional written and oral forward-looking statements, including statements contained in the company's filings with the Securities and Exchange Commission and our reports to shareholders. We do not undertake to update any forward-looking statement that may be made from time to time by us or on our behalf [12].

5.12 Jigsaw Academy and Analytics Vidhya Launch the Analytics and Big Data Salary Report 2016

Unlike large companies, which pay around 9.6 lakhs, Indian **startups** are willing to pay over Rs.**10.8 lakhs** per annum to attract the best talent in the analytics industry, according to the Analytics and Big Data Salary Report 2016 by Jigsaw Academy and Analytics Vidhya. The report's findings were based on information collected from **60,000+ analytics professionals** with advanced analytics / data science skills.

According to the report, analysts experience the biggest jump in salaries once they have clocked 5 years in the industry, and can expect a **raise of up to 70%** with an average pay of Rs.**12.3 lakhs p.a.**

The Analytics & Big Data sector has seen consistent growth over the last five years despite an increasingly uncertain global outlook. The market for advanced analytics is expected to grow at a **CAGR of 33.2% and Big Data at a CAGR of 26.4%, almost six to eight times that of the overall IT market.**

Commenting on the report findings, **CEO of Jigsaw Academy Gaurav Vohra** observed that, "The demand for data professionals has grown but a corresponding surge in supply has failed to happen. Experts estimate a shortfall of approximately 200, 000 data analysts in India by 2018. The extremely competitive pay scales reflect this incongruity. In 2005 entry level salaries were around 2-4 lakhs per year but today, pay scales have gone up phenomenally. Demand for big data and analytics professionals is rising because both domestic and international companies are relying upon India for the right talent. With data being generated at such a furious pace, I don't see the demand for big data analysis—or analysts—slowing down any time soon."

According to **Gaurav Vohra,** the start-up ecosystem is responsible for the creation of over 30,000 analytics & Big Data jobs every year across India. Being the startup capital of India, Bangalore sees at least 10,000 jobs being created in the data analytics sector annually, followed by Delhi with around 7000 jobs and Mumbai, with approximately 4000 jobs.

Puneet Gambhir, a key member of the **Analytics Leadership at Flipkart**, said "We are assiduously building up the analytics talent pool within Flipkart. Analytics enables us to create better and differentiated experiences for our customers at all touch-points of our business and hence the need to shore up on such skill sets."

Commenting on the report **Kunal Jain, Founder & CEO of Analytics Vidhya** had this to say:

This is one of the most exciting times to be alive for data science professionals. We are standing at an inflection point in history, after which analytics and data science will become an integral part of any product or service available. Our community comprises thousands of data scientists and we regularly look for trends in the industry. We are excited to release these findings for the benefit of a larger audience and hope that this helps people make the right career choices.

T.V. Mohandas Pai, Chairman of Manipal Global Education Services said that "Analytics is one of the most important skills required in today's professionals. Having analytics as a part of their skill portfolio will allow these professionals to easily scoop up the most lucrative jobs, as the market is hungry for such trained talent."

Other key highlights of the report: *Kolkata seems to be a clear winner for analysts, earnings-wise, when their salaries are adjusted to the cost of living. They enjoy a better quality of life here than in other cities. The average pay for analysts in Kolkata is projected to be Rs.9.35 lakhs per annum.Companies today are looking for employees who have knowledge of multiple tools. The highest recorded salary for 2015-2016 is Rs.12.75 lakhs p.a., the recipients of which are analysts with knowledge of more than one of these tools– SPSS, SAS, R & Python*

Companies are keen to hire individuals with business acumen and experience, which means that an MBA alone won't cut it. Candidates are also expected to know analytics to successfully land analytics/Big Data jobs

R remains the front-runner in the analytics race with salary packages of Rs.10.2lakhs per annum. Python, however, is hot on its heels.

Analysts who have Big Data and Data Science skill sets are paid 26% more than analysts with knowledge of just data science or Big Data.

Startups seem to be cashing in on professionals with R & SQL skills whereas larger organizations still seem to favour SAS, since they can afford to buy expensive proprietary software.

5.13   SAS for Academia and Management Schools

SAS India has partnered with different academic institutions including premier Business Schools, to deliver education in Business Analytics. SAS delivers it through several joint models depending on the skill readiness of the institutions. Some of them are listed below

- Joint Offering of Specialized Programs
- Industry based Management Development Programs (MDPs)
- Train the trainers programs
- Mentoring and assistance in Business Analytics Center of Excellence

SAS India actively participates and assists in the full life cycle of education programs including skill need assessment and analysis, analytics events & seminars, participants' personalized access to videos, extended learning e-access to participants post training, course content development, marketing assistance, industry use cases, BIG DATA sets, practice vouchers for participants, certification preparation sessions etc.

Following are the Institutes partnering with SAS. Please email us for more details.

Indian School of Business

Course Name: ISB Biocon Certificate Programme in Business Analytics (CBA)

The Indian School of Business (ISB), with campuses in Hyderabad and Mohali, launched its first 'hybrid' model executive education programme – ISB Biocon Certificate Programme in Business Analytics (CBA) - with the aim of creating the next generation of data management scientists. Supporting the ISB in this endeavour is Biocon Foundation which has extended full funding support towards developing and nurturing this programme.

IIM Lucknow

Course Name: Certificate Program in Business Analytics for Executives

This is jointly offered by IIM Lucknow, India, Kelley School of Business and Indiana University, USA in association with SAS Institute.

This Certificate Programme in Business Analytics for Executives (CPBAE) will impart cutting edge analytics knowledge using unique blend of online and in-class education. Classes will be conducted at IIM Lucknow campus and online over Internet.

IIM Bangalore

Course Name: Certificate Program in Business Analytics

IIM Bangalore has incorporated SAS Predictive Modeling training using Enterprise Miner into the certificate program in one of the executive education programs.

We are in discussions for further extending the relationship by partnering with various initiatives for IIM Bangalore Data Center and Analytics Lab.

VES Institute of Management Studies & Research

Course Name: PGDM - Specialization in Business Analytics

VESIM has designed a course in Business Analytics that covers all major areas like big data analytics, Statistical and predictive analytics, perspective and descriptive analytics, data mining and warehousing.

Program Objectives: The course is technology driven and designed to provide in-depth knowledge of the Business Analytics tools that are used for decision making.

- To impart education in all three segments of Business Analytics-Data Management, Data Analytics and Visualization for creating nbsp & Data Scientists.
- Understand the use of Business Analytics in strategy building and gaining competitive advantage for the organization.
- Learning about data through data visualization
- Learning to use advanced analytical tools to disintegrate complex problems under uncertainty into simpler ones and helping organization to find optimal solutions.
- Learning latest technology to locate sources of big data, and analyzing the same for drawing inferences.
- Developing the ability to collect and analyze unstructured data from social media.

Calcutta Business School

Course Name: Certificate Program in Business Analytics

This is jointly offered by CBS with SAS Institute. This Certificate Programme in Business Analytics at Calcutta Business

School will issue a 'Certificate in Business Analytics' along with transcripts.

On qualifying in the subsequent Predictive Modeling Certification Examination conducted by SAS Institute, participants will receive Certificate in Predictive Modeling which is globally valid.

NMIMS Hyderabad

Course Name: Certificate Program in Business Analyst - Hyderabad

Business analytics (BA) refers to the skills, technologies, applications and practices for continuous iterative exploration and investigation of past business performance to gain insight and drive business planning. Increases in computing power and the amount of data collected have led to the development and widespread adoption of analytics by numerous industries.

The proposed program on Business Analytics will combine coursework on developing analytical thinking, introductory and advanced statistical concepts, and applications across wide section of industry and functional domains.

In partnership with SAS, a 5-day 'Statistical Business Analyst' program will be conducted by SAS leading to SAS Certification as well. This program will be delivered by SAS at the end of the Certification Program offered by NMIMS. The students will be provided by the SAS course material and the necessary software package with validity over the training period.

NMIMS - School of Science, Mumbai

Course Name: Certificate Program in Business Analytics (Predictive Modeling)

SVKM's NMIMS, School of Science, Mumbai in association with SAS Institute India has amalgamated to offer a Certificate Program in Business Analytics consisting of: Statistical Concepts using Case Studies

- Training on Predictive Modeling using Enterprise Guide and Enterprise Miner.

In business, predictive models exploit patterns found in historical and transactional data to identify risks and opportunities. Models capture relationships among many factors to allow assessment of risk or potential associated with a particular set of conditions, guiding decision making for candidate transactions. Thus, School of Science, NMIMS with SAS offers this statistical programme to train the future "data analysts/data scientist's" so as to propel India's leap in Analytics.

NMIMS - Bangalore

Course Name: Certificate Program in Business Intelligence and Visual Analytics

SVKM's NMIMS, Bangalore in association with SAS Institute India is offering a Certificate Program in Business Intelligence and Visual Analytics. The proposed 6-day program will consist of advanced topics in Business Intelligence as well as Visual Analytics.

An effective business intelligence system can analyze the vast amount of data to provide information when it is needed. However, such systems are under pressure as data becomes bigger and more complex. Hence, there is an urgent need for developing innovative solutions that will enhance the effectiveness of traditional business intelligence systems.

Visual Analytics & nbsp is the science of analytical reasoning supported by interactive visual interfaces. This allows decision makers to combine human flexibility, creativity, and contextual knowledge to gain insights. It is an integrated approach combining visualization, human factors, and data analysis. Over the past decade, while many tools and techniques have been developed to support visual analytics, the awareness index and adoption is low. This programme is designed to help enhance the knowledge quotient on visual analytics and enable organizations take steps to accelerate its adoption for effective decision-making.

SHIV NADAR UNIVERSITY

Course Name: Master of Science in Data Analytics and P.G. Diploma in Business and Data Analytics.

This program covers analysis of business requirements, industry best practices and ability to assemble analysis flow diagrams using the rich tool set of SAS Enterprise Miner for both pattern discovery (segmentation, association, and sequence analyses) and predictive modeling (decision tree, regression, and neural network models).Offering a mix of real life examples, basic concepts for Predictive Analytics and the science of decision making shall be dealt with in this 4 day program. Faculty with more than a decade of experience in analytics education is in partnership with SAS Institute Consultants. Program delivery involves lectures, case studies, hands on sessions with real life data, online access to learning, certification preparation sessions etc [13].

5.14 Big Data Training Programme

SPONSORED BY: BIG DATA INITIATIVE (BDI) – DST INDIA

Big Data is everywhere. Several industries ranging from technology to finance to governments want to use Big Data Analysis techniques for knowledge discovery. Tools and techniques have been developed recently to handle various aspects of Big Data Analysis such as data aggregate tools, scalable storage, efficient retrieval, and faster analysis. It is important to get the awareness of this recent development in the area of Big Data Analytic tools and techniques. This course will look at the software and algorithms designed for coping with Big Data. We will train participant to get practical knowledge for Big Data Analysis.

Data Collections	Data Science basics	Faster Retrieval Techniques	Efficient Data Analysis	MapReduce and Hadoop
Databases and operational zing Big Data	Basic data models	Analyzing data in motion	Finding structures in data	Distributed and parallel computing using R
Scalable Storage	Advanced data models	Security Concern in Big Data Applications	Big Data case studies	Big Data Applications

We are excited to announce our first speaker - Sonal Gupta, B. Tech. IIT, Delhi

Title: Fuzzy Matching - Big Data for Analytics and Data Quality: Sonal is the founder, CEO at Nube Technologies (www.nubetech.co), a startup which makes tools for big data wrangling. Nube's product Reifier is built on Apache Spark and machine learning to fuzzily match different mentions of an entity across sources. Reifier helps enterprises in getting 360 views of customer and product data, data quality, fraud and security and data management for downstream analytics. Sonal is a regular speaker at international big data and machine learning conferences. Previously, she also opens sourced HIHO for Hadoop ETL and Crux reporting for Hbase at Github. Sonal holds a BTech from IIT Delhi.

Shweta Gupta, Senior Research Engineer, SnapDeal

Title: Scala and Spark for building Machine Learning on Big Data: Shweta has 5-6 years of experience in ML domain. She is working on deep learning (NLP area) focusing on big Data. She is interested in exploring scalable machine learning algorithm so that it can be applied to solve real world scenario. In Snapdeal, over a course of 16 months, she worked vividly on recommender systems, sentiment analysis using deep NLP. Prior to that, she worked as RA in IIT Roorkee RSL lab for a year, working on optimization problems.

Program Information

- Virtual Box
- Installation
- Setting HBase & Hadoop Environment

SlideCode

- CRUD Operations
- CAP Theorems
- JAVA API

SlideCode

- HDFS File System
- Map Reduce Program
- Java Program
- HDFS code

SlideCode

- Intro to Spark
- Comparison
- Filter Map

SlideCode

- Web Crawler
- Article Scraper
- Comment Extractor
- News Keyword Extractor
- Twitter API

SlideCode

- Sampling
- Normalization
- Transformation

SlideCode

- Clustering
- Classification
- Association Rule Mining
- WEKA

SlideCode

- Intro to Data Stream
- Intro to Apache Storm
- Use Cases
- Single Server Setup

SlideCode

- Intro to Thread
- Message Passing Interface (MPI)
- GPU Programming
- CUDA Programming

SlideCode

- Introduction
- Language Constructs
- Visualization
- Classification and Regression

SlideCode

Contact: Co-ordinator: Dr. Dhaval Patel Computer Science Department IIT Roorkee [14].

5.15 Big Data is a game-changer: TCS' Satya Ramaswamy

Big Data has become one of the top initiatives of TCS, says Ramaswamy.TCS is building a large Big data team at Silicon Valley in California, US.

Companies are increasingly focusing on big data, spending between $2.5 million and $500 million a year on analyzing large amounts of complex information that would help them improve their business strategies, *Tata Consultancy Services Ltd* (TCS) found in a recent study. Obviously, big data has become one of the top initiatives of TCS, India's largest software services provider, said **Satya Ramaswamy**, global mobility head and vice-president at the company. Ramaswamy, who joined TCS in 2010 after it bought Brightfon Inc., the mobile solutions firm he had founded, is helping TCS build a large big data team at Silicon Valley in California, US, he said in an interview at the Said Business School Oxford India Business forum on 5 April. Edited excerpts:

But how big is the TCS big data team?

At TCS, we believe we have one of the biggest big data and analytics team in the world, not only in size but also in talent. We have a training programme for big data, which we formally started one-and-a-half years back. Some of the players in the space like **Cloudera Inc.** (develops open source software on big data) is a pioneering start-up in the space. Cloudera now collaborates closely with TCS and we have the largest pool of Cloudera certified big data experts in the world. We have people who can talk in-depth about the origin of big data.

So what kind of products is TCS developing for big data?

Big data is one of the top most initiatives for TCS today. Our CEO (N. Chandrasekaran) has been articulating in every instance that he strongly believes in it. In big data, we are building products by placing a lot of emphasis on intellectual property development. It is a key part of our strategy in this fresh new space. The typical barriers you see in mature space are not there in big data, we are finding that it is an open space that is not occupied and we are creating IP (intellectual property)-led products there. We are conceptualizing these products in Silicon Valley with entrepreneurs there and then building it with our global engineering team in India. We are hiring entrepreneurs who have great ideas and we are building products based upon their entrepreneurial talent. We have very big ambitions for this space.

To what extent are companies spending on big data projects?

We commissioned a big data study (*The Emerging Big Returns on Big Data*, released on 21 March) to understand this space better and found that 53% out of 1,217 companies surveyed had a big data project and the other 47% will have a big data programme by year 2015. Some of them could be cautious as there are challenges like cultural issues (approving big investments), organizational issues (sharing information across organization) or technological issues (ability to handle large volume of data). One of the reasons we went out and did this research to understand why is people holding back? Now we have identified what these problems are. Currently, we have consulting offering around big data. But we have lot more insights now which we can leverage to have a very strong consulting offering for customers. We don't just want to grow ourselves but help the industry grow, give direction with these insights.

What are the other important insights of the big data study by TCS on its potential?

Big data is a game-changer. Customer want to implement big data because they have a performance barrier where big data can help them move up the bar. We had a gut instinct that it could but our survey clearly says it is so—46% return on investment is a powerful thing for clients. We will apply all that to make it a big part of TCS offering.

But in which division at TCS does big data fall under?

The larger picture is the digital space consisting of mobility, big data, social media, cloud, artificial intelligence and robotics. In this broader space, big data has a separate team which reports to me and I report to the chief executive officer. We have a team for mobility also. But cloud is fairly spread out because it has an infrastructure play. Social media too is integral part of everything we do. I also oversee the artificial intelligence, robotics and big data team. We also have a large analytics team like knowledge process outsourcing team and traditional analytics like business intelligence and performance management. Collectively, we have one of the biggest teams in the world.

Why has TCS set up its big data division in the US?

We believe big data is a global phenomenon and we are right at the source of this movement. We are positioned in Silicon Valley, which is the epicenter of big data when it was implemented by companies like **Google Inc.** and **Yahoo Inc**. Every single start-up here is contributing to the phenomenon and we at TCS contribute back by hosting meet-ups in Santa Clara. We are creating a global team from Silicon Valley and scaling it up rapidly [15].

5.16 Big Data Fellowships Fundraising Campaign

To recruit and train top talent in areas related to Big Data, we are raising funds to institute a set of Big Data Fellowships at II Sc. For details of how to sponsor a Fellowship, please feel free to contact us [16]. As a small token of appreciation, sponsors will continue to receive invitations to selected events and lectures related to Big Data at IISc throughout the Fellowship period, including possible participation in a Big Data Workshop in 2015/2016.

Organizing Team

The CSA Department at IISc has leading faculty in a wide spectrum of disciplines related to Big Data, including theory, algorithms, machine learning, optimization, parallel architectures, and visualization. The organizing team includes several of these faculty: Professors Shivani Agarwal, Arnab Bhattacharyya, Chiranjib Bhattacharyya, Uday Bondhugula, Ramesh Hariharan, Ravindran Kannan, Y. Narahari, Vijay Natarajan, and Chandan Saha; as well as Professor Chandra Murthy from the ECE Department and Professor Partha Pratim Talukdar from the SERC Department.

5.17 Data Science Online Training Courses

How to learn Big Data Analytics?

Well, examining Big Data i.e. extremely large data to uncover hidden patterns, and other useful information that can be used for make making a better decision is not something that could be done overnight. Here I've shared few Big Data Online Training Courses that one can opt to understand big data explicitly.

With growth of Big Data scope in recent years, companies are searching for data scientists. This specialized field demands multiple skills not easy to obtain through conventional curricula. Introduce yourself to the basics of big data and leave armed with practical experience extracting value from big data.

1. Udacity
2. EMC
3. Coursera
4. CalTech's learning from Data
5. MIT Open Courseware
6. Jigsaw Academy
7. Stanford's Open Classroom
8. Code School

These are the few courses that one can opt to enhance their big data analytics skills or just begun to get the basic idea of big data. Big data is here to stay and this field is on the way towards growth only and companies are desperately looking for qualified & skilled people. Grab any course from the above mentioned options to get started & to have a good knowledge of big data. There are some Prerequisites that a person should have in order to have a better understanding of the course. In recent years, with increase in scope of Big Data Technology, the demand of data scientists have increased gradually. All the big companies around the world are looking for skilled data scientists and ready to pay them big bucks. Well, it's just the initial stage; soon it will spread more to reach its peak. It won't be wrong to say that it's the right time to leverage various aspects of data science as the need for data scientists is increasing day by day.

If you are interested to learn data science and become a data science expert, check out the following courses to introduce yourself to the basics of data science and leave armed with practical experience extracting value from big data.

5.18 Top 5 Data Science Online Training Courses

1. Harvard

This course is taught by two Harvard Professors Hanspeter Pfister (Computer Science) and Joe Blizsten (Statistics). Here you'll be using Python programming language for programming assignments and projects through the class. To opt this course you must have some programming experience and working knowledge of Cs50 and Stat 100. This course isn't short and one has to spend 4 months of duration to finish it entirely. During the span of these 4 months you'll be introduces to the five major key aspects of Data Science.

- data wrangling, cleaning, and sampling
- data management to be able to access big data quickly and reliably;
- exploratory data analysis to generate hypotheses and intuition;
- prediction based on statistical methods such as regression and classification;
- Communication of results through visualization, stories, and summaries.

Quick Details

- **Course Duration**: 4 Months
- **Level:** Difficult
- **Programming Language:** Python
- **Instructor:** Hanspeter Pfister (Computer Science) and Joe Blizsten (Statistics)

2. <u>Analytics Edge</u>

To opt this course all you need is basic knowledge of Mathematics. Here everything from lectures to assignments is well structured to have a detailed knowledge of many different analytics methods, including linear regression, logistic regression, clustering, CART and data visualization. During the time span of 11 weeks you'll learn how to implement all the methods in R. If you want to have knowledge of an applied understanding of mathematical optimization, then opt this course.

Quick Details:

- **Course Duration**: 11 Weeks
- **Level:** Difficult
- **Programming Language:** R, Libre office/Excel
- **Instructor:** Dimitris Bertsimas and Allison Kelly O'Hair

3. <u>Coursera – Machine Learning Course</u>

Coursera offers Machine Learning course, an 11 week course where you'll be introduced to the theoretical & practical knowledge of most effective machine learning techniques, data mining, statistical pattern recognition and guide of how to make them work for yourself. For better understanding, it's good to have knowledge of Basic linear algebra and Calculus. This course will be taught in Octave programming language, videos of lectures are available there on how to use Octave.

Quick Details:

- **Course Duration**: 11 Weeks
- **Level:** Low
- **Programming Language:** Octave
- **Instructor:** Andrew Ng

4. <u>Udacity- Data Analyst Nano Degree</u>

Udacity offer Data Analyst Nano Degree where you can earn a certificate in 12 months (10 hours per week). Before taking this course you must have a knowledge of Descriptive statistics, Inferential statistics, R, machine learning, data wrangling, data science basics, data visualization, computer science basics. During this course you'll learn how to,

- Wrangle, extract, transform, and load data from various databases, formats, and data sources
- Use exploratory data analysis techniques to identify meaningful relationships, patterns, or trends from complex data sets
- Classify unlabeled data or predict into the future with applied statistics and machine learning algorithms
- Communicate data analysis and findings through effective data visualizations

Quick Details:

- **Course Duration**: 1 Year (10 hours per week)
- **Level:** Very High
- **Instructor:** Chen Hang Lee and Miriam Swords Kalk

5. <u>Coursera Intro to Data Science</u>

This course introduces to a various aspects of Data Science. In order to have a better understand during the class, it would be great if you already have knowledge of Basics of Python, statistics, basic knowledge of databases. Syllabus includes Introduction, Data Manipulation at Scale, Analytics, Communicating Results, and Special Topics. There will be four programming assignments: two in Python, one in SQL, and one in R.

Quick Details:

- **Course Duration**: 3 months
- **Level:** Intermediate
- **Programming Language:** Python and R
- **Instructor:** Bill howe

So these are the few courses that one can opt to enhance their data science skills or just begun to get the basic idea of data science. The demand of data scientist across the world is huge and this field is on the way towards growth only and companies are desperately looking for qualified & skilled data scientists. Grab any course from the above mentioned options to get started & to have a good knowledge of data science. These courses aren't free and one has to pay a particular amount as a fee and each course has some Prerequisites that a person should have in order to have a better understanding of the course [17].

5.19   Big Data Online Training Courses

Big Data Online Training Courses: Over the last few years, the activities around the internet have increased a lot which leads to gradual increase in the scope of Big Data. Examining Big Data i.e. extremely large data to uncover hidden patterns, and other useful information that can be used for making a better decision is not something that could be done overnight. Here I've shared few Big Data Online Training Courses that one can opt to understand big data explicitly.

With growth of Big Data scope in recent years, companies are searching for data scientists. This specialized field demands multiple skills not easy to obtain through conventional curricula. Introduce yourself to the basics of data science and leave armed with practical experience extracting value from big data.

5.20 8 Big Data Online Training Courses

1. Udacity

Udacity offers multiple courses well cut to ability levels for those who are completely new to technology. Learn data science from industry experts at Face book, Cloudera, MongoDB, Georgia Tech, and more. The courses that offered here are not free and one has to pay for them. The learning structure is well defined here, firstly you'll get to study Introduction to computer science, Inferential Statistics, and Descriptive Statistics, and then proceed to next step i.e. technology-special tutorials concentrated R, MongoDB, Machine Learning and more. To decide whether this course is apt for you, a 14 day free trial will be given to decide. Just to clear the fee criteria, around $150 per month will be charged for "Intro to Computer Science".

2. EMC

With continuous growth in big data technology, it's imperative for organization and industries to reconcile this new advancement for persistent growth of business. Fortunately, EMC are here to help you out by making you understand the big data technology. The good thing here is that you EMC will take you to a step by step guide i.e. from basic to advanced data analysis methods then guide of basic tools of the trade and the end to end analytic life cycle. It isn't cheap here; one has to pay a sum of $600 for starting and then for full course will land out in about $5000.

3. <u>Coursera</u>

Coursera is a MOOC (Massive Open Online Course) which is completely fee. Coursera is a fantastic free resource for those looking to take the first steps into data science exploration.

- Data Science with the University of Washington's Bill Howe
- Machine Learning with Stanford's Andrew Ng
- Statistics with Alison Gibbs & Jeffrey Rosenthal of the University of Toronto

As far as the course format is concerned, the class will consist of lecture videos about 8 to 10 minutes in length. These will contain 1-2 integrated quizzes per video. Some of these videos will be given by guest lecturers from the data science community.

4. <u>CalTech's Learning from Data</u>

CalTech's is another free source to learn introductory course to machine learning online taught by Professor Yaser Abu-Moustafa in the form of videos recorded from a live broadcast. CalTech offers courses in data science where you'll learn the basic theory and algorithms related to machine learning and can apply this learning to your big data needs. Filled with 8 homework sets and a final exam, discussion forum for participant, this platform offers everything to meet your learning goals.

5. <u>MIT Open Courseware</u>

Massachusetts Institute of Technology has taken this initiative to put all of their course material online to make it accessible to all the aspirants looking to learn Big Data Tactics online. Here are some course features that have been offered.

Course Features:

- Selected Lecture Notes
- Assignments(no solution)
- Exam (no solution)

6. Jigsaw Academy

Learn data science online with Jigsaw Academy. They offer courses in data science where you'll learn to solve data-rich problems and apply this knowledge to your big data needs. Whether you're new to the field or looking for additional training, we have introductory, advanced, and industry-specific courses to meet your learning goals.

7. Stanford's Open Classroom

Open Classroom offers fee online machine learning course, devised by Andrew Ng. They offer full courses in short videos where you'll learn about some of the most widely used and successful machine learning techniques, hands-on tricks and techniques (rarely discussed in textbooks) that help get learning algorithms to work well. The entire course has been broken down into six steps.

- Introduction
- Linear Regression I
- Linear Regression II
- Logistic Regression
- Regularization
- Naive Bayes

8. Code School

Code Schools have video tutorials, programming challenges, and screen casts that will surely help you in learning many courses offered on specific programming languages, such as R, Java, and a course on mastering Github. Few courses are free while for other one has to a specified amount of money. Code school has designed their course in various levels for better understanding.

For those looking to expand their big data skill or just begun to understand the basics of big data, the options specified on the list are good to start [18].

5.21 The Analytics Training Market in India

As mentioned in the overview section, this does not fall directly under data science industry, but is closely associated with the industry. Hence, I thought I would add some details on this as well. Lately, there has been an explosion in number of institutes (both recognized and new) offering data science trainings / courses in India. On one side, there are likes of ISB, Great Lakes, Praxis and IIMs offering several executive programs and on the other hand, there are several players providing short term certifications. I think the size of analytics training industry would be close to ~100 Crores p.a. and is increasing at approximately 20% p.a.

Though there has been an increase in the number of offerings to create industry professionals, till now the industry has not been opened to these candidates. Among the ones who undergo these trainings, only a few get placed in analytics roles within 3-6 months of finishing the training.

P.S. This is by no means saying that people don't get placed. I have seen many transition stories, but it takes time and effort. You can read this article for a more detailed view about transition into analytics.

So, there is a kind of imbalance in industry today, where on one hand there are trained people wanting to enter the industry and on the other hand companies are not able to find talent for the open positions they have.

So, there is a kind of imbalance in industry today, where on one hand there are trained people wanting to enter the industry and on the other hand companies are not able to find talent for the open positions they have. Normal cycle for filling up an analytics position in industry stands at staggering 6 – 12 months. And the more senior position you are looking for, the more difficult it is go get good people. Over time, I expect this gap to narrow, but there is clear need of improvement here.

5.22 Important Big Data Public Lectures by Indian Scientists-2016

To increase awareness and build a strong ecosystem around Big Data in India, a series of public lectures will be delivered by leading experts.

Venue: Faculty Hall, Indian Institute of Science.

Registration: Free, open to all (limited to 250 seats per lecture)

Prof. Partha Talukdar, Assistant Professor, CDS and CSA, II Sc

From Big Text to Big Knowledge

Abstract: Knowledge harvesting from Web-scale text datasets has emerged as an important and active research area over the last few years, resulting in the automatic construction of large knowledge graphs (KGs) consisting of millions of entities and relationships among them. This has the potential to revolutionize Artificial Intelligence and intelligent decision making by removing the knowledge bottleneck which has plagued systems in these areas all along. In this talk, I shall provide an overview of research in this exciting and emerging area.

Prof. Vijay Natarajan, Associate Professor, CSA, II Sc

Symmetry in Scientific Data: An Approach to Feature-Directed Visualization

Abstract: Several natural and man-made objects exhibit symmetry in different forms, both in their geometry and in the material distribution. The study of symmetry plays an important role in understanding both the structure of these objects and their physical properties. In this talk, I will introduce the problem of symmetry detection in scientific data, where the data is represented as a scalar field. The goal is to identify regions of interest within the domain of a scalar field that remain invariant under transformations of both domain geometry and the scalar values. I will present algorithms to detect symmetry and discuss applications to visualization, interactive exploration, and visual analysis of large and feature-rich scientific data.

Dr. Mayur Thakur, Data Analytics Group, Goldman Sachs,

Leveraging Big Data Analytics for Compliance in Financial Institutions

Abstract: It is critical for a financial institution to comply with government regulations. The cost of non-compliance can result in criminal indictment, multi-billion dollar fines and loss of banking and other licenses. Employees of Compliance departments are responsible for implementation of proper policies, procedures and monitoring to ensure compliance with regulations. This discussion will focus on how Compliance leverages large quantities of data to establish monitoring controls. In particular, we will discuss specific business problems and show how they map into problems in natural language processing, outlier detection, and graph analytics. No prior knowledge of finance will be assumed.

Dr. Mayur Datar, Principal Data Scientist, Flipkart

Machine learning challenges in E-commerce

Abstract: In this talk, we will look at what it means to be doing Big Data research in industry. Why is Big Data critical for success of companies and also examples when it is not needed? We will look at a selection of problems from the e-commerce space that is well served by standard machine learning constructs. We will take a breadth first view of around a dozen problems from e-commerce, some of which are applicable to the larger area of consumer internet. Time permitting; we will also discuss the new emerging field of deep learning (aka Deep Neural Networks) and their applicability to Big Data.

Prof. Shubhabrata Das, Professor, IIM Bangalore

Selected Problems in Sports Analytics

Abstract: Application of more advanced statistical methods in the domain of sports has been on steady rise, leading to academic conferences and journals dwelling exclusively on this domain. In this talk, we would discuss briefly a few such problems. 1) Not out scores in cricket. In cricket, batting average has always been used as the primary measure of performance of a batsman. But traditional batting average exhibits serious limitation in reflecting the true performance of a batsman in light of not out innings. Treating not outs as censored data, adaptation of Kaplan-Meir estimator provides a more reasonable solution, but it still suffers both from conceptual as well as operational problems at certain situations. A generalized class of geometric distribution (GGD) is proposed in this work to model the runs scored by individual batsmen, with the generalization coming in the form of hazard of getting out changing from one score to another. We consider the change points as the known or specified parameters and derive the general expressions for the restricted maximum likelihood estimators of the hazard rates under the generalized structure considered. Given the domain context, we propose and test ten different variations of the GGD model and carry out the test across the nested models using the asymptotic distribution of the likelihood ratio statistic. We propose two alternative approaches for improved estimation of batting average on the basis of the above modeling. 2) Tracking the progress in a round-robin tournament (World Cup football, hockey, and cricket). The up-to-date position of competing teams based on points obtained by them in the middle of any round-robin (stage of) tournament may inadequately reflect their actual relative position, because of the strength of the opposition faced till that stage. To help the followers of the game, as well as to possibly help the teams to strategize, a simple probably matrix based approach followed up by computation of the expected points may easily bring clarity to the situation. While an unstructured or unconstrained way of updating these probabilities, reflecting individual perspective, at successive stages of the tournament may be an acceptable approach, this method, being ad-hoc, suffers from arbitrariness and may lack consistency. In that context, we explore how a model based Bayesian adaptation can work effectively. 3) New models for repeated tournaments (Illustration with NCAA College basketball). The primary objective here is to model the win-loss records of matches in a repeated tournament, using strengths of the teams. Of particular focus is the case of a standard knockout tournament with teams ranked a priori and National Collegiate Athletic Association (NCAA) men and women basketball tournament data are considered for demonstration. The work considers modifications of Bradley-Terry (BT) model that are consistent with ranks of the participating teams. The BT model with restricted maximum likelihood strengths involves estimation of too many parameters and strength estimates typically lack strict monotonicity. A proposed class of rank-based percentile BT models from different parametric family provides an excellent fit to the past data using only few parameters and this validates the ranking procedure adopted by NCAA. Parameter estimation, goodness-of-fit using suitably framed test statistic and its null distribution, selection between nested models in the change point framework, as well as other estimation aspects are discussed. Adaptive variations of the model, that allow strength to alter, are also considered. The discussed model and analysis can be extended in more general tournament structures, as shown through an analysis of results from Indian Premiere League. The work has potential application in the wider domain of paired comparison. 4) Seeded Contests and Betting Odds (Illustration with tennis). We next develop a model to predict the outcome (win-loss) of a game based on the rank of the participating players and the betting odds set by the bookmakers. The model is based on Bradley Terry framework where the participating players are linked by a measure of their competitive ability. We illustrate the application of our model with a data set comprising records from international tennis tournament for women and men. Bayesian approach has been adopted to make inferences about the parameters in the model. The estimates are also used to infer the margin by which the 'true-odds' may be altered by the bookmakers. Prediction based on the estimated model is compared with true observation for the games played in the year 2015. Various strategies of selecting bets based on the model have been discussed. We propose two very promising betting strategies that have yielded positive result, albeit in short run.

<u>Dr. Rajeev Rastogi</u>, Director of Machine Learning, Amazon India - *Machine Learning @Amazon*

Abstract: In this talk, I will first provide an overview of the key Machine Learning (ML) applications we are developing at Amazon. I will then describe a matrix factorization model that we have developed for making product recommendations – the salient characteristics of the model are: (1) It uses a Bayesian approach to handle data sparsity, (2) It leverages user and item features to handle the cold start problem (3) It introduces latent variables to handle multiple personas associated with a user account (e.g. family members). Our experimental results with synthetic and real-life datasets show that leveraging user and item features, and incorporating user personas enables our model to provide lower RMSE and perplexity compared to baselines.

<u>S. Anand</u>, Chief Data Scientist, Gramener

Visualizing Big Data

Abstract: Today, more information is produced every year than the entire history of human civilization until 2000. This offers a unique opportunity - the ability to use this information to intelligently guide us. It also poses a challenge: how does one understand such vast quantities of data - which are well beyond most supercomputers' comprehension, let alone the human mind? Yet, analytics and visualization research has made great strides. With modern visualizations such as tree maps, over 150 pages of productivity reports have been compressed into a single sheet without loss of information or insight. With animated visualizations, 100 years of weather data has been compressed into half a minute video. A confluence of programming, statistics and design gives us new ways to visualize, experience, and interact with a world of information. This talk will cover - How organizations use visuals to comprehend large scale data. What kind of decisions can be driven through data, and how to enable this techniques and support mechanisms are available in the market today.

Anurag Agrawal, Principal Scientist, CSIR Institute of Genomics & Integrative Biology (IGIB)

The Role of Big Data in Public Health and Medicine

Abstract: Public health and medical decision support occupies an interdisciplinary space that lies between Medical, Biological, Mathematical, and Engineering Sciences. Interdisciplinary marriages remain uncommon and multidisciplinary marriages even more so. I will discuss recent efforts where we used information technology, systems biology visualization tools, and Bayesian frameworks to gain novel understanding of public health in India, while creating a framework for integrating transparent and effective healthcare delivery with big data collection for tomorrow's medicine.

Ramesh Hariharan, CTO, Strand Life Sciences and Adjunct Professor, CSA, II Sc

Using Data to Understand Biological Systems

Abstract: Hidden inside a living organism are a large number of molecular entities, all working in concert to make, and sometimes break, the organism. We are slowly learning to tease out information about these entities, less and less via direct observation, and more and more via indirect data generation. This talk will provide an introduction to the area and outline various challenges in generating this data, priming it for analysis, interpreting its meaning, and using it to impact lives.

Arnab Bhattacharyya, Assistant Professor, CSA, II Sc

Spectral graph theory and graph partitioning

Abstract: Clustering is one of the most widely used techniques for big data analysis. This fundamental algorithmic primitive has found applications in biology, natural language processing, sociology, business analytics and many other fields. In this talk, I will describe how to cluster using spectral methods and the reasons behind the success of spectral partitioning. This algorithm has become the method of choice in many domains and can be implemented efficiently by standard linear algebra software. The talk will be for a general audience and not require prior mathematical background.

Rajesh Sundaresan, Associate Professor, ECE, II Sc

Belief Propagation for Large-Scale Optimization on Graphs

Abstract: Belief propagation algorithms pass messages along the edges of a graph and update them via local computations at the nodes of the graph. They are used for decoding error correcting codes in communication systems, for probabilistic inference in Bayesian networks, and for solving certain combinatorial optimization problems. The talk will give an overview of these algorithms and the challenges involved in showing their validity.

Chiranjib Bhattacharyya, Associate Professor, CSA, II Sc

Learning from Big Data: Using Statistics to tame the Complexity

Abstract: The problem of learning Statistical models from Data can be posed as Optimization programs. These programs often become unwieldy, in the Big Data setting, as the number of variables and constraints grow with number of data-points. Distributed Optimization, requiring expensive parallel hardware, is the current state of the art remedy for such problems. However, in Statistics growth of data points is often welcomed as it yields more understanding. This then begs the question: Are there alternatives to distributed processing where statistical understanding, gleaned from large volumes of data, can be used for taming the computational complexity of optimization programs? Following this paradigm we present two ideas for solving classification problems: the first involving resembling constraints and the second involving chance constraint programming. Time permitting we will show how these ideas can be leveraged to build large scale focused crawlers.

Jayant Haritsa, Professor, SERC and CSA, II Sc

Big Data, Small Testing?

Abstract: Big Data has become the buzzword of choice in recent times, especially in the software industry. The accompanying hoopla has spawned frenetic claims foretelling the development of great and wondrous solutions to Big Data challenges. However, there is very little said about the testing of such systems, an essential pre-requisite for deployment. In this talk, we will discuss the research challenges involved in the testing process, especially from the database perspective. We will also present CODD, a graphical tool that takes a first step towards the effective testing of Big Data deployments through a new metaphor of "data-less databases". CODD is currently in use at industrial and academic institutions worldwide.

Chandra Murthy, Associate Professor, ECE, II Sc

Role of Sparse Signal Recovery in Big Data Analytics

Abstract: In this talk, we start with providing a brief overview of some of the signal processing challenges that arise in big data analytics. We then discuss the mathematical models that are commonly employed to address these challenges, and argue that sparsity and sparse signal recovery methods naturally arise as promising solutions to a variety of big data problems. We also discuss some of the recent sparse signal recovery algorithms that may be applicable to big data. We present example studies on the use of these techniques in distributed sparse signal recovery, spectrum cartography, and, time permitting, wideband channel estimation in wireless communications.

Y. Narahari, Professor and Chairman, CSA, II Sc

Mechanism Design for Strategic Networks, Crowds, and Markets

Abstract: Social networks, crowd sourcing, and Internet markets represent modern institutions that present many big data challenges. A distinctive feature of these institutions is the presence of human agents who exhibit strategic, possibly manipulative, behaviour. In this talk, we address the following question: can we ensure that the strategic agents behave honestly? and, can we realize social goals in the presence of these self-interested agents? A clear answer to this question has far-reaching implications for solving numerous economic and algorithmic problems in areas such as electronic commerce, online auctions, public procurements, Internet advertising, social network monetization, and crowd sourcing. A perfect answer to this question is still elusive; however, the discipline of game theory and mechanism design provides a principled way of addressing this question. In this talk, we bring out, through many examples, the fundamentally different way in which mechanism design combined with machine learning can enable design of solutions and algorithms to problems involving strategic networks, crowds, and markets.

Uday Bondhugula, Assistant Professor, CSA, II Sc

Scalable Programming Technologies and Architectures for Big Data

Abstract: This talk will present challenges associated with developing programs for big data along with some useful programming techniques and paradigms. Big data has a strong connection with high performance computing due to the need to extract parallelism when dealing with large amounts of data. We will highlight the problem of data movement and the need to exploit data locality and minimize data communication. We will also look at the relative strengths and weaknesses of various approaches: automatic compiler/runtime-based, domain-specific tools and code generators, tuned library-based, and completely manual. At a high level, we will also understand the merits and weaknesses of languages that provide a higher level of abstraction for expressive and productive programming at the expense of performance -- from C to R.

N. Viswanadham, INSA Senior Scientist, CSA, II Sc

Big Data Based Decision making in Manufacturing Supply Chains

Abstract: Decision making in supply chains is based on optimization models and the data from past sales. Software tools such as ERP, CRP, TMS, and WMS have been developed and used in the

Industry. The aim is to deliver quality products to the customers at the right cost. Currently, there are several new trends that are happening in the supply chain arena. Globalization has created dispersed supply chains which are vulnerable and dependent on entities and factors that are exogenous to the supply chain. Also, technologies such as Big data, Cloud computing, Blogs, Social Media, Internet of Things and Mobility have become sources of large volumes and several varieties of data. In this lecture, I would first present some recent big data start-ups that are revolutionizing or disrupting the traditional manufacturing networks. We then discuss how the new developments in tagging, sensing and embedding effects the four important supply chain processes: procurement, manufacturing, maintenance & repair and retail. Next, we present the big data ecosystem model: big data service chain, institutions (governments and social groups) and their influence on data availability, resources (natural, human, financial, and industry inputs) and delivery service infrastructure (communication and decision). This leads us to the question: what data should I collect, and what algorithms should I use to make decisions that would result in better business outcomes. Data based decision making, particularly with unorganized and non-numerical data is a relatively unexplored area of research with abundant opportunities. The takeaways from this lecture are opportunities for both research and start-ups in this evolving area.

References:

[1] http://www.jigsawacademy.com

[2] http://www.analyticstraining.com/

[3] http://www.datasciencecentral.com/profiles/blogs/how-do-i-become-a-data-scientist

[4] http://bigdatasciencetraining.com/learn-big-data-analytics/

[5] http://bigdatasciencetraining.com/big-data-training-in-noida/

[6] http://www.databrio.com/courses/data-science/

[7] https://www.edx.org/course/introduction-python-data-science-microsoft-dat208x#!

[8] http://www.analyticsvidhya.com/blog/2014/12/top-analytics-programs-india-2014-2015/

[9] http://bigdatasciencetraining.com/hadoop-tutorial-for-beginners-youtube-videos/

[10] http://www.analyticsvidhya.com/blog/2015/12/top-business-analytics-programs-india-2015-2016/

[11] http://www.jigsawacademy.com/bocconi-business-analytics-program-mumbai/

[12] http://www.wipro.com/newsroom/press-releases/Wipro-launches-WiSTA-data-scientist-academic-program-for-fresh-graduate-hires/

[13] http://www.sas.com/en_in/training/home/academic-program.html

[14] http://www.iitr.ac.in/media/facspace/patelfec/16Bit/index.html

[15] http://www.livemint.com/Companies/VntdSjSnNsPFmtagpdt QZJ/Big-data-is-a-gamechanger-TCS-Satya-Ramaswamy.html

[16] http://drona.csa.iisc.ernet.in/~bigdata/

[17] http://bigdatasciencetraining.com/data-science-online-training-courses/

[18] http://bigdatasciencetraining.com/big-data-online-training-courses/

Chapter 6: Best Data Science and Big Data Courses Offered Abroad

6.1 The Best Data Science Courses

Here we present a list of the top programs with the best reviews, as well as a short-list of other data science boot camps with a strong reputation. This list of courses is by no means exhaustive, but we wanted to narrow it down to provide students with a starting point of well-reviewed, vetted data science courses. As more data comes in for different schools, we will update our list. We will not be covering master's degrees in this article - we have a follow up article about the differences between boot camps vs. degree programs.

6.2 Top courses in the USA - Educational Institutes at USA

NYC Data Science Academy 5 stars (6 reviews)

The Manhattan-based full-time boot camp runs for 12 weeks and seeks to help students learn practical skills needed for a career in data science. During the course, students will learn how to solve real-world business and industry problems as well as beginner and intermediate levels of Data Science (R, Python and Hadoop) and R packages R(Shiny, Knitr, rCharts and more). Students will also complete a 2-week hands-on project and have help from the school with job support and preparation in the last week. Applicants are expected to have a Masters or PhD in science, technology, engineering or math, or at least have equivalent experience in quantitative science or programming.

Overall Satisfaction	(5.0)
Location	New York
Number of Reviews	7
Subjects	Data Science, R, Python, Hadoop, Spark
Price Range	$
Courses	Big Data with Hadoop and Spark, Data Science with R: Machine Learning, Data Science with R: Data Analysis and Visualization, Data Science with Python: Data Analysis and Visualization, Data Science with Python: Machine Learning.

Data Science Boot camp was the best experience in my career. Instructors were not only helpful in teaching the regular materials but also guide you to establish your confidence in yourself to be a Data Scientist. They will help you even after completing your boot camp. Nice and honest environment.

Check out more NYC Data Science Academy reviews on Switch.

Galvanize 5 stars (11 reviews)

A 12-week immersive boot camp in San Francisco, Galvanize teaches data science tools, techniques and fundamental concepts. By working through messy, real-world data sets, students will gain experience in data munging, exploration, modelling, validation, visualization, communication and more. Among those teaching the classes are world-class instructors, data scientists and industry leaders. The school not only boasts an immersive education, a collaborative environment and world-class networking, but also a 93 percent placement rate, $115,000 average salary and job placement within six months. The boot camp difficulty is intermediate, so all applicants are required to have programming experience. (Note: Zipfian Academy was acquired by Galvanize.)

Overall Satisfaction	(5.0)
Location	Denver, Boulder, Fort Collins, San Francisco, Seattle
Number of Reviews	11
Subjects	HTML, CSS, Ruby on Rails, Java script, Data Science
Price Range	$$$$
Courses	Galvanize Full Stack, Galvanize Data Science, Galvanize U.

This was probably the largest single propeller of a career that I've ever heard of. After attending the course I was given a ton of resources and opportunities for face time with companies in the area. I had a job two days before graduating and I absolutely love it.

Check out more Galvanize reviews on Switch.

General Assembly 4 stars (40 reviews)

The 11-week data science technology course is one of General Assembly's part-time boot camps. It runs twice a week in the evenings. Some core skills students should expect to walk away with include knowing how to apply math and programming skills to make meaning out of large data sets, learning how to analyze and manipulate data with Python and learning how to make predictions about data using fundamental modelling techniques. The course must be done in person and takes place a General Assembly's many locations.

Overall Satisfaction	(4.1)
Location	New York City, Los Angeles, San Francisco, Boston, Atlanta, Seattle, Washington D.C., Austin, Chicago, London, Hong Kong, Sydney, Melbourne, Singapore
Number of Reviews	39
Subjects	Web Development (Full-stack: Java script, Ruby, Rails), Web Design, UI/UX Design, Product Management, Digital Marketing, Analytics, Front-end (HTML, CSS, Java script), Back-end (Ruby, Ruby on Rails), Data Science
Price Range	$
Courses	User Experience Design Immersive, Data Science, Back End Web Development, Web Development Immersive, Front End Web Development, Digital Marketing, Mobile Development, Product Management, Product Management Immersive, Visual Design, Analytics,

I've not only taken the 11 week Data Science course but have attended many workshops and watched many courses online. Overall,

GA has really helped me stay current with my skills and helped me innovate in my company.

Check out more General Assembly reviews on Switch.

Métis 5 stars (9 reviews)

After 12 weeks of the intensive, in-person data science boot camp, Métis grads should expect to be fully qualified for an entry-level data scientist position. At the New York City boot camp, students will receive 100% in-person instruction with experts from Data scope Analytics as well as career coaching during and after the course and job placement support upon completion. All applicants are expected to have some previous experience in programming and statistics. By the end of the course, students will be capable coding in Python and at the command line, understand data science tools and applications, know the fundamentals of data visualization; have introductory exposure to modern big data tools; and more.

Overall Satisfaction	(4.6)
Location	New York, San Francisco
Number of Reviews	9
Subjects	Data Science, Python, Data Visualization, JavaScript, D3, NLP, Naive Bayes,
Price Range	$$$
Courses	Data Science,

I had full career support throughout my job search, even after I graduated from the boot camp, and I definitely couldn't have found my awesome job without taking this course. Check out more Métis reviews on Switch.

Short List Courses

Here is a list of date science programs that have also made it onto our shortlist, but do not currently have a lot of alumni reviews.

Bit Boot camp

Bit Boot camp is based in New York. Both the 12-week Algorithm Training course and 4-week Big Data/Hadoop Training course are immersive and use diverse methods -- live instruction, class collaboration and technical fundamentals -- to cover much more than basics of data science. By the end of the course, students will not only have a portfolio of real-world projects but will also have access to a network of employers and career preparation. Prospective students are expected to have familiarity with SQL and programming like Java, C# and C++, as well as solid math and problem solving skills.

The Data Incubator

The Data Incubator is an intensive fellowship that seeks to transform scientists and engineers into data scientists and quants. The fellowship is seven weeks long and includes training in technical skills, like software engineering, statistics, data visualization, databases and parallelization, and soft skills like communication techniques and networking. It also provides mentorship opportunities, employer-paid scholarships and access to innovative employers. Fellows can either attend the program full time in person in New York City, San Francisco or Washington, D.C., or part time online.

Data Science Dojo

Unlike some of the other boot camps that span several weeks, Data Science Dojo is a 5-day immersive data science boot camp. Because they believe the two concepts should be taught together, both data science and data engineering are a part of the curriculum. After completing the course, graduates will be connected with the boot camp's hiring partners and the school has an active job board to help students who want to find jobs on their own. The only requirement for students is to have knowledge of at least one programming or scripting language, and the boot camp recommends the knowledge of R or Python programming. The boot camp takes place all over, from Silicon Valley to Sydney.

Data Science for Social Good

The Eric & Wendy Schmidt Data Science for Social Good Fellowship is a University of Chicago program that runs for 12 weeks in the summer. The program trains aspiring data scientists to work on data mining, machine learning, big data, and data science projects with social impact. In the program, fellows work to help governments and nonprofits solve real-world problems dealing with education, health, transportation, economic development and more. Prospective fellows are expected to be graduate students or at least seniors in college and have a passion for solving problems with social impact.

Microsoft Research Data Science Summer School

An intensive 8-week introduction to data science, the Microsoft Research Data Science Summer School is a course for college students in the New York City area. Course work includes both data science and group research projects, and classes are taught by leading scientists at Microsoft Research. In an effort to increase diversity, the school encourages women, minorities and individuals with disabilities to apply. Each student receives a $5,000 stipend and a laptop.

Slide Rule

Slide Rule's Intro to Data Science course isn't your typical boot camp. First, it's all done online; second, it's completed at the student's own pace (though, it's worth noting that tuition adjusts depending on how long it takes to complete; and third, students get a weekly call from an expert industry mentor. The curriculum includes probability and statistics, R basics, exploratory data analysis, data visualization, data wrangling and analysis techniques. During the course, students will be able to create and kick start their portfolio and network with industry experts.

Insight Data Engineering

The intensive, 7-week fellowship touts itself as the bridge to a career in data engineering. It takes place in New York City and Silicon Valley and is open to anyone with a strong background in math, computer science and software engineering fundamentals. They also seek fellows who come from positions in the industry or directly from degree programs (bachelor's, masters and PhD). In the program, students will be able to participate in project-based learning and work with top industry mentors [1].

6.3 *University of California* - Berkeley, AD Featured Online Programme

Start your search with a respected online program that's recruiting data science students from around the US.

The UC Berkeley School of Information offers an **online Master of Information and Data Science** to prepare the next leaders in data science. The interdisciplinary curriculum integrates the latest tools and analytical methods to derive insights from data, communicate findings, and solve complex challenges. The online platform seamlessly brings the UC Berkeley experience to students around the world.

<u>Click here for admissions information.</u>

- Data analytic methods;
- data exploration;
- R programming language;
- statistical methods;
- visualization techniques

This chapter introduces the basic functionality of the R programming language and environment. The first section gives an overview of how to use R to acquire, parse, and filter the data as well as how to obtain some basic descriptive statistics on a dataset. A useful way to detect patterns and anomalies in the data is through the exploratory data analysis with visualization. Exploratory data analysis is a data analysis approach to reveal the important characteristics of a dataset, mainly through visualization. The chapter discusses how to use some basic visualization techniques and the plotting feature in R to perform exploratory data analysis. Visualization is useful for data exploration and presentation, but statistics is crucial because it may exist throughout the entire Data Analytics Lifecycle. The final section of the chapter focuses on statistical inference, such as hypothesis testing and analysis of variance in R.

6.4   Educational Institutes at United Kingdom

Data Science Goldsmiths, University of London

Department name: Computing
Qualification, duration, mode: M.Sc., 12, FT
Months of entry: September

Entry requirements: You should have an undergraduate degree of at least upper second class standard in computing, engineering or mathematical sciences, and an interest in and capability for working in interdisciplinary contexts.

Course description

The M.Sc. in Data Science will provide you with the technical and practical skills to analyze the big data that is the key to success in future business, digital media and science.

The rate at which we are able to create data is rapidly accelerating. According to IBM, globally, we currently produce over 2.5 quintillion bytes of data a day. This ranges from biomedical data to social media activity and climate monitoring to retail transactions. These enormous quantities of data hold the keys to success across many domains from business and marketing to treating cancer or mitigating climate change.

The pace at which we produce data is rapidly outstripping our ability to analyze and use it. Science and industry are crying out for a new generation of data scientists who combine the statistical skills of data analysis and the computational skills needed to carry out this analysis on a vast scale. M.Sc. Data Science provides you with these skills. Studying M.Sc. Data Science, you will learn the mathematical foundations of statistics, data mining and machine learning, and apply these to practical, real world data. As well as these statistical skills, you will learn the computational techniques needed to efficiently analyze very large data sets. You will apply these skills to a range of real world data, under the guidance of experts in that domain. You will analyze trends in social media, make financial predictions and extract musical information from audio files. The Masters will culminate in a final project in which you will you can apply your skills and follow your specialist interests. You will do a novel analysis of a real world data of your choice.

Funding: Please visit http://www.gold.ac.uk/pg/fees-funding/ for details.

Contact name: Course Enquiries
Contact email: course-info@gold.ac.uk
Contact phone: +44 (0)20 7078 5300
Contact web: http://www.gold.ac.uk/pg/msc-data-science/ *[7]*.

Data Science, University of Glasgow

Department name: School of Computing Science

Qualification, duration, mode: M.Sc., 12, FT 24, PT * PG Dip 9, FT 21, PT

Months of entry: September

Entry requirements: A minimum of a 2.1 Honours degree or equivalent (e.g. GPA 3.0 or equivalent) with computing as a major subject. Further information regarding academic entry requirements: student.recruitment@glasgow.ac.uk

Information for International Students

For applicants whose first language is not English, the University sets a minimum English Language proficiency level. International English Language Testing System (IELTS) Academic module (not General Training): overall score 6.5; no sub-test less than 6.0. IBTOEFL: 92; no sub-test less than 20

Course description: The Masters in Data Science provides you with a thorough grounding in the analysis and use of large data sets, preparing you for responsible positions in the Big Data and IT industries. As well as studying a range of taught courses reflecting the state-of-the-art and the expertise of our internationally respected academic staff, you will undertake a significant programming team project, and develop your own skills in creating a project proposal and in conducting a data science project.

Why Glasgow? The University of Glasgow's School of Computing Science is consistently highly ranked achieving 1st in Scotland and 2nd in the UK (Guardian University Guide 2014)

· The School is a member of the Scottish Informatics and Computer Science Alliance: SICSA. This collaboration of Scottish universities aims to develop Scotland's place as a world leader in Informatics and Computer Science research and education.

· With a 97% overall student satisfaction in the National Student Survey 2014, the School of Computing Science continues to meet student expectations combining both teaching excellence and a supportive learning environment.

· You will have opportunities to meet industrial speakers who contribute to our professional skills & issues course. Employers also come to make recruitment presentations, and often seek to recruit our graduates during the programme.

· You will benefit from having 24-hour access to a computer laboratory equipped with state-of-the-art hardware and software.

Programme Structure: Modes of delivery of the MSc in Data Science include lectures, seminars and tutorials and allow students the opportunity to take part in lab, project and team work.

Projects: To complete the MSc degree you must undertake a project worth 60 credits. This is a project chosen by you to investigate a challenging but constrained Data Science problem.

·The project will integrate the subject knowledge and generic skills that you will acquire during your Masters.

We offer a wide range of projects, and each student is normally allocated a different project. We take your preferences into account when we allocate the projects.

You will also have the opportunity to propose your own project, subject to academic approval.

Here are some typical project titles:

- ❖ Big Data modern database showdown
- ❖ Support for PBS batch jobs in Hadoop 2.0
- ❖ Real-time corroboration of information from Twitter using follower graphs
- ❖ A Hybrid Learning to Rank Approach for an Effective Web Search Engine
- ❖ Fair pricing models for the Big Data era

Furthermore for students hoping to continue into research, we have seven major research groups: computer vision and graphics; embedded, networked, and distributed systems; formal analysis, theory, and algorithms; human computer interaction; inference, dynamics, and interaction; information retrieval; software engineering and information security. Most MSc students choose projects offered by these groups, giving them an opportunity to go on to PhD study.

UK students' fees: £6800

International students' fees: £18200

Funding: http://www.gla.ac.uk/postgraduate/taught/datascience/

Contact name: Dr Ron Poet

Contact email: Ron.Poet@glasgow.ac.uk

Contact web: http://www.gla.ac.uk/postgraduate/taught/datascience/

Apply online http://www.prospects.ac.uk/search_courses_details/university of_ Glasgow/data science/109843

6.5 Review of the Coursera Data Science Specialization: Posted on Thursday, September 10, 2015

I recently completed the 10th and final course in the Data Science Specialization offered by Coursera in conjunction with Johns Hopkins University. My background is as a computer scientist and programmer looking to learn more about statistical analysis and machine learning — I have always had an interest in data analysis and machine learning but never actually studied it. I used the Data Science Specialization acted as a starting point to learn more about the field and become familiar with typical problems and solutions that data scientists encounter in the field. This article describes my experience with the specialization and answers the question of whether or not it is worth the time.

The Data Scientist's Toolbox

The specialization opens with The Data Scientist's Toolbox, providing a broad overview of the specialization itself and of the tools and technologies that will be covered throughout the course. You will learn the basics of Git, GitHub, Markdown and R. With tutorials on how to install RStudio and R packages.

The Data Scientist's Toolbox is basic to the point of being remedial. A large portion of the course is spent reviewing what the upcoming courses will cover. It seems disingenuous to charge $50 for a course that explains what additional courses will cover. The concrete material in this course could easily be relegated to pre-requisites of other courses. If you complete a basic tutorial on Git and Markdown and know how to install software you will have completed all the requirements for this course.

Verdict

Skip. If you know absolutely nothing about software development this course may be useful. Otherwise, skip it.

R Programming

The R Programming course provides an overview of R as a programming language. It covers basic R syntax and data structures and offers an opportunity to practice writing basic R functions.

Given background in other programming languages the R Programming course will not provide you with much benefit. I would recommend following some R programming introductory tutorials at your own pace. If, however, you do not have much programming experience this course will explain the fundamentals and teach you to think programmatically. This is one of the few courses that come with a recommended textbook. Unfortunately, the textbook covers advanced R material and would only be useful after becoming familiar with R programming. The pace of the book does not match the expectations of the course.

Verdict

Take. There is enough R specific material to make this course worthwhile. Just don't expect revelations — you will not be an expert in R after this course. An additional textbook would be wonderful.

Getting and Cleaning Data

Getting and Cleaning Data covers reading files into R from a variety of sources: CSV, MySQL, HDFS, among others. You will learn how to reshape data using R and how to generate summary statistics of your data.

While getting and cleaning data is a necessary process in data analysis, the material covered in this course is basic and disjointed. I would have vastly preferred covering how to load one or two different file types and spent more time on manipulating and preparing data with R.

Verdict

Skip. This material can easily be learned when needed using specific Google searches on how to load a particular file with R. Consider taking this course if you need additional practice in R.

Exploratory Data Analysis

The Exploratory Analysis course covers plotting in R using the base plotting system, the lattice package and ggplot2. It then moves on to explain k-means, dimensionality reduction and principal components analysis.

The material on plotting is great. I only wish that the coverage of the lattice package were removed and more time dedicated to ggplot. I've yet to see any lattice plots in the real world — it seems like ggplot is the de facto standard in this area and should be covered more thoroughly. The course provides a cursory overview of k-means and principal components analysis as a way to summarize data. This material could have used a lot more explanation and motivation.

Verdict

The ggplot is must and this course will get you started on the right path to plotting. The statistical material on k-means and principal components analysis deserved more in-depth treatment and could almost be a course in itself. I wished for more material in these areas.

Reproducible Research

Reproducible research provides the motivation for making research reproducible. It then follows with coverage of R specific technologies that can aid in producing reproducible research: knitr, RPubs, and slidify.

I have mixed feelings about this course. It's great that coverage of reproducible research is included in the specialization but four weeks is too much for this particular topic. Most of the course seems like filler and following a quick tutorial on knitr would provide much the same benefit as taking this course. I also do not see the benefit in covering both RPubs and slidify when they do basically the same thing. I would much prefer seeing more in-depth coverage of one technology — anything learned in one technology could be easily applied to the other when it is needed.

Verdict

Skip. The coverage of each technology is cursory at best. Reading the documentation of knitr would provide more detail for less time and effort than taking this course. Not recommended.

Statistical Inference

The statistical inference course covers they key concepts of statistical inference: probability, confidence intervals, hypothesis testing and common statistical distributions. The course is math heavy, covering the theory behind each statistical method before providing R code for using the method in practice.

The course is a jarring departure from the rest of the specialization so far. Previous courses have covered practical considerations and mostly focused on becoming proficient with R and the RStudio environment. The mathematical treatment of statistics and statistical models can be overwhelming at times and the videos are unevenly paced with complex topics being covered with only one or two slides. The course highlights one of the key failings of the specialization: lack of supplementary material. I would have loved a companion text and problem set to help work though the details.

Verdict

Skip. The material in this course is fundamental. Unfortunately you will need a better source to learn it from. It's a shame that so much material is crammed into this four week course with no additional material to draw from. I would recommend picking up a basic statistics book rather than taking this course.

Regression Models

Regression models continue the discussion of statistical methods, this time focusing on linear regression, log-linear regression and how to interpret the results of a regression model using residuals.

The regression models course fall victim to the same shortcomings as the statistical inference course. Namely, the theoretical nature of the course without supplementary resources makes it difficult to fully dive into the technical details. One or two slides and a video as a format for learning complex material is unrealistic.

Verdict

Skip. This course attempts to cover a very broad range of material in a short time frame. Unfortunately, not having a supplementary text to work from means, the coverage of the material is spotty and incomplete.

Practical Machine Learning

The practical machine learning course eases off from the theoretical underpinnings of prediction to introduce the caret package in R and walks through some typical machine learning algorithms. It starts with a discussion of what prediction is and how to measure if a prediction model is accurate or not, then dives in to linear regression, prediction trees, and random forests.

The caret package is becoming the de facto standard interface for machine learning in R. As such, the course has some great material focusing on the practical aspects of the caret package. The course also provides a discussion of how to evaluate a prediction model for accuracy and how to compare models against one another. I wish there was more of this material as it seems like such a fundamental problem in machine learning.

Verdict

Take. This course provides a solid introduction to the caret package and should guide the student to further areas of study. You will not be an expert in machine learning after taking this course but it should give you a starting point to learn additional details whenever they are needed.

Developing Data Products

This course focuses on using R to create presentations and web apps as a means of showcasing your models. This course covers Shiny,

RStudio presenter and slidify, among other technologies. Each technology for presenting your work is introduced along with a minimal tutorial. Once that tutorial is complete, a new technology is introduced.

I wish this course focused more on one or two technologies and expanded more deeply on how they work and what can be accomplished with them. As it stands, it's hard to recommend a course that simply re-implements existing documentation for each technology that could easily be gotten in other, more complete, forms from the respective technologies websites. The course instructor even admits that most of the material is the exact examples from the technologies documentation.

Verdict

Skip. Just read the tutorial for the technologies that interest you.

Data Science Capstone

The capstone project involves creating a Shiny web application that, given a sequence of input words, predicts the next word in the sentence. This project requires some understanding of NLP, data management, Shiny, and RPubs.

The project provided a good experience of what being a data scientist entails. It necessitated a lot of research, data mangling, and performance tuning that are common in the field. The end product is useful and the skills required to make it run well are novel and useful. My only issue with the project was that there was little use of statistical methods.

Verdict

Take. The capstone brings together a lot of elements of the course and ties it all together. I feel like I learned a lot about data science simply by taking the capstone project.

Summing up it appears that the individual reviews of the courses follow a definite trend: uneven coverage of material and technologies. That trend continues for the specialization as a whole. I don't think anyone doing actual data science would believe that a topic such as statistical inference should be given the same weight as a topic such as git. Although git is definitely something that is valuable for a data scientist, it is not essential to the field. As such, the course would be a great introduction to data science from the perspective of a statistician. It would teach the statistician basic programming techniques, version control, and how to deploy your code via a Shiny application.

Another failing of the course is the lack of supplementary material. Not everyone learns best from watching videos and if you need to go back and review material at a later date then you need to either find the correct place in the video or look at only a few bullet points in a set of slides. As it stands, the specialization does provide a broad overview of the field of data science.

6.6 Review-of-top-10-Online-Data-Science-Courses/

As more and more of life's day-to-day work and personal activities are being simplified by Big Data technologies, the need for data scientists has risen remarkably for the past several years. Companies around the world scamper desperately to grab people with data science skills, and are willing to shell out big bucks to keep these data-crazed workers in their payroll. Experts agree that data science is still in its fledgling state, it will become a pervasive force pretty soon. If you want to learn data science and become a data science expert, check out our reviews of the following courses!

6.7 Harvard Data Science Course

The course is a combination of various data science concepts such as machine learning, visualization, data mining, programming, data munging, etc. You will be using popular scientific Python libraries such as Numpy, Scipy, Scikit-learn and Pandas throughout the course. I suggest you to complete machine learning course on Coursera before taking this course, as machine learning concepts such as PCA (dimensionality reduction), k-means and logistic regression are not covered in depth. But remember, you have to invest lot of time to complete this course; especially the home work exercises are very challenging.

If you are good at statistics and programming take this course. 2014 version of Harvard data science course is going on. You can access the lecture videos here.

Prerequisites:	Cs50 and Stat 100
Programming Language:	Python
Course Length:	4 months
Difficulty:	Very high
Taught By:	Hanspeter Pfister and Joe Blizsten

Reviews by others:

- Vincent granvelli has written a detailed review about this course.
- What is it to take cs109 — on Quora
- Ms. Natalia has written a review about this course.

Analytics Edge

The course gives a good intro to R and also gives hands on experience with statistical modelling techniques. The course has real world examples of how analytics have been used to significantly improve a business or industry. The workload is high, but the lectures and problem sets are well organized and structured. If you're interested in learning some practical analytic methods that don't require a ton of math background to understand, this is the course for you.

Prerequisites:	Basic knowledge of mathematics
Programming Language:	R, Libre office/Excel
Course Length:	11 weeks
Difficulty:	High
Taught By:	Dimitris Bertsimas and Allison Kelly O'Hair
Reviews by others:	Course Talk.

6.8 Machine Learning Course on Coursera

Data science and machine learning are closely related. Apart from machine learning the course shows you how to handle high dimensional data (Pca), introduces to map reduce, bias vs. variance, learning curves, etc. The course is taught using Octave (alternative for mat lab), there are set of videos that shows you how to use octave. It is better to have some knowledge of calculus before taking this course, so Consider taking MIT multivariable calculus course.

Prerequisites:	Basic linear algebra and Calculus
Programming Language:	Octave
Course Length:	11 weeks
Difficulty:	Low
Taught By:	Andrew Ng

Reviews by others:

- Class Central Machine learning course Review
- Course Talk Machine learning course Review

6.9 List of Machine Learning Certifications and Best Data Science Boot camps

Everyone has a different style of learning. Hence, there are multiple ways to become a data scientist. You can learn from tutorials, blogs, books, hackathons, videos and what not! I personally like self paced learning aided by help from a community – it works best for me. What works best for you?

If the answer to above question was **class room / instructor led certifications**, you should check out **machine learning certifications** and **data science boot camps**. They offer a great way to learn and prepare you for the role and expectations from a data scientist. More: 11 things you should know as a Data Scientist.

In this article, listed down the essential resources to master the basic and advanced version of data science using:

Global Machine Learning Certifications – This list highlights the widely recognized & renowned certifications in machine learning which can add significant weight to your candidature, thereby increasing your chances to grab a data scientist job.

Data Science Boot camps – You can think of boot camps as online / offline classroom training which are held periodically. The motive of these boot camps is to empower aspiring data scientists with necessary skills & knowledge highly sought by potential employers, in a short duration of time. These are like concentrated shots of learning consumed along with a bunch of fellow (aspiring) data scientists.

Free Resources for Machine Learning – This list highlights the free course material available on machine learning & related concepts. Interesting part is, I have included some resources from the top universities of the world which are not so commonly mentioned, but can turn out to be great if you follow them seriously.

Please note that this is simply a list of best certifications / boot camps / resources. You should look at them as the best options available and choose what fits you the best. They are not ranked.

6.10 Data Analyst Nano Degree Udacity

A Nano degree, provided by Udacity and AT&T, is an online certification that you can earn in 6-12 months (10-20 hours/week) for $200/month. Udacity's Data Science track teaches R, Python, MongoDB and Hadoop. The courses cover both theory and practice of Data Science, and every course ends with a project that allows you to demonstrate what you learned. The projects can be the start of your portfolio of work to share with others, especially recruiters. The prerequisites are pretty high; you need a variety of skills before taking this course.

Prerequisites:	Descriptive statistics, Inferential statistics, data wrangling, R, machine learning, data visualization, data science basics, computer science basics.
Course Length:	12 months (10 hours/ week)
Difficulty:	Very high
Taught by:	Chen Hang Lee and Miriam Swords Kalk

6.11 Introduction to Computational Thinking and Data Science

The course provides a brief introduction to plotting, stochastic programs, probability and statistics, random walks, Monte Carlo simulations, modeling data, optimization problems, and clustering. Even if you have little programming experience you can learn a lot from this course. The course serves as a motivation for the beginners in Python and data science.

Prerequisites:	Introduction to computer science and python programming
Programming Language:	Python
Course Length:	9 weeks (12 hours/week)
Difficulty:	Intermediate
Taught by:	John Guttag, Eric Grimson, Ana Bell
Reviews about the course:	Mooctivity

6.12 Coursera Intro to Data Science Course

The class gives a broad introduction to various concepts of data science. The first programming exercise "Twitter Sentiment Analysis in Python" is challenging, and rest of the assignments requires less time commitment. Professor Bill Howe assumes that you know statistics, Python, and SQL; you really need to know them because the lectures are so poor. Before taking this course, go through Stanford's data base course, learn Python programming concepts from code academy, learn basic statistics, and basics of machine learning. Don't expect this course to introduce you to these concepts. Despite its shortcomings, the course explains a lot about relational databases, Map Reduce and No -SQL. The course is not intended for beginners.

Prerequisites:	Basics of Python, statistics, basic knowledge of databases.
Taught by:	Bill Howe
Programming language:	Python and R
Length:	3 months
Difficulty:	Intermediate
Reviews about the course:	Course Talk and Quora

6.13 Johns Hopkinson Data Science Course

R programming, exploratory data analysis and cleaning data modules are really well taught and practical. The statistical inference and regression model structure modules are not well organized; they have too much material for someone new to it. Data scientist tool box module is a waste of time; you can see the reviews of this module here: data science tool box.

Project swirl is a fun way to learn R. Most time the professor just reads the slides without adding any additional information. Certain concepts are not clearly explained, so you will spend more time googling and learning those concepts. It is too traditional and too heavy in statistics in particular.

Prerequisites:	Working knowledge of mathematics up to algebra and some programming knowledge.
Taught by:	Brian Caffo
Programming language:	R
Length:	12 months
Difficulty:	Intermediate
Reviews about the course:	Tech Powered math

6.14   Foundations of Data Analysis

The course focuses only on statistics and gives hands on experience with descriptive and inferential statistical concepts in R. If you want to learn R and statistical concepts, then this course is for you. You will be working with well formatted data sets, so you won't be learning data munging in this course. At end of this course you will be comfortable using different statistical techniques to solve your own problems about your own data using R.

Prerequisites:	None
Taught by:	Micheal J. Mahometa
Programming language:	R
Length:	13 weeks (3-6 hours/week)
Difficulty:	Intermediate
Reviews about the course:	Course Talk

Data Science in Action

The course is based on the book *"Process Mining"* written by professor *Wil van der Aals.* If you are a business professional and don't have prior programming experience, then this course is for you. The course acts as a classical divide between "business" and "IT". The course uses many examples using real-life event logs to illustrate the concepts and algorithms. After taking this course, you will be able to run process mining projects and have a good understanding of the Business Process Intelligence field.

Prerequisites:	A basic understanding of logic, sets, and statistics (at the undergraduate level).
Taught by:	Wil Van Der Aalst

Programming Language/Tools: ProM, Disco, Rapid Miner
Length: 13 weeks (3-6 hours/week)
Difficulty: Easy

6.15 Mining Massive Datasets

The class will introduce you to fundamental algorithms and techniques to deal with Big Data, such as MapReduce, Locality Sensitive Hashing, Page Rank, and algorithms for Large Graphs and Data Streams. It will teach you how to apply these tool-kits to important practical applications, such as Web Search, Recommender Systems and Online Advertising. This course gives a special attention to dimensionality reduction. A book based on this course is available for free. The course expects you to have good knowledge of database and algorithms.

Prerequisites: Basic course on algorithms, data structures and databases
Taught by: Jure Leskovec, Anand Rajaraman, Jeff Ulman
Programming Language/Tools: SQL
Length: 7 weeks
Difficulty: Intermediate
Reviews about the course: Quora

Finally, some of the upcoming courses in data analysis are computational methods for data analysis, data analysis and statistical inference, coding the matrix. Data camp is a great place to learn R. To learn Python for data analysis, you can check out my post.

So, what other courses are worth taking if you want to get a good education in data science? [2].

References:

[1]   https://www.switchup.org/research/best-data-science-bootcamps

[2]   http://bigdata-madesimple.com/review-of-top-10-online-data-science-courses/

Chapter 7: Ways to become Data Scientist by oneself

7.1   The Road to Data Science

A lot of people ask me: **how do I become a data scientist?** I think the short answer is: as with any technical role, it isn't necessarily easy or quick, but if you're smart, committed and willing to invest in learning and experimentation, then of course you can do it. Data Science is a hybrid role that combines the "applied scientist" with the "data engineer". Many developers, statisticians, analysts and IT professionals have some partial background and are looking to make the transition into data science. And so, how does one go about that? Your approach will likely depend on your previous experience. Here are some perspectives below from developers to business analysts.

Java Developers

If you're a Java developer, you are familiar with software engineering principles and thrive on crafting software systems that perform complex tasks. Data science is all about building "data products", essentially software systems that are based on data and algorithms.

A good first step is to understand the various algorithms in machine learning: which algorithms exist, which problems they solve and how they are implemented. It is also useful to learn how to use a modelling tool like R or Matlab. Libraries like WEKA, Vowpal Wabbit, and OpenNLP provide well-tested implementations of many common algorithms. If you're not already familiar with Hadoop — learning map-reduce, Pig and Hive and Mahout will be valuable.

Python Developers

If you're a Python developer, you are familiar with software development and scripting, and may have already used some Python libraries that are often used in data science such as NumPy and SciPy.

Python has great support for data science applications, especially with libraries such as NumPy/Scipy, Pandas, Scikit-learn, IPython for exploratory analysis, and Matplotlib for visualizations.

To deal with large datasets, learn more about Hadoop and its integration with Python via streaming.

7.2 Self Learning of skill to become a good Data Scientist

Data science is big landscape and self-learning is the necessary skill if anyone wants to become a good data scientist. MOOCs had been Major source of treasure for the data scientist. Though there are many sites offering MOOCs, but Coursera, Edx and Udacity have been leaders. Whether, your language is R, python, Java or C/C++ we have captured all of them. If, you are a beginner and understanding what data science is exactly or you are an expert looking for your next frontiers. You can search through this exhaustive list as per needed.

Some general guidelines about the source details:

- The level of the course is decided by considering the prerequisites, the efforts required and duration of the course.
- All courses assume basic background in the statistics.

- The courses are arranged with respect to level of expertise, i.e. beginners courses are listed ahead of expert level courses.
- The tools are considered as a programming language, or software tools used in the course.

7.3 Data Science (Harvard Extension School)

Level:	Beginners-Expert
Effort:	7-12 hrs/week
Status:	Archived
Duration:	16 weeks
Prerequisite:	None
Tools:	Python, d3

Excellent course, recommended to all the data science aspirants. This course introduces methods for five key facets of an investigation: data wrangling, cleaning, and sampling to get a suitable data set; data management to be able to access big data quickly and reliably; exploratory data analysis to generate hypotheses and intuition; prediction based on statistical methods such as regression and classification; and communication of results through visualization, stories, and interpretable summaries.

7.4 Introduction to Data Science (University of Washington)

Level:	Beginner-Intermediate
Effort:	10-14 hrs/week
Status:	Archived
Duration:	10 weeks
Prerequisite:	Programming
Tools:	Python, R, SQL

Introduce yourself to the basics of data science and leave armed with practical experience extracting value from big data. This course teaches the basic techniques of data science, including both SQL and NoSQL solutions for massive data management (e.g., MapReduce and contemporaries), algorithms for data mining (e.g., clustering and association rule mining), and basic statistical modelling (e.g., linear and non-linear regression).

7.5 How to Become a Data Scientist for Free

Big Data, Data Sciences, and Predictive Analytics are the talk of the town and it doesn't matter which town you are referring to, it's everywhere, from the White House hiring DJ Patil as the first chief data scientist to the United Nations using predictive analytics to forecast bombings on schools. There are dozens of Start-ups springing out every month stretching human imagination of how the underlying technologies can be used to improve our lives and everything we do. Data science is in demand and its growth is on steroids. According to LinkedIn, "Statistical Analysis" and "Data Mining" are two top-most skills to get hired this year. Gartner says there are 4.4 million jobs for data scientists (and related titles) worldwide in 2015, 1.9 million in the US alone. One data science job creates another three non-IT jobs, so we are talking about some 13 million jobs altogether. The question is what YOU can do to secure a job and make your dreams come true, and how YOU can become someone that would qualify for these 4.4 million jobs worldwide.

There are at least 50 data science degree programs by universities worldwide offering diplomas in this discipline, it costs from 50,000 to 270,000 US$ and takes 1 to 4 years of your life. It might be a good option if you are looking to join college soon, and it has its own benefits over other programs in similar or not-to-so similar disciplines. I find these programs very expensive for the people from developing countries or working professionals to commit X years of their lives.

Then there are few very good summer programs, fellowships and boot camps that promise you to make a data scientists in very short span of time, some of them are free but almost impossible to get in, while other requires a PhD or advanced degree, and some would cost between 15,000 to 25,000 US$ for 2 months or so. While these are very good options for recent Ph.D. graduates to gain some real industry experience, we have yet to see their quality and performance against a veteran industry analyst. Few of the ones that I really like are Data Incubator, Insight Fellowship, Metis Boot camp, Data Science for Social Goods and the famous Zipfian Academy programs.

Let me also mention few paid resources that I am a fan of before I tell you how to do all that for free. First one is the Explore Data Science program by Booz Allen, it costs 1,250 $ but worth a single penny. Second one is recorded lectures by Tim Chartier on DVD, called Big Data: How Data Analytics is transforming the world, it costs 80 bucks and worth your investment. The next in the list are two courses by MIT, Tackling the Big Data Challenges, that costs 500$ and provides you a very solid theoretical foundation on big data, and The Analytics Edge, that costs only 100 bucks and gives a superb introduction on how the analytics can be used to solve day-to-day business problems. If you can spare few hours a day then Udacity offers a perfect Nano degree for Data Analysts that costs 200$/month can be completed in 6 months or so, they offer this in partnership with Face book, Zipfian Academy, and MongoDB. ThinkFul has a wonderful program for 500$/month to connect you live with a mentor to guide you to become a data scientist.

Ok, so what one can do to become a data scientist if he/she cannot afford or get selected in the aforementioned competitive and expensive programs. What someone from a developing country can do to improve his/her chances of getting hired in this very important field or even try to use these advanced skills to improve their own surroundings, communities and countries.

7.6   Videos for Self Learning

How Data Science is Preventing College Dropouts and Advancing Student Success

Educational institutions have a wealth of data around student demographics, admissions, academic per…Tags: Predictive Analytics, Big Data Tim Matteson on **Wednesday 216 views**

DSC Webinar Series: From Visual Analysis to Presentation

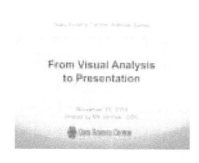

While most of us understand how to analyze our data using visualization quite well, and well aware…Tags: Visualization, Data Story Telling Tim Matteson **Nov 10186 views**

DSC Webinar Series: Data Analytics with Amazon Red shift: A Success Story

In today's latest DSC Webinar series you will learn how business intelligence and systems integrity… Tags: Sager Creek, Amazon Red shift Tim Matteson **Oct 28255 views**

DSC Webinar Series: Data Science Driven Approaches to Malware Detection

Malware detection within enterprise networks is a critical component of an effective information se... Tags: Anirudh Kondaveeti, Malware Detection Tim Matteson Oct 13210 views

DSC Webinar Series: Democratizing Data and Predictive Analytics While Ensuring Governance & Transparency

As organizations empower more users to fully leverage advanced and predictive analytics to "democrat... Tags: Data Visualization, Governance Tim Matteson Oct 7228 views

DSC Webinar Series: 100 Years of Data Visualization – It's Time to Stop Making the Same Mistakes

In 1914, New Yorker Willard Brinton wrote Graphic Methods for Presenting Facts, the first book on t... Tags: DSC, Big Data Tim Matteson Oct 1294 views

Tim Sep 15279 views

DSC Webinar Series: 5 Things Your Organization Needs to Succeed in Data Science

What does it take to succeed in the world of Data Science and Analytics? It takes the right culture... Tags: Big Data, Analytics

DSC Webinar Series: When is the right time for real-time? Architectural best practices for Hadoop

Real-time processing is an important part of your Hadoop architecture, but is it always the best ap... Tags: Analytics, Big Data Tim Matteson Aug 20138 views

DSC Webinar Series: How Do We Know That? An Introduction to Visualization Research

Matteson Aug 4405 views

Pie charts are bad, right? Bar charts are good, but stacked bars aren't. And there are lots of the... Tags: Big Data, Robert KosaraTim

IoT: How Data Science-Driven Software is Eating the Connected World

The Internet of Things (IoT) will forever change the way businesses interact with consumers Tags: Predictive Analytics, Big Data Tim Matteson Jul 21455 views

DSC Webinar Series: Faster Predictive Insight with Data Blending

Predictive analytics is only as good as the data you are working with. This can be a challenge in t... Tags: BI, Big Data Tim Matteson Jul 8276 views

Deriving Analytic Insights from Machine Data and IoT Sensors

Hadoop and The Internet of Things have enabled data driven companies to leverage new data sources. Tags: Predictive Analytics, Data Tim Jun 25258 views

DSC Webinar Series: From Insight to Action – Predictive and Prescriptive Analytics from IBM

Predictive analytics has become an imperative for organizations as they strive to incorporate data-...Tags: BI, Data Tim

Jun 2336 views

DSC Webinar Series: 7 Reasons to combine SPSS Statistics and R

According to the Rexer survey,* R is the analytic software of choice for data scientists, business...Tags: Analytics, Modeling Tim May 26336 views

DSC Webinar Series: The Beautiful Science of Data Visualization

Seeing and understanding data is richer than creating a collection of queries, dashboards, and work... Tags: Cognitive Science, Data Viz Tim Matteson Apr 28828 views

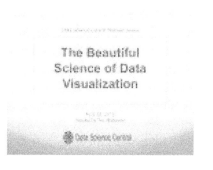

The Science of Segmentation: What Questions Should You Be Asking Your Data?

Enterprise companies starting the transformation into a data-driven organization often wonder. ... Tags: Predictive Models Tim Matteson Apr 14744 views

DSC Webinar Series: Learn How to Work with Large Datasets to Build Predictive Models with Microsoft's Analytics Toolkit

In today's webinar we will use a case study of NY taxi data to discuss

and cover how: • Azure provides...Tags: Big Data, Predictive Models Tim Matteson **Apr 1651 views**

DSC Webinar Series: Data Lakes, Reservoirs, and Swamps: A Data Science and Engineering Perspective

In the fast paced and ever changing landscape of Hadoop based data lakes, there tends to be varying... Tags: Big Data, Data Scientist Tim Matteson **Mar 24450 views**

DSC Webinar Series: Predictive Analytics – Rethinking how you process your Big Data

Newer, Faster, Better...The tools that are coming to the Big Data market seem to reflect this quick d... Tags: Big Data, Data Integration Tim Matteson **Mar 17810 views**

DSC Webinar Series: Better Risk Management with Apache Hadoop and Red Hat

The risk management systems that each firm operates must respond not only to new reporting requirement... Tags: Analytics, Hortonworks Tim Matteson **Mar 3126 views** [1].

7.7   The Best Free Courses

My Slide Rule – Complete Learning Path: Data Analysis Learning Path by Claudia Gold- *(This prepares you enough)*

One of best all-in-one Box: The Open Source Data Science Masters

Extensive and Intensive **DSE Track**: Page on bitly.com *(In depth, complete mastery of every concept in analytics landscape)*

Fast Track on Data Tools: Page on coursera.org *(R, R Studio, Version Control, Real Projects)*

Roadmaps: Metacademy - Roadmaps *(Another awesome source)*

Sources by Components

Intensive Hadoop Specialization Hadoop Tutorial -- with HDFS, HBase, MapReduce, Oozie, Hive, and Pig (Right from installing until deploying Big Data apps) Hadoop Tutorial - YDN (Yahoo Tutorial) Page on cloudera.com (Fast Track Hadoop from Cloudera) Big Data University(A to Z free course of Big Data) Welcome to Apache™ Hadoop®! (From Hadoop itself)

For DB, Various Analytics, Machine Learning and other related Courses and Training on Analytics, Data Mining, and Data Science (exhaustive free list) DataTau (Latest Must Dos/Must Know from Analytics World) Page on www.hakkalabs.co (Data pipeline from Scratch) Machine Learning With R (ML with R)

Real World Problem Sets: Data Science: What are some good toy problems in data science? Find, Use and Share Numerical Data

Data Result Presentation and Data Visualization Tutorials \ Processing.org Tableau Public (Tableau) Big Data Analytics with Tableau Great tools for data visualization

Your Data Repository, Program and App Repository, and Result Portfolio Check-In Build software better, together

Real-World Competitions Competitions | Kaggle

7.8   Most Sought After Skills Employers Are Looking For Data Scientist Positions

Here are the most sought after skills employers are looking for Data Scientist positions, based on analysis performed on job postings (I also included some free resources I found for each skill):

1. Python

- Web Programming Beginners Course – Learn Python Programming
- Python
- Learn Python - Free Interactive Python Tutorial

2. Machine Learning

- Machine Learning on coursera

3. R

- Learn R Programming Language & RStudio Basics in 1 Hour
- R Programming Language - Code School
- Introduction to R | Data Camp

4. Big Data

- Big Data University
- Big Data and Hadoop Essentials - Udemy
- Basic overview of Big Data Hadoop - Udemy

5. Hadoop

- Big Data and Hadoop Essentials - Udemy
- Basic overview of Big Data Hadoop - Udemy
- Hadoop Training & Certification Course | Udemy

6. SQL

- Interactive Online SQL Training for Beginners
- Sachin Quickly Learns (SQL) - Structured Query Language
- SQL Tutorial

7. Statistics

- Statistics One on coursera
- Statistics and Probability
- Probability & Statistics

8. Java

- Learn Java: The Java Programming Tutorial For Beginners
- Learn Java - Free Interactive Java Tutorial
- Learn Java Programming From Scratch - Udemy

9. Data Mining

- Data Mining and Web Scraping: How to Convert Sites into Data
- Data Mining on coursera

A great way to acquire new skills and to grow your professional network is to attend meet ups: Data Science Meetups

You can learn more about the required skills to become a data scientist and get relevant resources here.

Statistical analysis and data mining were the top skills that got people hired in 2014 based on LinkedIn analysis of 330 million LinkedIn member profiles. We live in an increasingly data driven world, and businesses are aggressively hiring experts in data storage, retrieval, and analysis. Across the globe, statistics and data analysis skills were highly valued. In the US, India, and France, those skills are in particularly high demand.

7.9   Top-10-Online-Data-Science-Courses

As more and more of life's day-to-day work and personal activities are being simplified by Big Data technologies, the need for data scientists has risen remarkably for the past several years. Companies around the world scamper desperately to grab people with data science skills, and are willing to shell out big bucks to keep these data-crazed workers in their payroll. Experts agree that data science is still in its fledgling state, it will become a pervasive force pretty soon. If you want to learn data science and become a data science expert, check out our reviews of the following courses!

1) Harvard Data Science Course

The course is a combination of various data science concepts such as machine learning, visualization, data mining, programming, data munging, etc. You will be using popular scientific Python libraries such as Numpy, Scipy, Scikit-learn and Pandas throughout the course. I suggest you to complete machine learning course on coursera before taking this course, as machine learning concepts such as PCA (dimensionality reduction), k-means and logistic regression are not covered in depth. But remember, you have to invest lot of time to complete this course; especially the home work exercises are very challenging.

If you are good at statistics and programming take this course. 2014 version of Harvard data science course is going on. You can access the lecture videos here.

Prerequisites:	Cs50 and Stat 100
Programming Language:	Python
Course Length:	4 months
Difficulty:	Very high
Taught By:	Hanspeter Pfister and Joe Blizsten
Reviews by others:	Vincent granvelli has written a detailed review about this course. What is it to take cs109 — on Quora? Ms. Natalia has written a review about this course.

2) Analytics Edge

The course gives a good intro to R and also gives hands on experience with statistical modeling techniques. The course has real world examples of how analytics have been used to significantly improve a business or industry. The workload is high, but the lectures and problem sets are well organized and structured. If you're interested in learning some practical analytic methods that don't require a ton of math background to understand, this is the course for you.

Prerequisites:	Basic knowledge of mathematics
Programming Language:	R, Libre office/Excel
Course Length:	11 weeks
Difficulty:	High

Taught By:	Dimitris Bertsimas and Allison
	Kelly O'Hair
Reviews by others:	Course Talk.

3) Machine Learning Course on Coursera

Data science and machine learning are closely related. Apart from machine learning the course shows you how to handle high dimensional data (Pca), introduces to map reduce, bias vs. variance, learning curves, etc. The course is taught using Octave (alternative for matlab), there are set of videos that shows you how to use octave. It is better to have some knowledge of calculus before taking this course, so Consider taking MIT multivariable calculus course.

| Prerequisites: | Basic linear algebra and Calculus |
Programming Language:	Octave
Course Length:	11 weeks
Difficulty:	Low
Taught By:	Andrew Ng
Reviews by others:	Class Central Machine learning course Review
	Course Talk Machine learning course Review

4) Data Analyst Nano Degree Udacity

A Nano degree, provided by Udacity and AT&T, is an online certification that you can earn in 6-12 months (10-20 hours/week) for $200/month. Udacity's Data Science track teaches R, Python, MongoDB and Hadoop. The courses cover both theory and practice of Data Science, and every course ends with a project that allows you to demonstrate what you learned. The projects can be the start of your portfolio of work to share with others, especially recruiters. The prerequisites are pretty high; you need a variety of skills before taking this course.

Prerequisites:	Descriptive statistics, Inferential statistics, data wrangling, R, machine learning, data visualization, data science basics, computer science basics.
Course Length:	12 months (10 hours/ week)
Difficulty:	Very high
Taught by:	Chen Hang Lee and Miriam Swords Kalk

5) Introduction to Computational Thinking and Data Science

The course provides a brief introduction to plotting, stochastic programs, probability and statistics, random walks, Monte Carlo simulations, modeling data, optimization problems, and clustering. Even if you have little programming experience you can learn a lot from this course. The course serves as a motivation for the beginners in Python and data science.

Prerequisites:	Introduction to computer science and python programming
Programming Language:	Python
Course Length:	9 weeks (12 hours/week)
Difficulty:	Intermediate
Taught by:	John Guttag, Eric Grimson, Ana Bell
Reviews about the course:	Mooctivity

6) Coursera Intro to Data Science Course

The class gives a broad introduction to various concepts of data science. The first programming exercise "Twitter Sentiment Analysis in Python" is challenging, and rest of the assignments requires less time commitment. Professor Bill Howe assumes that you know statistics, Python, and SQL; you really need to know them because the lectures are so poor. Before taking this course, go through Stanford's data base course, learn Python programming concepts from code academy, learn basic statistics, and basics of machine learning. Don't expect this course to introduce you to these concepts. Despite its shortcomings, the course explains a lot about relational databases, Map Reduce and No -SQL. The course is not intended for beginners.

Prerequisites:	Basics of Python, statistics, basic knowledge of databases.
Taught by:	Bill howe
Programming language:	Python and R
Length:	3 months
Difficulty:	Intermediate
Reviews about the course:	Course Talk and Quora

7) Johns Hopkinson Data Science Course

R programming, exploratory data analysis and cleaning data modules are really well taught and practical. The statistical inference and regression model structure modules are not well organized; they have too much material. Data scientist tool box module is a waste of time; you can see the reviews of this module here: data science tool box.

Project swirl is a fun way to learn R. Most time the professor just reads the slides without adding any additional information. Certain concepts are not clearly explained, so you will spend more time goggling and learning those concepts. It is too traditional and too heavy in statistics in particular.

Prerequisites:	Working knowledge of mathematics up to algebra and some programming knowledge.
Taught by:	Brian Caffo
Programming language:	R
Length:	12 months
Difficulty:	Intermediate
Reviews about the course:	Tech Powered math

8) Foundations of Data Analysis

The course focuses only on statistics and gives hands on experience with descriptive and inferential statistical concepts in R. If you want to learn R and statistical concepts, then this course is for you. You will be working with well formatted data sets, so you won't be learning data munging in this course. At end of this course you will be comfortable using different statistical techniques to solve your own problems about your own data using R.

Prerequisites:	None
Taught by:	Micheal J. Mahometa
Programming language:	R
Length:	13 weeks (3-6 hours/week)
Difficulty:	Intermediate
Reviews about the course:	Course Talk

9) Data Science in Action

The course is based on the book "*Process Mining*" written by professor *Wil van der Aals.* If you are a business professional and don't have prior programming experience, then this course is for you. The course acts as a classical divide between "business" and "IT". The course uses many examples using real-life event logs to illustrate the concepts and algorithms. After taking this course, you will be able to run process mining projects and have a good understanding of the Business Process Intelligence field.

Prerequisites:	A basic understanding of logic, sets, and statistics (at the undergraduate level).
Taught by:	Wil Van Der Aalst
Programming Language/Tools:	ProM, Disco, Rapid Miner
Length:	13 weeks (3-6 hours/week)
Difficulty:	Easy

10) Mining Massive Datasets

The class will introduce you to fundamental algorithms and techniques to deal with Big Data, such as MapReduce, Locality Sensitive Hashing, Page Rank, and algorithms for Large Graphs and Data Streams. It will teach you how to apply these tool-kits to important practical applications, such as Web Search, Recommender Systems and Online Advertising. This course gives a special attention to dimensionality reduction. A book based on this course is available for free. The course expects you to have good knowledge of database and algorithms.

Prerequisites:	Basic course on algorithms, data structures and databases
Taught by:	Jure Leskovec, Anand Rajaraman, Jeff Ulman

Programming Language/Tools: SQL
Length: 7 weeks
Difficulty: Intermediate
Reviews about the course: Quora

Some of the upcoming courses in data analysis are computational methods for data analysis, data analysis and statistical inference, coding the matrix. Data camp is a great place to learn R. To learn Python for data analysis, you can check out my post.

So, what other courses are worth taking if you want to get a good education in data science? [2].

References:

[1] http://www.datasciencecentral.com/video/video/listFeatured

[2] http://bigdata-madesimple.com/review-of-top-10-online-data-science-courses/

Chapter 8: Prospect of Data Science

8.1   Introduction

Data Science is different from other areas such as mathematics or statistics. Data Science is an applied activity and data scientists serve the needs and solve the problems of data users. Before you can solve a problem, you need to identify it and this process is not always as obvious as it might seem. Data Science is a flourishing industry. Countries and companies around the world are continuously experiencing a rush in the amount of data collected. They are determined to hire experts who can work on their data and improve their lives. Such experts are known by many names. Most popular is 'Data Scientist'. Among others include Data Engineers, Data Architects and Statisticians etc. But, how many of us are clear about the difference in these roles and designations?

Figure 32: Prospect of Data Science

As I've experienced, people are confused between a Data Scientist, Data Engineer and Statistics. Some end up concluding, all these people do the same job, its just their names are different. I got astonished at hearing such answers. With these thoughts in mind, I decided to create a simple info graphic to help you understand the job roles of a Data Scientist vs. Data Engineer vs. Statistician. This will help you to decide the best job role for you in coming future.

8.2   The Hot Job of the Decade

Hal Varian, the chief economist at Google, is known to have said, "The sexy job in the next 10 years will be statisticians. People think I'm joking, but who would've guessed that computer engineers would've been the sexy job of the 1990s?"

If "sexy" means having rare qualities that are much in demand, data scientists are already there. They are difficult and expensive to hire and, given the very competitive market for their services, difficult to retain. There simply aren't a lot of people with their combination of scientific background and computational and analytical skills.

Data scientists today are akin to Wall Street "quant" of the 1980s and 1990s. In those days people with backgrounds in physics and math streamed to investment banks and hedge funds, where they could devise entirely new algorithms and data strategies. Then a variety of universities developed master's programs in financial engineering, which churned out a second generation of talent that was more accessible to mainstream firms. The pattern was repeated later in the 1990s with search engineers, whose rarefied skills soon came to be taught in computer science programs.

One question raised by this is whether some firms would be wise to wait until that second generation of data scientists emerges, and the candidates are more numerous, less expensive, and easier to vet and assimilate in a business setting. Why not leave the trouble of hunting down and domesticating exotic talent to the big data start-ups and to firms like GE and Wal-Mart, whose aggressive strategies require them to be at the forefront?

The problem with that reasoning is that the advance of big data shows no signs of slowing. If companies sit out this trend's early days for lack of talent, they risk falling behind as competitors and channel partners gain nearly unassailable advantages. Think of big data as an epic wave gathering now, starting to crest. If you want to catch it, you need people who can surf [1].

8.3   The Sexiest Job of the 21st Century

Thomas Davenport and D.J. Patil brought the data scientist into the national spotlight in their October 2012 Harvard Business Review article: Data Scientist: The Sexiest Job of the 21st Century. Job trends data fromIndeed.com confirms the rise in popularity for the position, showing that the number of job postings for data scientist positions increased by 15,000% between the summers of 2011 and 2012.

When I asked Bruno Aziza last year how he would best describe a data scientist, his answer still sticks with me today. "Think of a data scientist more like the business analyst-plus," he told me. Part mathematician, part business strategist, these statistical savants are able to apply their background in mathematics to help companies tame their data dragons. But these individuals aren't just math geeks, per se.

"A data scientist is somebody who is inquisitive, who can stare at data and spot trends. It's almost like a Renaissance individual who really wants to learn and bring change to an organization." — *Anjul Bhambhri, Vice President of Big Data Products, IBM*

Tips for aspiring data scientists: If this sounds like you, the good news is demand for data scientists is far outstripping supply.

Nonetheless, with the rising popularity of the data scientist – not to mention the highly-competitive companies that are typically hiring for these positions – candidates will have to be at the top of their fields to get the jobs. Here are some quick tips for career success.

For students about to graduate: Focus on academics before (and after) graduation. Successful data scientists come from a number of different disciplines: biostatistics, econometrics, engineering, computer science, physics, applied mathematics, statistics, machine learning, and other interrelated disciplines. Experience applying the scientific method to many disciplines and areas of research will provide fruitful in the field of data science. And as important as academics are during school, it's just as important to stay up-to-date with current research trends and discoveries within academia, even after graduation, for instance by subscribing to academic journals.

For career entrants: Focus on business acumen. While programming and statistical expertise is the foundation for any data scientist, a strong background in business and strategy can help jettison a younger scientist's career to the next level.

Krishna Gopinathan, founder of Global Analytics Holdings, recently recounted to me how he has built some of his most exceptional data scientist teams. The secret, in his opinion, was to build teams around data scientists that ask the most questions about:

- ➢ How the business works
- ➢ How it collects its data
- ➢ How it intends to use this data
- ➢ What it hopes to achieve from these analyses.

These questions were important to Gopinathan because data scientists will often unearth information that can "reshape an entire company." Obtaining a better understanding of the business' underpinnings not only directs the data scientist's research, but helps them present the findings and communicate with the less-analytical executives within the organization.

While it's important to understand your own business, learning about the successes of other corporations will help a data scientist in their current job–and the next.

8.4   Data Scientist Job Outlook

In an oft-cited 2011 big data study, McKinsey reported that by 2018 the U.S. could face a shortage of 140,000 to 190,000 "people with deep analytic skills" and 1.5 million "managers and analysts with the know-how to use the analysis of big data to make effective decisions."

The ensuing panic has led to high demand for data scientists. Companies of every size and industry – from Google, LinkedIn and Amazon to the humble retail store – are looking for experts to help them wrestle big data into submission. Starting salaries are astronomical.

The bubble is bound to burst, of course. In a 2014 Mashable article, Roy Lawrence, the managing director of New York University's Centre for Data Science program, is quoted as saying "anything that gets hot like this can only cool off." But even as demand for data engineers surges, job postings for big data experts are expected to remain high.

There are also some indications that the roles of data scientists and business analysts are beginning to merge. In certain companies, "new look" data scientists may find themselves responsible for financial planning, ROI assessment, budgets and a host of other duties related to the management of an organization.

"Why Spotify just bought a data science start up." http://fortune.com/2015/06/24/spotify-data-acquisition/

ESPN, June, 2015. "Gaming Your Brain." http://espn.go.com/ espn/story/_/id/13065280/video-game-data-science-profit

Bloomberg, June, 2015 "Data Scientists are the new Kings of the Silicon Valley!" http://telecom.economictimes.indiatimes.com/ news/industry/data-scientists-are-the-new-kings-of-the-silicon-valley/47582013

Bednorz Ann, "Big Data, Big Pay: 10 Data Jobs with Climbing Salaries." Network World, March 18, 2014. Accessed January 18, 2015 http://www.networkworld.com/article/2286529/big-data-business-intelligence/144797-Big-data-big-pay-10-data-jobs-with-climbing-salaries.html.

Columbus, Louis, "Where Big Data Jobs Will Be In 2015", Forbes, December 29, 2014; Accessed January 18, 2015. http://www.forbes.com/sites/louiscolumbus/   2014/12/29/where-big-data-jobs-will-be-in-2015.

Idea, Ian. "Big Data: Career Opportunities Abound in Tech's Hottest Field." Mashable, October 5, 2014; Accessed January 18, 2015. http://mashable.com/2014/ 10/05/big-data-careers.

Platt, John R. "Landing a Job in Big Data." IEEE, September 8, 2014; Accessed January 18, 2015. http://theinstitute.ieee.org/career-and-education/career-guidance/ landing-a-job-in-big-data.

Violino, Bob. "The Hottest Jobs In IT: Training Tomorrow's Data Scientists." Forbes, June 26, 2014; Accessed January 18,

2015. http://www.forbes.com/sites/emc/ 2014/06/26/the-hottest-jobs-in-it-training-tomorrows-data-scientists
[2]
.

8.5   Hot Career: The number of Data Scientists has doubled over the last 4 years

A new study of LinkedIn LNKD-1.24% profiles by RJMetrics has found that the number of data scientists has doubled over the last 4 years . This reflects the increasing demand for sophisticated data analysis skills, combining computer programming with statistics, and the growth in the popularity of the term "data science" both in job openings and the words people use to describe their work on LinkedIn. At least 52% of all current 11,400 data scientists on LinkedIn have added that title to their profiles within the past 4 years .

In the chart above, the cumulative number of data scientists in any given year corresponds to the number of present-day data scientists who started their first job that year. We can safely assume that those who started their first jobs between 1995 and 2009 were not called then "data scientists," but the data shows the cumulative growth in the number of professionals who have this title today. *Here are the other highlights of the study*:

The high-tech industry (LinkedIn classification: Information Technology and Services industry, Internet and Computer Software industries) employs 44.9% of the professionals identified on LinkedIn as data scientists, followed by education (8.3%, probably employed mostly by universities), Banking and Financial Services (7.2%), and Marketing and Advertising (5.2%).

Top ten companies employing data scientists: Microsoft MSFT-1.85%, Face book FB-1.92%, IBM IBM +0.00%, GlaxoSmithKline, Booz Allen Hamilton, Nielsen, GE, Apple, LinkedIn, and Teradata. Note that Google is not at the top ten, possibly because the data science Googlers on LinkedIn adheres to the title Google bestows on them: quantitative analyst. Both Microsoft and Face book, according to RJMetrics' analysis, appear to be on a hiring spree, accelerating their data scientist recruiting during the 2014 calendar year by at least 151% and 39%, respectively, when compared to 2013. But given the scarcity of experienced data scientists, it's a revolving door, with Microsoft also losing the largest number of data scientists over that period [3].

Data Scientist

Some companies treat the titles of "data scientist" and "data analyst" as the same thing and they are often used interchangeably. However, in general, there are some distinctions between the two. *A data scientist's work* usually needs more complicated analysis and a stronger understanding of the fundamentals of statistics. A strong background in college and graduate level statistics coursework is needed for a career as a data scientist. Usually job listings will require a master's degree in quantitative finance, statistics, or some relevant field.

While *a data analyst* simply may be doing work in excel to present summary statistics of small datasets, a data scientist will be managing larger data sets from different sources. They'll likely be comfortable with Python and R programming and using advanced statistical models and tools like STATA and SPSS. SQL and basic scripting languages are a must-know for data scientists. Data scientists are often employed by technology and financial sectors, where huge volumes of data are being processed every day. As new data comes in and new problems come up, these data scientists are employed to find ways to optimize a company's marketing campaign, optimize a hedge fund's trading algorithm, or come up with new ways to predict or model consumer behaviour. The end goal is to make full use of the company's data to help generate profits and make the products better.

Note that in different industries, often times they require specialized knowledge. For example, in the medical industry they require knowledge of biostatistics and bio-statistical models, which can be different to financial statistics and financial modelling.

Data Engineer

A data engineer is very different to a data scientist. Think of a data engineer as more of a computer scientist who specializes in building systems to manage data. They focus on creating robust data systems that can aggregate, process, clean, transform, and store large amounts of data. Typically in large corporations a data engineer builds a robust, fault-tolerant data pipeline that cleans, transforms, and aggregates unorganized and messy data into databases or data sources. Data engineers are typically software engineers by trade. Instead of data analysis, data engineers are responsible for compiling and installing database systems, writing complex queries, scaling to multiple machines, and putting disaster recovery systems into place.

Data engineers essentially lay the groundwork for a data analyst or data scientist to easily retrieve the needed data for their evaluations and experiments.

Skills and tools: Data engineers need to have strong knowledge of core computer science principles and software development experience. In addition, they need to have expertise in new technologies that help manage large datasets. These technologies and concepts include MapReduce, NoSQL databases, MongoDB, SQL, Hadoop, Storm, and other various Dev Ops tools like Chef. You will need the ability to learn whatever technology the company is using to manage their data systems, and there are a wide variety of them, although the core underlying principles are very similar.

Salary Ranges

According to Data Jobs, national salary ranges for the following data job are as follows:

Data analyst (entry level): $50,000-$75,000
Data analyst (experienced): $65,000-$110,000
Data scientist: $85,000-$170,000
Database administrator (entry level): $50,000-$70,000
Database administrator (experienced): $70,000-$120,000
Data engineer (junior/generalist): $70,000-$115,000
Data engineer (domain expert): $100,000-$165,000

[4].

8.6   How Companies are using Analytics

Telecom services providers such as **Bharti Airtel Ltd** and **Vodafone Business Services**, for instance, analyze usage and charging patterns with the help of predictive analytics. So do online travel agencies, e-commerce firms and car makers.

According to **Sharat Dhall**, president of online travel agency **Yatra.com**, his firm "is leveraging a combination of in-house and third-party technologies to develop a more holistic and consolidated view of customers and offer more personalized experiences to customers".

India's biggest automobile companies including **Maruti Suzuki India Ltd**, **Tata Motors Ltd** and two-wheeler make **Hero MotoCorp Ltd**, have been sifting through large pools of data that they collect during customer interactions to accelerate decision-making, improve efficiency and sell more vehicles.

During a panel discussion organized by *Mint* in March, **Amitabh Misra**, vice-president (engineering) of online retailer **Snapdeal**, said that "every single decision that we make internally is based on analytics". He pointed out that about 31% of the e-commerce company's orders come through our analytics-driven systems.

Indian companies have the advantage of "picking up learning's from global clients", according to Khanna, who pointed out that some Indian government departments too "are using Big Data analytics amazingly well". He cited the examples of improved weather and storm forecasts by the country's meteorological department.

According to Khanna, however, it's only big companies in India that are applying data analytics to better customer experience and increase revenue while others "are simply learning to store Big Data in data warehouses".

Banks, for instance, could potentially "map the lives of users" if they analyze all the data they have, such as credit card usage in the country and abroad, ATM usage and online and mobile banking transactions. "With all this data, banks will know my income, food habits, brands I like, shopping habits, my preference for cash or credit cards, investments I make, etc. A smart decision maker can use all this data to provide me with better offers but as of now, it's mostly global banks and global retailers that use Big Data analytics effectively," said Khanna.

8.7 Market Opportunity

The market potential, meanwhile, is huge for vendors of Big Data analytics services.

In a 5 September report, software lobby body Nasscom and CRISIL Global Research and Analytics forecast the global Big Data market opportunity to touch $25 billion by 2015 from $5.3 billion in 2011, and the Indian industry to grow five-fold from the current level of $200 million to touch $1 billion by 2015.

The report added that the information technology services segment will be the major contributor to the Big Data services market.

A 27 June report by software lobby body Nasscom and Blue ocean Market Intelligence pegged the Indian analytics market to cross the $2 billion mark by fiscal 2018.

"The availability of humongous un-interpreted data (Big Data), created through global connectivity via smart phones and other smart devices and the need for analysis of consumer behaviour has thrown up plethora of opportunities for the IT sector, which we believe will be the next growth driver," according to a 30 January report by **Edelweiss Securities Ltd**.

The report added that "...going by investments in these technologies, we prefer **Infosys Ltd**, **HCL Technologies Ltd**, **Tata Consultancy Services Ltd**, **Tech Mahindra Ltd** and **Persistent Systems Ltd**."

Wipro Ltd's "analytics and information management" service has been growing ahead of the group's revenue, according to a 23 April report by brokerage **Prabhudas Lilladher Pvt. Ltd**.

On 18 April, **Wipro** said it has increased its stake in US-based Big Data and analytics company Opera Solutions to 12.5%. It had acquired a 6.5% stake in Opera in May 2013 for about $30 million, and analysts said the company might have spent a similar amount to pick up the additional stake. Wipro did not disclose the amount.

Challenges

Companies have to understand what data to collect, and how to integrate it. Moreover, implementing the right solutions to accurately analyze and interpret the data, and reacting in a timely fashion to insights as they arise, are equally important challenges for companies.

For vendors, the success of Big Data will also depend on a large skilled talent pool. However, the shortage of skilled professionals may prove to be the biggest challenge for the industry.

The US alone is expected to witness a shortage of 190,000 data scientists by 2018. In India, Big Data analytics and related IT services will create an estimated 15,000-20,000 specialist jobs by 2015 [5].

8.8 What about Jobs? Are Analytics Jobs increasing by the day?

I am sure you have heard the headline here. The famous McKinsey report quotes a shortfall of up to 190,000 data scientists and 1.5 Mn data managers in the U.S. alone. The shortage obviously increases when you look at the situation across the globe. Let us add more texture to this.

Google Trends speaks about searches related to analytics jobs across the globe. The global trend is quite evident and India is the most significant in heat map of Google searches, the trend in India looks to have lot more noise. Here is how it looks specifically for India.

Looking at regional searches with in India, Gurgaon & Bengaluru seem to have the highest search for analytics jobs, while Bengaluru, Hyderabad and Chennai seem to have most searches for Big Data jobs. This is also in sync with our experience with jobs in industry. As per our estimate, Bengaluru would have 30 – 40% jobs market share, Delhi NCR would have 25 – 30% market share and then the remaining cities. Here is a heat map of the same.

8.9   Data Scientist Salary

Mean annual salary for data scientists in North America: $89,000

Salaries for data scientists and related positions:

- Business Analyst: $78,000
- Business Intelligence Analyst: $84,000
- SAS Data Analyst: $84,000
- IBM Data Analyst: $84,000
- *Data Scientist: $89,000*
- Data Mining Engineer: $93,000
- Machine Learning Engineer: $94,000
- Big Data Scientist: $97,000
- Data Architect: $107,000
- Business Intelligence Architect: $110,000
- Enterprise Data Architect: $110,000
- Big Data Architect: $111,000
- Hadoop Engineer: $112,000
- Data Warehouse Architect: $113,000
- Senior Data Scientist: $130,000
- Senior Big Data Analyst: $138,000

The business intelligence & analytics field has practically unlimited earning potential. Highly talented, educated and experienced big data scientists can earn well over $250,000 per year with salary plus incentives. The hourly salary range for data scientist contract positions is $30-$85, dependent upon skills and project requirements.

Source: Indeed.com

References:

[1]   https://hbr.org/2012/10/data-scientist-the-sexiest-job-of-the-21st-century?cm_sp=Article-_-Links-_-Top%20of%20Page%20Recirculation

[2]   https://www.wpi.edu/academics/datascience/career-outlook.html

[3]   http://www.forbes.com/sites/gilpress/2015/10/21/the-number-of-data-scientists-has-doubled-over-the-last-4-years/

[4]   https://www.udemy.com/data-science/

[5]   http://www.livemint.com/Industry/bUQo8xQ3gStSAy5II9lxoK/Are-Indian-companies-making-enough-sense-of-Big-Data.html

----------------------END----------------------

About the Author

Award winning Key Note Speaker at International Level, Professor Ajit Kumar Roy is an acclaimed researcher and consultant. Prof. Roy obtained his M.Sc.degree in Statistics and joined Agricultural Research Service (ARS) of Indian Council of Agricultural Research (ICAR) as a Scientist (Statistics) in 1976. In recent past was engaged as National Consultant (Impact Assessment), for East & North Eastern States of India at National Agricultural Innovation Project (World Bank funded) of ICAR. Prior to that he had served as a Consultant (Statistics) at Central Agricultural University, Agartala. Earlier had served at CIFA, ICAR, as Principal Scientist and was involved in applied research in the areas of ICT, Statistics, Bioinformatics Analytics, and Economics. At International level he served as a Computer Specialist at SAAR Agricultural Information Centre (SAIC), Dhaka, Bangladesh for over 3years. The author with over 45 years of research and teaching experience in Statistical Analysis, Analytics, and information & Knowledge management edited eighteen books and several conference proceedings. Besides, published over 100 articles in refereed journals. His recent best-sellers are 'Applied Big Data Analytics'; 'Impact of Big Data Analytics on Business, Economy, Health Care and Society'; 'Data Science - A Career Option for 21st Century'; 'Self Learning of Bioinformatics Online';' Applied Bioinformatics, Statistics and Economics in Fisheries Research' and 'Applied Computational Biology and Statistics in Biotechnology and Bioinformatics'. *Presently Member,* Organizing Committee Board for the *5th International Conference on 'Biometrics and Biostatistics'* to be held during, October 20-21, 2016, Houston, Texas, USA. *Editorial Board Member*, **Jacobs Journal of Biostatistics,** Jacobs Publishers, 900 Great Hills, Trail # 150 w, Austin, Texas. He now works as Visiting Professor, question setter and examiner of four Indian Universities.

www.ingramcontent.com/pod-product-compliance
Lightning Source LLC
Chambersburg PA
CBHW071358050326
40689CB00010B/1687